Animating SwiftUI Applications

Create visually stunning and engaging animations for iOS
with SwiftUI

D1563690

Stephen DeStefano

BIRMINGHAM—MUMBAI

Animating SwiftUI Applications

Group Product Manager: Rohit Rajkumar

Publishing Product Manager: Nitin Nainani

Senior Editor: Hayden Edwards

Technical Editor: Joseph Aloocaran

Copy Editor: Safis Editing

Project Coordinator: Aishwarya Mohan

Proofreader: Safis Editing

Indexer: Rekha Nair

Production Designer: Nilesh Mohite

Marketing Coordinator: Nivedita Pandey

First published: March 2023

Production reference: 1100323

Published by Packt Publishing Ltd.

Livery Place

35 Livery Street

Birmingham

B3 2PB, UK.

ISBN 978-1-80323-266-9

www.packtpub.com

To my family, who have always been my source of love, support, and encouragement. Your unwavering belief in me has been my foundation, and I am eternally grateful for everything you have done for me. This book is dedicated to each and every one of you with heartfelt love and gratitude.

And to my best friend, Akiko, who has been my faithful companion on our life journey together. Thank you for your love, support, and endless laughter.

With love and admiration,

Stephen DeStefano

Foreword

SwiftUI has come a long way since it was first introduced in 2019. At first, the framework was nothing more than a novelty, but it has grown significantly over the past few years. The tools have been improved and all the bugs have been fixed, but perhaps the most important aspect of this evolution is that the framework is now forging its own path, introducing tools that didn't exist before, such as widgets and charts, and integrating old technologies in a way that makes it easy for developers to build professional applications. Performing complex tasks such as file and database management, or adding personal touches that set your application apart, is now easier than ever.

However, nothing represents these innovations better than animation, giving the user interface a professional look that cannot be achieved with static elements. Creating an animation with previous frameworks required dozens of lines of code and setting multiple parameters. SwiftUI has always included built-in support for animation, but the feature has now been enhanced and extended to allow developers to create stunning user interfaces with ease.

In this book, Stephen DeStefano shows you how to create SwiftUI animations and how to implement them to achieve the look and feel you have always wanted for your application. With clear and easy-to-follow examples, Stephen explains all the aspects of the technology, from animating simple views to creating complex animations for custom graphics, allowing you to focus on your project and get results fast.

J.D. Gauchat

Author of SwiftUI for Masterminds

Contributors

About the author

Stephen DeStefano is a seasoned SwiftUI programmer with over a decade of experience in teaching beginners the fundamentals of Apple's Swift language. His passion for programming, specifically SwiftUI and animations, is evident in his work, including several in-depth and comprehensive courses featured on Udemy and other platforms.

Throughout his career, he's had the privilege of working with some of the leading Swift and SwiftUI programmers in the field, including Paul Hudson and J.D. Gauchat, but his own unique approach of blending best practices and industry standards with hands-on tutorials and exercises has attracted over 30,000 students, solidifying him as a sought-after SwiftUI educator.

About the reviewers

Nimesh Neema is a passionate programmer who loves well-designed software. He is proficient with Apple developer technologies and has written apps for iPhone, iPad, Mac, Apple Watch, and Apple TV. He has an excellent understanding of shell scripting, version control, and software engineering principles.

In his career spanning over 15 years, he has worked with teams of diverse sizes and backgrounds and has experience writing utility, payment, gaming, hospitality, and low-level system apps.

He runs a software engineering consultancy, Perspicacious Solutions Private Limited, with clients from around the world. He takes up corporate training and speaking gigs and is one of the highly rated Apple development experts on `Codementor.io`.

Scotti Dscyre is a highly accomplished and dedicated iOS developer with strong experience in developing and maintaining large-scale applications at the production level. He possesses in-depth knowledge of the iOS ecosystem and his expertise embraces a wide range of technologies and tools, including Swift, Objective-C, UIKit, SwiftUI, Swift Concurrency, Combine, RxSwift, CoreData, CoreAnimation, XCTest, MVVM, clean architecture, composable architecture, the Swift Package Manager, CocoaPods, fastlane, Git, and Bitrise.

He is also devoted to open source contributions and has distributed a number of open source packages, including ShuffleIt and SwiftTheming on GitHub.

Table of Contents

10

Creating an Ocean Scene   243

11

Animating an Elevator   271

12

Creating a Word Game (Part 1)   295

13

Creating a Word Game (Part 2)   327

14

Creating a Color Game   359

15

Integrating SpriteKit into Your SwiftUI Projects   393

Preface

Welcome to *Animating SwiftUI Applications*, a book designed to help you create engaging and interactive user experiences using SwiftUI animations.

SwiftUI is a modern, declarative, and intuitive framework for building user interfaces on Apple platforms, and it comes with a powerful and easy-to-use animation system that lets you add motion and life to your apps effortlessly.

With SwiftUI animations, you can add dynamic transitions, smooth movements, and delightful effects to your app's UI elements, making them more engaging and intuitive for users. You can animate anything from simple buttons and text fields to complex layouts and custom shapes, all with just a few lines of code.

In this book, you will learn how to use SwiftUI animations to create various types of effects, including transitions, gestures, and even SpriteKit animations. You'll explore different animation techniques, such as implicit, explicit, and combined animations, and learn how to apply them to create stunning and responsive user interfaces. By the end of the book, you'll be able to create beautiful and engaging animations and apps that really stand out from the crowd.

Who this book is for

This book is aimed at those who have a basic working knowledge of Swift but are a beginner when it comes to SwiftUI. The book starts with some basics of the SwiftUI framework, and then proceeds with simple animation examples, before moving on to more advanced topics.

What this book covers

In *Chapter 1, Exploring the Fundamentals of SwiftUI*, you will receive a comprehensive overview of the two distinct programming styles: imperative and declarative. Then, we will delve into the Xcode interface, the free application provided by Apple, where all our development work will take place. Finally, we will examine the fundamental SwiftUI structures required for creating applications, laying the groundwork for advancing with animations.

In *Chapter 2, Understanding Animation in SwiftUI*, we will examine the mechanics of animations, covering essential topics such as timing curves and animatable properties. This will establish a solid foundation for the projects we will construct.

In *Chapter 3*, *Creating a Breathing App*, we will harness the power of SwiftUI's user-friendly modifiers and design tools to effortlessly rotate, scale, and move views. Moreover, we will utilize the `animation` modifier to smoothly interpolate between start and end values, producing a seamless animation.

In *Chapter 4*, *Building a Record Player*, we will incorporate images from the Asset Catalog into our code. Then, we will create standalone files for creating various views that can be seamlessly integrated into the main view for display. Furthermore, we will add a button to trigger the animation and incorporate sound into the project.

In *Chapter 5*, *Animating Colorful Kaleidoscope Effects*, we will explore the animation of colors using the `hueRotation` modifier, where `hue` pertains to the colors of the object and `rotation` signifies the rotation or animation of these colors. We will construct a straightforward project that showcases various images, and then utilize `hueRotation` to alter the color of the images, producing a kaleidoscope-like effect.

In *Chapter 6*, *Animating a Girl on a Swing*, we will investigate the process of cutting up images into separate parts, and then using code to animate these separate parts together in creative and unique ways. Additionally, we will utilize a new modifier, `mask`, to help disguise and hide specific areas of our animation that we don't want to see.

In *Chapter 7*, *Building a Series of Belts and Gears*, we will generate a "marching ants" effect by employing the `stroke` modifier, and then examine how to neatly organize code using Pragma Marks and Groups. We will also animate objects along all three axes, *x*, *y*, and *z*, by utilizing the `rotation3Deffect` modifier.

In *Chapter 8*, *Animating a Flower*, we will construct the illusion of a bouquet of flowers breathing through the use of modifiers such as `blur`, `scale`, and `rotationEffect`. Additionally, we will examine the `UIViewRepresentable` protocol and the `CAEmitter` class to incorporate falling snow into the scene.

In *Chapter 9*, *Animating Strokes around Shapes*, we will delve into the process of converting bitmap images into vector files, and then transform these vector files into code that we can utilize in a SwiftUI project. Furthermore, we will animate a stroke around various shapes through the use of the `stroke` modifier and timers.

In *Chapter 10*, *Creating an Ocean Scene*, we will utilize the `Shape` protocol to craft an oceanic scene featuring undulating waves, a buoy that bobs in the water, a flashing light, and accompanying sounds.

In *Chapter 11*, *Animating an Elevator*, we will employ `GeometryReader` and the `proxy` constant to insert images into the project and position them appropriately. This will enable the images to be dynamically resized based on the device in use. Furthermore, we will create a `DataModel` to store the app's data and functions and make use of timers to activate doors and light animations at various points in the scene.

In *Chapter 12, Creating a Word Game – Part 1*, we will commence with the construction of a word-based game that allows players to input words to play using three different languages, with validations in place to verify their choices.

In *Chapter 13, Creating a Word Game – Part 2*, we will add the finishing touches to our word game by organizing its properties and functions within `DataModel` and creating distinct header and footer views to display information to the user. Additionally, we will incorporate user feedback in three different forms: pop-up alerts, haptic feedback, and audio.

In *Chapter 14, Creating a Color Game*, we will develop an RGB color-matching game that keeps track of the score and displays a celebratory confetti animation upon the player achieving a perfect score. We will also examine the integration of Swift packages into the project.

In *Chapter 15, Integrating SpriteKit into your SwiftUI Projects*, we will create six separate projects that showcase SpriteKit and a variety of particle systems. We will learn how to blend realistic and fluid animations seamlessly with your SwiftUI code.

To get the most out of this book

To get the most out of this book, a working knowledge of the Swift programming language is required. Knowledge of the fundamentals of SwiftUI is helpful, but not required.

You will also need a Mac computer and have downloaded the free software, Xcode (Xcode runs well on most versions of macOS, so it should work with the version you have).

We will build our projects for iOS devices.

If you are using the digital version of this book, we advise you to type the code yourself or access the code from the book's GitHub repository (a link is available in the next section). Doing so will help you avoid any potential errors related to the copying and pasting of code.

If you prefer to learn through video tutorials, I recommend my Swift and SwiftUI courses over at `udemy.com`. Other highly recommended resources that can help to build your coding skills fast are Paul Hudson's works at `hackingwithswift.com`, and J.D. Gauchat's *SwiftUI for Masterminds* book.

Download the example code files

You can download the example code files for this book from GitHub at `https://github.com/PacktPublishing/Animating-SwiftUI-Applications`. If there's an update to the code, it will be updated in the GitHub repository.

We also have other code bundles from our rich catalog of books and videos available at `https://github.com/PacktPublishing/`. Check them out!

Download the color images

We also provide a PDF file that has color images of the screenshots and diagrams used in this book. You can download it here: `https://packt.link/O1ZYe`.

Conventions used

There are a number of text conventions used throughout this book.

`Code in text`: Indicates code words in text, database table names, folder names, filenames, file extensions, pathnames, dummy URLs, user input, and Twitter handles. Here is an example: "He is very thorough as well, and you can find his work at `jdgauchat.com`."

A block of code is set as follows:

```
struct ContentView: View {
    var body: some View {
        HStack {
            Text("Hello")
            Spacer()
```

When we wish to draw your attention to a particular part of a code block, the relevant lines or items are set in bold:

```
struct ContentView: View {
    var body: some View {
        VStack(alignment: .leading)  {
        Text("Hi, I'm child one in this vertical stack")
        Text("Hi, I'm child two in this vertical stack")
```

Bold: Indicates a new term, an important word, or words that you see onscreen. For instance, words in menus or dialog boxes appear in **bold**. Here is an example: "We will be using the first option, which is **Create a new Xcode project**, for all of our projects, so select that."

> **Tips or important notes**
> Appear like this.

Get in touch

Feedback from our readers is always welcome.

General feedback: If you have questions about any aspect of this book, email us at customercare@packtpub.com and mention the book title in the subject of your message.

Errata: Although we have taken every care to ensure the accuracy of our content, mistakes do happen. If you have found a mistake in this book, we would be grateful if you would report this to us. Please visit www.packtpub.com/support/errata and fill in the form.

Piracy: If you come across any illegal copies of our works in any form on the internet, we would be grateful if you would provide us with the location address or website name. Please contact us at copyright@packt.com with a link to the material.

If you are interested in becoming an author: If there is a topic that you have expertise in and you are interested in either writing or contributing to a book, please visit authors.packtpub.com.

Share Your Thoughts

Once you've read *Animating SwiftUI Applications*, we'd love to hear your thoughts! Scan the QR code below to go straight to the Amazon review page for this book and share your feedback.

https://packt.link/r/1-803-23266-8

Your review is important to us and the tech community and will help us make sure we're delivering excellent quality content.

Download a free PDF copy of this book

Thanks for purchasing this book!

Do you like to read on the go but are unable to carry your print books everywhere?

Is your eBook purchase not compatible with the device of your choice?

Don't worry, now with every Packt book you get a DRM-free PDF version of that book at no cost.

Read anywhere, any place, on any device. Search, copy, and paste code from your favorite technical books directly into your application.

The perks don't stop there, you can get exclusive access to discounts, newsletters, and great free content in your inbox daily

Follow these simple steps to get the benefits:

1. Scan the QR code or visit the link below

https://packt.link/free-ebook/9781803232669

2. Submit your proof of purchase
3. That's it! We'll send your free PDF and other benefits to your email directly

1

Exploring the Fundamentals of SwiftUI

Welcome to *Animating SwiftUI Applications*! If you picked up this book, then there's a good chance you are a developer – or aspiring to be one – and you want to learn more about SwiftUI animations. Or maybe you're fascinated by animations and how they work like I am. I know for me that the first time I played a video game (before the home computer was even available) and saw objects collide and bounce off each other on the screen, I was hooked by animations and the code behind how they worked. Whatever the reason you're here though, together we will explore the amazing things we can make happen on an Apple device by leveraging the power of SwiftUI's animation classes, methods, and properties.

This chapter starts with a brief look at the two programming styles, imperative and declarative, and will give you an idea of why Apple introduced the declarative SwiftUI way of coding to the development world. Then, we'll explore the Xcode interface, the free application from Apple, where we do all of our work. Finally, we'll look at the SwiftUI structures needed to develop apps, which is the foundation for proceeding further with animations.

In this chapter, we will cover the following topics:

- Understanding imperative and declarative programming
- Exploring the Xcode interface
- Understanding the state
- Understanding SwiftUI structures

Technical requirements

In order to write code that can run on Apple devices, first, we need an Apple computer. This can be any of their models, but the MacBook Pro is the most popular for coding because of its power and speed.

Once we have the hardware, then the next bit of tech we need to write code is the software. Apple has put together a very comprehensive set of tools all bundled into one program called Xcode, which is free to download from the App Store. Those two things are everything you need to start writing code on Apple, but if you want to upload your finished app to the App Store, then you will need an Apple Developer account. This currently costs $99 a year to maintain, but it is necessary to be able to sell your apps to the world. Go to `developer.apple.com` and sign up for an account there.

You should also have a working knowledge of the Swift programming language so that you feel comfortable writing code, but you don't have to be an expert by any means; it's just that it is very helpful if you understand, or at least recognize, the syntax of the Swift language and the fundamentals of **object-oriented programming (OOP)** so that you can follow along with the projects better.

With that said, if you are a complete beginner to writing code, you might be a bit confused here – but not to worry, when Apple introduced the Swift programming language in 2014, they held fast to their goal of making one of the easiest-to-pick-up and most user-friendly programming languages to date. And for the most part, the Swift language reads like English sentences, so you can progress very quickly.

Here is what I recommend when you're just starting out learning Swift:

Start with the Swift tutorials offered by Paul Hudson. He is a brilliant Swift programmer, and one of the most prolific in the industry. He has put together tons of free Swift training tutorials and videos that get you to write code fast. I have worked with Paul on many projects, and you would be hard-pressed to find a better and more thorough teaching style – he's also just an all-around nice guy. Check out all his stuff at `hackingwithswift.com`.

Someone else I have worked with (and continue to work with) is John D. Gauchat. He has put together a Swift and SwiftUI Mastermind series of books that can serve as both a reference and a guide/cookbook of code for when you need to remember the syntax or how to implement something fast. He is very thorough as well, and you can find his work at `jdgauchat.com`.

Finally, if you like structured video courses, I have translated many of Paul's and John's Swift and SwiftUI books into video courses, and they are available over at `udemy.com` – just search for my name to see them all, including the video version of this book (which includes extra projects).

OK, that's enough of those shameful plugs, but if you are a complete beginner, I want you to learn the Swift programming language from the very best, and those two guys are; this way, you will be ready to follow along and code in no time. So, go get some Swift knowledge under your belt, and come back here. I'll wait…

Finally, to access all of the code in this book, go to the following GitHub repository: `https://github.com/PacktPublishing/Animating-SwiftUI-Applications`.

Understanding imperative and declarative programming

SwiftUI is a fairly new framework introduced by Apple in 2019 that includes intuitive new design tools that help make building great-looking interfaces almost as easy as dragging and dropping... almost. With its modular approach, it's estimated that you can build the same projects previously built in Xcode using about five times less code. Also, SwiftUI was Apple's solution for building apps that can easily be used on all of their other platforms – so, an app can be built once, and it will perform perfectly on iOS, tvOS, macOS, and watchOS.

The SwiftUI interface, which we will cover shortly, uses editor and canvas preview windows that work in tandem. As you code in the Xcode editor, the new design canvas displays everything completely in sync and renders in real time as you type. So, any change you make in the editor is immediately reflected in the canvas preview, and vice versa.

I mentioned the ease of drag and dropping in code earlier; this is because those nice engineers at Apple must have spent countless nights working hard putting together a huge selection of pre-made chunks of code called views and modifiers that you can drag and drop right into the editor. This includes things such as buttons, labels, menus, lists, pickers, forms, text fields, toggle switches, modifiers, events, navigation objects, effects, and well, much more, but you get the point. Unlike UIKit and Storyboards, when you drop a view or a modifier into the editor or on the canvas, SwiftUI generates the code for that view automatically.

The SwiftUI approach to app development is known as **declarative programming**, and it has become widely popular in the last few years. Examples of declarative programming would include frameworks such as React and cross-platform development frameworks such as React Native and Flutter. So, now it's Apple's turn to offer its own completely native declarative UI framework, SwiftUI.

But what does declarative programming actually mean? Well, to best describe declarative programming, let's first understand what imperative programming is.

Imperative programming has been the oldest programming paradigm since the dawn of computer languages. The word "imperative" has its origin in the Latin word "imperare", which means "to command," and it was first used to express a command – for example: "do it"! (Hmm, I wonder whether Nike borrowed that imperative command and tweaked it a little...) This style of programming is what iOS developers used before SwiftUI came out.

Imperative programming is a programming paradigm that uses statements that change a program's state. These statements are executed in a specific order, and they usually involve assignment statements, loops, and control structures that specify how the computation should be carried out.

In imperative programming, the programmer specifies exactly how the computation should be carried out, using statements that tell the computer what to do. This can make imperative programs more complex because the programmer has to specify all of the steps of computation. However, it can also make them more flexible because the programmer has more control over the details of the computation.

Here is an example of imperative programming using the UIKit framework in iOS:

```
let button = UIButton(frame: CGRect(x: 0, y: 0, width: 100,
height: 50))
button.setTitle("Button", for: .normal)
button.setTitleColor(.black, for: .normal)
button.addTarget(self, action: #selector(buttonTapped), for:
.touchUpInside)
view.addSubview(button)
```

This code creates a new UIButton, sets its title and title color, and adds an action to be performed when the button is tapped. It then adds the button to the view hierarchy. This code is imperative because it specifies the exact steps needed to create and configure the button and add it to the view.

Now, this same code could also be written in a declarative style using a library such as SwiftUI, ReactiveCocoa, or RxSwift, which allows you to specify the desired behavior of the button rather than the steps needed to achieve it. Here is the same example written using SwiftUI:

```
import SwiftUI
struct ContentView: View {
    var body: some View {
        Button(action: {
            // action to be performed when button is tapped
        }) {
            Text("Button")
                .font(.title)
                .foregroundColor(.black)
        }
    }
}
```

In this example, the Button view is declarative, because it specifies the desired behavior of the button (displaying text and performing an action when tapped), rather than the steps needed to create and configure the button.

SwiftUI uses a declarative style of programming, which can make it easier to understand and maintain your code because you don't have to specify all of the intermediate steps needed to achieve the desired behavior. It also allows your code to automatically update when the underlying data changes because you specify the desired outcome rather than the steps needed to achieve it.

So, declarative programming is a programming paradigm in which a program specifies what it wants to achieve, rather than how to achieve it. The focus is on the "what" rather than the "how." Declarative programs are usually easier to understand because they don't require the programmer to specify every single step of the computation. They can also be more concise because they don't need to specify all of the intermediate steps.

There are many different programming languages and technologies that support declarative programming, including SQL, HTML, and functional programming languages such as Haskell and Lisp. In general, declarative programming is well suited to tasks that involve defining data relationships or specifying a desired output, rather than specifying the steps needed to achieve something.

To clarify, let's use the analogy of an artist: imperative languages paint by numbers to reach the desired result, a finished painting, but declarative languages use the finished painting and let background algorithms (functions and methods) automatically choose the appropriate colors and brush strokes to achieve the desired result. Also, by using this declarative approach, SwiftUI minimizes or eliminates programming side effects, usually caused by tracking the state of the program.

> **Note**
> You will want to keep in mind that in many cases, code will be a mixture of both imperative and declarative styles, so it's not always one or the other.

With a better understanding of SwiftUI now, we will proceed to an overview of the Xcode interface.

Exploring the Xcode interface

In this section, we will take a tour of the Xcode interface. I'm assuming that you have used Xcode before, practicing your Swift skills, which means you have a good handle on many of the things here in the interface. However, there are a few new additions to accommodate SwiftUI.

When you first start up Xcode, you see the welcome screen. On the right is a list of recent projects, and on the left, there are buttons to start a new project, open an existing project, or clone one saved in a repository.

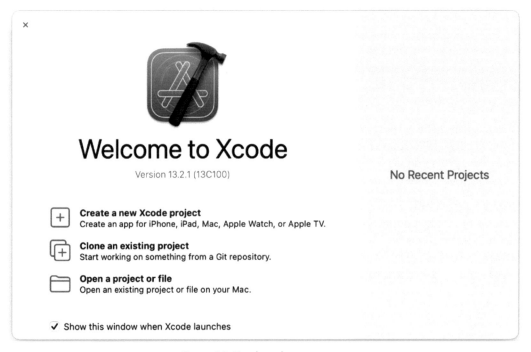

Figure 1.1: Xcode welcome screen

We will be using the first option, which is **Create a new Xcode project**, for all of our projects, so select that.

The next screen lets us choose options for the project:

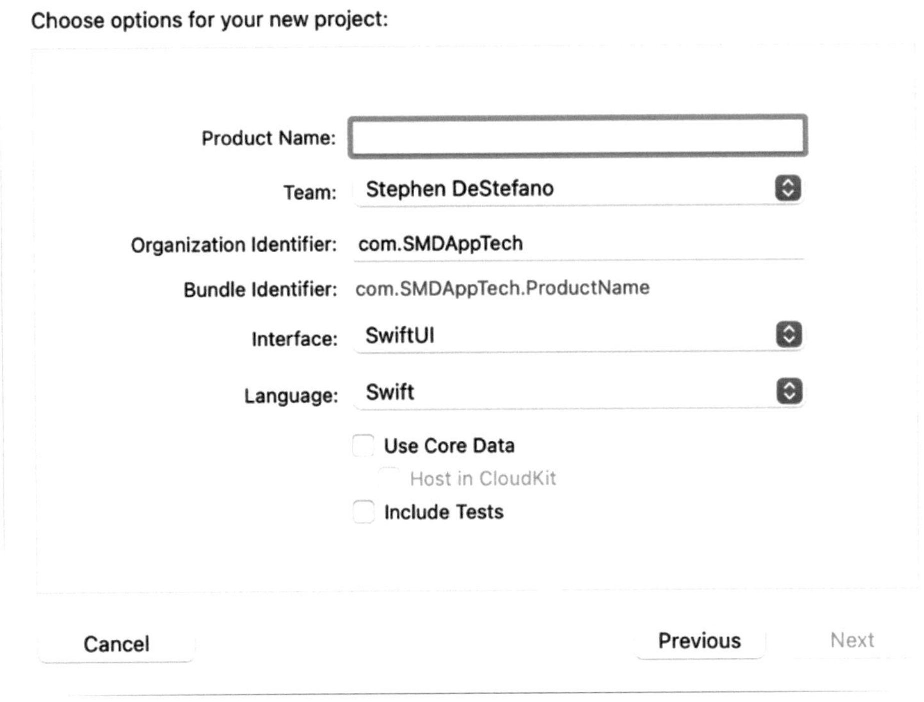

Choose options for your new project:

Figure 1.2: Project options

Let's look at these options:

- **Product Name**: This will be the name of the project. You should select a name that is directly related to what the project will do.

- **Team**: This will be the developer account you created with your Apple ID at `developer.apple.com`, or a company account if you have one.

- **Organization Identifier**: Xcode will take this value and add it to the project's name to create a unique bundle identifier for your app. It is recommended to write the identifier out with an inverted domain, as I did in the example (`com.SMDAppTech`).

> **Note**
>
> If you were wondering why Apple requires this reverse notion, here's a deeper explanation. Reverse domain name notation (or reverse DNS) is a system used to map an IP address to a domain name. Reverse DNS strings are based on registered domain names, with the order of the components reversed for grouping purposes. Here is an example: if a company making a product called MyProduct has the domain name `exampleDomain.com`, they could use a reverse DNS string of `com.exampleDomain.MyProduct` as an identifier for that product. Reverse DNS names are a simple way of eliminating namespace collisions since any domain name is globally unique to its registered owner.

- **Interface**: This is where we select the technology we will use to design the UI. From the drop-down list, you can choose **SwiftUI** or **Storyboard**. SwiftUI is a system that lets us declare the interface from code, while Storyboard is a graphical system that allows us to drag and drop many components and controls onto a storyboard to create the user interface – we want to select **SwiftUI**.

  A quick note: even though we drag and drop onto the storyboard in that option, the code is not generated after you drop an object onto the board. You still have to write out the code for each object and make connections for buttons and other controls. Whereas in SwiftUI, you can drag and drop similar components, and the code is automatically propagated in the editor for you. You then fill out the body with what you want it to do.

- **Language**: This is the coding language; here, we will select **Swift**.

- We don't need to use core data, which is a way of persisting your data so it always loads back up again, and we don't need to include tests for any of the projects.

When we hit **Next**, we're asked where to save the project. I like to save it on the desktop, but you can choose any location you want.

And now we are in the Xcode interface:

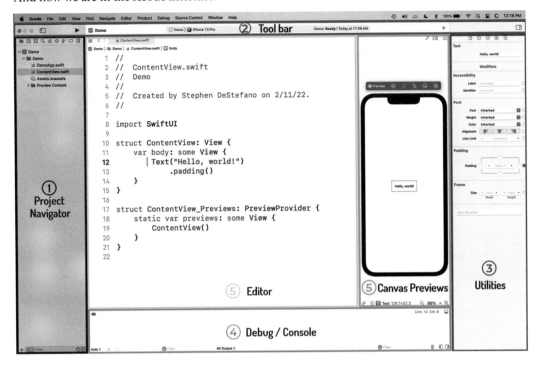

Figure 1.3: Xcode interface

The Xcode interface is the part of Xcode where we do all of our coding. It is split up into different sections; here are those sections explained:

- **Project Navigator (1)**:

  This is a collapsible space that contains all the project files. A file called ContentView is here, into which we can write our code, and we can create more files as the project grows. If you have worked in Xcode before with UIKit, then the ContentView file is analogous to UIKit's View Controller, where it had the ViewDidLoad method, in which we would usually load some user interface code. Here, we put the UI code in the ContentView struct and create other structs as needed. We can also organize all these files by creating and naming new groups and folders. There's another file here called Assets.xcassets (also called the Assets catalog), where we place the images and colors needed for our project.

  Looking at the top of the **Project Navigator** section, you'll see a blue icon, followed by the name of your project; here, it's Demo. This is the main folder of your project into which everything else is placed, including the new Swift files that you create. Clicking on that takes us to many different options and settings to configure the app, things such as the deployment target, signing, capabilities, build settings, and more.

- **Tool bar** (2):

  Let's look at the toolbar (after the traffic light buttons), starting from left to right:

  - There is a navigator toggle button that opens and closes the **Project Navigator** pane that we just looked at, to give you more working space when you need it.

  - To the right of the navigation button is a play button that runs and stops the project.

  - Next, you will see the title of your project. However, if you click on it, this is a drop-down list, allowing you to select the scheme and various different simulators or devices to run your project in. A scheme is a destination for running the app. For example, Xcode lets us run the project on different simulators, on a device, in a window on the Mac computer, on an Apple watch, on an iPad, or on an Apple TV if we are building for those. We are building for the iPhone, so you can select any of the iPhone simulator models from the list, or connect your iPhone to your computer and you will see it appear in the list. If you select your iPhone, you can see what your app looks like running on an actual device.

  - After that, there is a display area to show any errors or warnings, as well as the app's current status.

  - To the right on the toolbar is a plus button that opens up a library of tools that we use to help create the user interface, things such as modifiers, views, controls, and code snippets.

  - And finally, there's another button at the far right to show or collapse the Utilities Inspector, again, for more screen real estate when needed.

- **Utilities** (3):

  The **Utilities** Inspector is a collapsible area that offers more options to edit and configure the interface and its elements. There are five tabs at the top for this; from left to right, they are as follows:

  - **File Inspector** is used to adjust the parameters for the file you are working in

  - **History Inspector** is used to view your project's history (this is not used much in a SwiftUI project)

  - **Quick Help Inspector** will give you a description/definition of the code selected in the editor

  - **Accessibility Inspector** is for configuring things such as voiceover, Braille reading, and other settings related to making your app more accessible

  - **Attributes Inspector** gives you the option to change any of the attributes of a particular view, modifier, or other control that you have selected

- **Debug/Console** (4):

  This is a collapsible space that appears and disappears by toggling the button on the bottom right. The area can also be divided into two sections. When split, the section on the left provides information for debugging, and the right is a console used to display any relevant information when we run the code, as well as warnings and errors.

- **Editor** (**5**):

  This is the area in which we write our code. This section of Xcode is not collapsible, but we can split it into two or more sections by clicking the button at the far right just underneath the toolbar. It can be positioned at the top or the bottom depending on how you like to write code.

  There is also a feature called the mini-map, a miniature map of the code file, which offers a helpful view of the entire file, and makes it easy to reference and navigate around your code, especially if you have very large files. We can enable it by clicking on the little hamburger icon at the top right and choosing **Mini Map**.

- **Canvas Previews** (**6**):

  The canvas is its own collapsible section of Xcode that features a graphical simulator called a preview, that has a real-time connection to the code within the editor. Any changes we make in the editor will be reflected in the preview. There is a **Run** button on the preview to test out what you've done so far, but the preview is a great visual aid that helps speed up development.

That's the XCode interface in a nutshell. It may look daunting at first, but as you code along through the projects, you will become more comfortable and start to learn where everything is.

Let's continue and look at the concept of the state, which is data that can change. We hold our data in variables, and that data changes many times when we animate something in SwiftUI; when the data changes, SwiftUI helpfully will handle updating the animations for us by using the state to refresh the views.

Understanding the state

In SwiftUI, a state is a piece of data that can change. When the state changes, the view that depends on the state is automatically refreshed.

You can declare a state in a SwiftUI view by using the `@State` property wrapper. For example, see the following:

```
struct ContentView: View {
    @State private var name: String = "Bella"
}
```

Here, `name` is a state that is stored as a string. You can then use this state to display dynamic content in your view:

```
struct ContentView: View {
    @State private var name: String = "Bella"
```

```
    var body: some View {
        Text("Hello, \(name)")
    }
}
```

To change the state, we can assign a new value to the `@State` property. For example, see the following:

```
struct ContentView: View {
    @State private var name: String = "Bella"
        var body: some View {
        VStack {
            Text("Hello, \(name)")
            Button(action: {
                name = "Jack"
            }) {
                Text("Change name")
            }
        }
    }
}
```

When the button is tapped, the name state is changed to `"Jack"` and the view is automatically refreshed to display the new name.

Let's continue now and look at what makes up SwiftUI and helps it works so well.

Understanding SwiftUI structures

SwiftUI gives us views, controls, modifiers, and layout structures for declaring the user interface. The framework also includes event handlers for providing taps, gestures, and other kinds of input for our app, as well as tools for managing the flow of data coming from your app's models.

But what's a model? A **model** is simply a folder we create in the **Project Navigator** window where we usually keep the app's data; for example, if we are working on a weather app, we can keep our wind, temperature, precipitation, and snow accumulation data in the app's model after it has been received from the internet through an **Application Programming Interface** (**API**) call, which is prebuilt software that talks to other programs for us. That data will then be processed and sent down to the views and controls that the user will see and can interact with.

SwiftUI allows us to avoid using Interface Builder and Storyboards to design the app's user interface, as we can use the preview canvas and the editor instead. We can inspect the user interface as we write code, and also generate code when dragging and dropping views/controls into the canvas. The code within the editor and the canvas preview are side by side; changing one will update the other.

When building our apps, we use **views**. Nearly everything is a view in SwiftUI, and they are the building blocks of our apps, things such as text boxes, buttons, toggles, pickers, shapes, colors (yes, even colors are a view), stacks, and more. We add them to the canvas by dragging them out of the view's library, or by typing out the code in the editor, and then setting their properties with modifiers. Each view will have its own unique set of properties and modifiers, and many views will also share those same properties and modifiers too.

The following are the SwiftUI structures we will look at so you can get a good foundation for completing this book's projects:

- Computed properties
- Stacks (`VStack`, `HStack`, and `ZStack`)
- The `Spacer` view
- The `Divider` view
- The `padding` modifier
- Closures
- `GeometryReader`

Let's go through each of these now.

Computed properties

One of the first things we will look at is **computed properties** because that is how views are made. Here is a look at the template code that we see when we first create a new SwiftUI project:

```
struct ContentView: View {
    var body: some View {
        VStack {
            Image(systemName: "globe")
                .imageScale(.large)
                .foregroundColor(.accentColor)
            Text("Hello, world!")
        }
        .padding()
    }
}
```

If we run that code, this is what we see in the preview window:

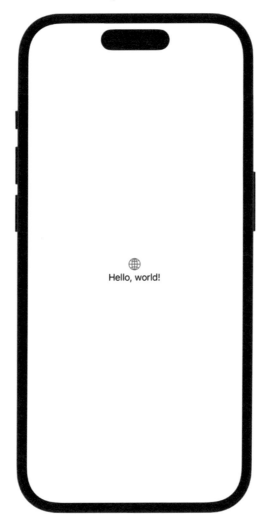

Figure 1.4: Running the template code

The **Hello, world!** string is displayed in the middle of the screen.

Looking at the code, we see that it includes a `struct` object called `ContentView`, which is the basic building block struct that SwiftUI creates for us. Inside that is a computed property called `body` – it has open and close parentheses, and yes, it has a body where you place your code to be executed, as does any function in Swift. Computed properties do not store values as a regular stored property or variable would. Instead, this property will compute the code you place in between the parentheses and then return the result.

Computed properties can have getters and or setters. They can either get and return a value, set a new value, or do both. However, if it just has a getter, then it's known as a read-only property because it will only return the computed properties value.

You might be wondering if this is a computed read-only property, where are the getter and return keywords? Well, this code is actually the shorthand version of a computed property. It's optional to write out the longhand version, but we could if we wanted more readable and descriptive code; if we did, it would look like this:

```
struct ContentView: View {
    var body: some View {
        get {
            return VStack {
                Image(systemName: "globe")
                    .imageScale(.large)
                    .foregroundColor(.accentColor)
                Text("Hello, world!")
            }
            .padding()
        }
    }
}
```

This code does the same thing as before: it returns the **Hello World!** text view, and the image view, but I've just added the two keywords, get and return. Again, they are optional, so you will see the shorthand version in most cases, because less code is, well, less code, which makes life easier. Still, many developers prefer the clarity of adding those keywords... it's up to you.

There's another curious bit of syntax here and that's the some View keyword. The some keyword indicates that an opaque type will be returned, and View is the opaque type in this instance. Opaque refers to something that's not clear or not easily understood. So, what's not clear? That would be the type that this view will return. That's because, being an opaque type, it hides the type and its implementation from us. All it cares about is that a single view will be returned, which is important because only one view can be returned to satisfy the some keyword's requirements. The view's type that will be returned is determined by what we put into the body of the computed property. In the code, there is a Text view there, so that's the type that is returned.

When we create custom views, we just have to make sure that it conforms to the View protocol. To do that, we just need to implement the required body computed property, then we can add whatever view we want to display, things such as buttons, toggles, pickers, shapes, colors, and so on, but again, just one view.

Another bit of syntax to look at is `.padding()`, called a layout modifier – it modifies the layout of the text view by placing 20 points of padding (that's the default amount when we don't choose a value) all around the text view. Many different modifiers are grouped into different categories, such as text modifiers, image modifiers, list modifiers, and more.

Have a play around and experiment with them by clicking on the plus button on the top right in Xcode and then selecting the **Modifiers** tab. You will quickly get to know the many different modifiers as you start building the projects.

Let's now turn our attention to the organizational layout of these views on the screen.

Stacks

Remember I said that the `some View` protocol has one requirement, and that is to return just one view when we run the code. That's fine in very simple apps, but more often than not, we need to return more than one view – several views might need to be displayed on the screen for the user to interact with in fact, such as a button, a text field, some images, text, and so on. We need to organize these views vertically and horizontally on the screen, as well as on the *z*-axis (placing views on top of each other).

To achieve this, SwiftUI gives us vertical, horizontal, and zed stacks, or `VStack`, `HStack`, and `ZStack` for short. These are container views that can hold 10 views inside them. The views inside them are know as **child views**. Let's look at each now.

VStack

A **VStack** is simply a container view that arranges its children in a vertical line. Looking at the previous code, when we press the **Run** button, one view is returned, the `Text` view, and it displays **Hello World!** on the user's screen.

But what if we want to have more than one view returned from inside the body computed property? Maybe we want to have a `Button` *and* a `Text` view on the screen, as in this code example:

```swift
struct ContentView: View {
    @State var myText = ""
    @State var changeText = false
    var body: some View {
        Text(myText)
            .padding()
        Button("Button") {
            changeText.toggle()
            if changeText {
                myText = "Hello SwiftUI!"
            } else {
```

```
                myText = "Hello World!"
            }
        }
    }
}
```

If we press *Command + B* to build this code, it builds cleanly and error-free.

But even though this code is error-free, nothing appears in the previews, so it won't do anything when we press the play button to run it. The code won't do anything because there are two views inside the body computed property: a Text view and a Button view. This violates the View protocol, which only wants some View returned (singular), not some Views (plural).

Now, look at the same code with a minor change made to it:

```
struct ContentView: View {
    @State var myText = ""
    @State var changeText = false

    var body: some View {
        VStack {
            Text(myText)
                .padding()
            Button("Button") {
                changeText.toggle()
                if changeText {
                    myText = "Hello SwiftUI!"
                } else {
                    myText = "Hello World!"
                }
            }
        }
    }
}
```

I have put all of the code inside the VStack. Now, when we run it, everything works as expected, and the two views can coexist inside the body computed property without any issues. If we press the button, the text will change depending on the value in the changeText property:

Figure 1.5: VStack

The VStack can hold 10 child views and is still considered to only return one view itself, so the some View protocol is satisfied. If you need more than 10 children, you can nest VStacks inside each other to add even more views.

The VStack, as you might imagine, will stack all of its children vertically, but you can also set an optional alignment and spacing within the VStack initializer too.

Alignment

By default, everything in the VStack is center-aligned, but if you want all of its child views aligned to the leading edge or trailing edge, you can use the alignment parameter like this:

```
struct ContentView: View {
    var body: some View {
```

```
    VStack(alignment: .leading) {
  Text("Hi, I'm child one in this vertical stack")
  Text("Hi, I'm child two in this vertical stack")
  Text("Hi, I'm child three in this vertical stack")
  Text("Hi, I'm child four in this vertical stack, I'm the
    best")
    }
}}
```

All the child views are now aligned to the leading edge within the `VStack`:

Figure 1.6: Leading alignment

You can also align the views to the trailing edge or the center. To do that, we use dot syntax to access those other enumeration values: .leading, .trailing, or .center are the options available for alignment.

Spacing

The other parameter inside the VStack is the spacing option. This will put some space between all the child views:

```
struct ContentView: View {
    var body: some View {
        VStack(alignment: .leading, spacing: 10) {
            Text("Hi, I'm child one in this vertical stack")
            Text("Hi, I'm child two in this vertical stack")
            Text("Hi, I'm child three in this vertical stack")
            Text("Hi, I'm child four in this vertical stack,
                I'm the best")
        }
    }
}
```

The code puts 10 points of space between each child view, as we can see here:

Figure 1.7: VStack spacing

That's how the VStack works; let's continue and look at the HStack now.

HStack

In contrast to a VStack, an **HStack** displays its children horizontally. Here's an example:

```
struct ContentView: View {
    var body: some View {
        HStack() {
            Text("0")
            Text("1")
            Text("2")
            Text("3")
            Text("4")
            Text("5")
            Text("6")
            Text("7")
            Text("8")
            Text("9")
        }.font(.headline)
    }
}
```

The number views are now all stacked horizontally:

Figure 1.8: HStack

Adding a font modifier to the entire parent stack will affect all the children inside it, but to affect an individual child view, you need to place the modifier on it directly. Here is an example of doing that:

```
struct ContentView: View {
    var body: some View {
        HStack() {
            Text("0")
            Text("1")
            Text("2")
            Text("3")
            Text("4").font(.title)
```

```
            Text("5")
            Text("6")
            Text("7")
            Text("8")
            Text("9")
        }.font(.headline)
    }
}
```

As a result, the Text view number of 4 has now been altered to have a larger font:

Figure 1.9: Modifying the child

Let's look at another important stack, the ZStack.

ZStack

A **ZStack** is a stack that will overlay its children, one on top of another. With this stack, we can create a hierarchy of views, where the first view in the stack will be placed at the bottom, and subsequent views will be stacked up on top of each other in sequential order. Take a look at this example:

```
struct ContentView: View {
    var body: some View {
        ZStack() {
            Image(systemName: "rectangle.inset.filled.and.
                person.filled")
                .renderingMode(.original)
                .resizable()
                .frame(width: 350, height: 250)

            Text("SwiftUI")
                .font(.system(size: 50))
                .foregroundColor(.yellow)
                .padding(.trailing, 80)
        }
    }
}
```

The code contains two views:

- The first is the Image view, which accepts images that you have imported into the Assets catalog, and makes it possible to display the images on the screen. By using the systemName parameter, we can choose a system image from Apple's stock of pre-made images, from many different categories.

  To use a system image in your projects, download the **SF Symbols** app – this is free from Apple and contains thousands of images to use in Xcode from your developer portal. Simply look through the app, pick one, copy its name, and paste it into the Image parameter called systemName. For my example, I've used an image called rectangle.inset.filled. and.person.filled and have placed it at the beginning of the ZStack; any view added underneath it will be placed on top of that image.

- The second view is a Text view, placed on top of the system image by the ZStack. Again, because the code for the Text view is added under the code that creates the Image view, it is placed on top of the Image view when we run the app.

Then, I use a little bit of padding, and we can position that text where we want it. You can also use the `offset` modifier to place views anywhere on the screen.

You can see the result of the code in the following figure:

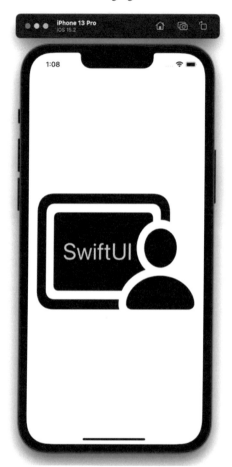

Figure 1.10: ZStack

There are also three modifiers in this code that we will look at in more depth when we start building the projects – that's the `renderingMode`, `resizable`, and `frame` modifiers. They are used here because we need to render and resize the image correctly.

Combining stacks

Now that we have seen how the three stacks can be used to display multiple views and position them where we want them on the screen, let's look at an example that combines all three stacks, and the child views inside them, to produce a varied layout:

```
struct ContentView: View {
    var body: some View {
        VStack {
            ZStack() {
                Image(systemName: "cloud.moon.rain.fill")
                    .foregroundColor(Color(.systemOrange))
                    .font(.system (size: 150))
                Text("Stormy").bold()
                    .font(.system(size: 30))
                    .offset(x: -15, y: -5)
                    .foregroundColor(.indigo)
            }
            HStack() {
                Image(systemName: "tornado")
                    .foregroundColor(Color(.systemBlue))
                    .font(.system (size: 50))

                VStack(alignment: .leading) {
                    Text("Be prepared for anything")
                        .font(.system(size: 25))
                        .fontWeight(.bold)

                    Text("With the Stormy Weather app")
                        .font(.system(size: 16))
                }
            }
        }
    }
}
```

Let's break down this code to get a clear understanding of what we are doing.

First is the VStack. This will be our main stack and will hold all of our code. Using the VStack in this way means we can squeeze 10 child views inside it, but we only need to place a couple of views inside for this example.

Next is the ZStack. Inside are its two child views – a Text view and an Image view. Since the Image view comes first in the code, the Text view gets placed on top of it.

Notice how each child view in the ZStack has its own set of modifiers that are indented; these are to style these child views with colors and sizes and to position them on the screen.

The next stack is the HStack. Remember that this arranges its children horizontally, and it has two child views, including an Image view and VStack. Notice how we can nest stacks inside of other stacks as we are doing here, with this VStack inside of a HStack. The HStack places its first child view to the left – that's the tornado image – and then places its second child view to the right – that's the VStack. If we look inside the VStack now, it has two child views of its own. They will be placed vertically, with the smaller text on the bottom.

Don't worry if this nesting of stacks seems a bit confusing at first; as we start building projects, you will train your brain to think and see in hierarchies, and this will become very natural to you.

By nesting the different stacks, we can make all kinds of interesting layout scenes. Here is the result of our example:

Figure 1.11: Combining and nesting stacks

Stacks are great for helping to organize and lay our views out on the screen, but there is another container view we can use that offers even more flexibility. That's the GeometryReader view. However, we will look at that at the end of the chapter.

For now, let's look at a Spacer view – this is a view that helps with spacing out the layout in our UI design.

Spacer views

A **Spacer view** does exactly what its name says: it creates space between your views by pushing other components to the edges of a container or helps fill empty space between components. For example, when placed within a HStack, a Spacer view expands horizontally as much as the stack allows, moving sibling views out of the way within the limits of the stack's size.

This is the Spacer initializer: Spacer(minLength: CGFloat). This initializer creates a flexible space. The minLength argument sets the minimum size that the space can take. If the argument is left empty, the minimum length is zero.

Here's an example of using a Spacer view in a HStack:

```
struct ContentView: View {
    var body: some View {
        HStack {
            Text("Hello")
            Spacer()
            Text("World")
        }.padding()
    }
}
```

This will create a horizontal stack with **Hello** on the left, **World** on the right, and a flexible space in between. The Spacer view will take up all of the remaining space so that the two pieces of text are pushed to the edges of the container:

Figure 1.12: Spacer

The Spacer view can also be used in the VStack, and it will expand and push the child views apart vertically instead of horizontally. The Spacer view won't do anything within the ZStack though, as that stack deals with the depth of a view on the z-axis, front to back.

Where `Spacer` separates views by creating space between them, another object called a `Divider` view separates views with a thin line, either vertically or horizontally.

Divider views

A **Divider view** is a visual element, a dividing line, that can be used to separate content either horizontally or vertically. You can also alter the divider's thickness. Let's look at some examples.

Horizontal

The following code creates a horizontal divider:

```
struct ContentView: View {
    var body: some View {
        VStack(alignment: .leading, spacing: 10) {
            Text("Hi, I'm child one in this vertical stack")
            Text("Hi, I'm child two in this vertical stack")
            Text("Hi, I'm child three in this vertical stack")
            Text("Hi, I'm child four in this vertical stack")
            Divider().background(Color.black)

            Text("Hi, I'm child five in this vertical stack")
            Text("Hi, I'm child six in this vertical stack")
            Text("Hi, I'm child seven in this vertical stack")
            Text("Hi, I'm child eight in this vertical stack")
        }.padding()
    }
}
```

As you can see, we have added a horizontal dividing line and set its color to black using the `background` modifier:

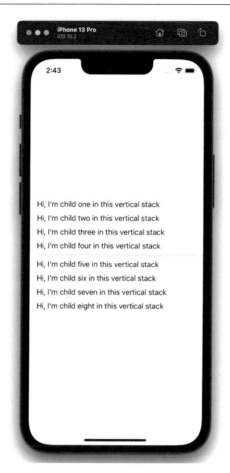

Figure 1.13: Divider

Vertical

If we want to change the horizontal line to a vertical one, then we can pass the `width` parameter using a smaller number, and the `height` parameter using a larger number, as in this example:

```
struct ContentView: View {
    var body: some View {
        VStack(alignment: .leading, spacing: 10) {
            Text("Hi, I'm child one in this vertical stack")
            Text("Hi, I'm child two in this vertical stack")
            Text("Hi, I'm child three in this vertical stack")
            Text("Hi, I'm child four in this vertical stack")
```

```
        Divider().frame(height: 200).frame(width:
          3).background(Color.blue)
        Divider().frame(height:200).frame(width:
          3).background(Color.blue).offset(x: 300, y: 0)

        Text("Hi, I'm child five in this vertical stack")
        Text("Hi, I'm child six in this vertical stack")
        Text("Hi, I'm child seven in this vertical stack")
        Text("Hi, I'm child eight in this vertical stack")
      }.padding()
    }
  }
```

Using the `offset` modifier lets us place the line anywhere on the screen, or on any view for that matter. Here is the result:

Figure 1.14: Vertical Divider view

Thickness

We can change the thickness of the dividing line using the `frame` modifier, like so:

```
struct ContentView: View {
    var body: some View {
        VStack(alignment: .leading, spacing: 10) {
            Text("Hi, I'm child one in this vertical stack")
            Text("Hi, I'm child two in this vertical stack")
            Text("Hi, I'm child three in this vertical stack")
            Text("Hi, I'm child four in this vertical stack")
            Divider().frame(height: 20).frame(width: 300).
                background(Color.blue)

            Text("Hi, I'm child five in this vertical stack")
            Text("Hi, I'm child six in this vertical stack")
            Text("Hi, I'm child seven in this vertical stack")
            Text("Hi, I'm child eight in this vertical stack")
        }.padding()
    }
}
```

Then, by using the `height` and `width` parameters of the `frame` modifier, we can change the dimensions of the `Divider` view, so we can make a line as long and wide as we want. The result of our example can be seen here:

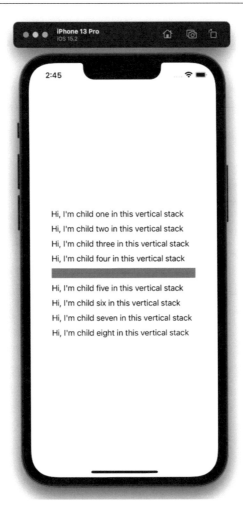

Figure 1.15: Divider thickness

That's pretty much all the configuring we can do with the `Divider` view. Let's now look at one of the most frequently used modifiers in SwiftUI – the `padding` modifier.

The padding modifier

You may have noticed that we have used the **padding modifier** quite a bit already without really explaining it yet.

Every view has its own dimensions and space that it takes up on the screen. For example, we can place two views side by side and they will be very close to each other, separated by only a few points.

Points and pixels refer to different ways of measuring the size of the views on the screen.

Points are used to specify the size of text and other UI elements, and they are independent of the resolution of the device's screen. This means that a point will always be the same size on any device, regardless of the screen's resolution.

Pixels, on the other hand, are the individual dots that make up the screen of an iPhone (or any other device). Pixels are used to measure the physical resolution of a device's screen.

When you add a `padding` modifier to a view, it adds a small amount of empty space all around that view by default, and that space is measured in points. The `padding` modifier by default adds eight points of empty space around a view, but if you want to be more specific about the amount of space with which to pad your view, then you can pass in a value (an integer) for a custom amount of padding. Let's look at an example:

```
struct ContentView: View {
    var body: some View {
        VStack{
            VStack(alignment: .leading, spacing: 10) {
                Text("There is padding all around this view")
                Text("There is padding all around this view")
                Text("There is padding all around this view")
                Text("There is padding all around this view")

            }.background(Color.yellow)
                .padding(30)
                .background(Color.red)
        }
    }
}
```

In this code, there are four `Text` views inside the `VStack`. At the end of the VStack's closing brace is a call to the `background` modifier, which will color the background yellow so that you can see the `padding` modifier at work. Next, I added the `padding` modifier and passed in 30 points, which will be applied around the `VStack` equally. Finally, I colored the padding red, again, using the `background` modifier, so you can see the padding directly. In the example, the padding will look like a red frame around `VStack`, as shown in the following screenshot:

Figure 1.16: Padding

Let's look at some of the other `padding` options. The modifier allows us to choose from predefined enum values if we only want to pad one side, as in the following code:

```
struct ContentView: View {
    var body: some View {
        VStack{
            VStack(alignment: .leading, spacing: 10) {
                Text("The leading edge has been padded")
```

```
        }.padding(.leading, 75)
    }
}
}
```

This code pads only the `leading` edge of each `Text` view by 75 points of space:

Figure 1.17: Padding options

We can also choose other padding options by typing in a dot for the `alignment` parameter and selecting from many different options, including `trailing`, `top`, `bottom`, `horizontal`, `infinity`, and others.

Looking at the previous code, notice the placement of the `padding` modifier; it has been put on the closing brace of the `VStack`. When placed like this, all the children inside the `VStack` have the padding applied to them, but if we want to pad the child views individually, we can do so by placing modifiers directly on them:

```
struct ContentView: View {
    var body: some View {
        VStack{
            VStack(alignment: .leading, spacing: 10) {
                Text("I'm padded on the leading edge").padding
                    (.leading, 75)
                Text("I'm padded on the trailing edge").padding
                    (.trailing, 75)
                Text("I'm padded on the leading edge").padding
                    (.leading, 75)
                Text("I'm padded on the trailing edge").padding
                    (.trailing, 75)
                Text("I'm padded on the leading edge").padding
                    (.leading, 75)
                Text("I'm padded on the trailing edge").padding
                    (.trailing, 75)
                Text("I'm padded on the leading edge").padding
                    (.leading, 75)
                Text("I'm padded on the trailing edge").padding
                    (.trailing, 75)
            }
        }
    }
}
```

As you can see, you can add modifiers to child views individually, styling them as you need for your layout. The result is as follows:

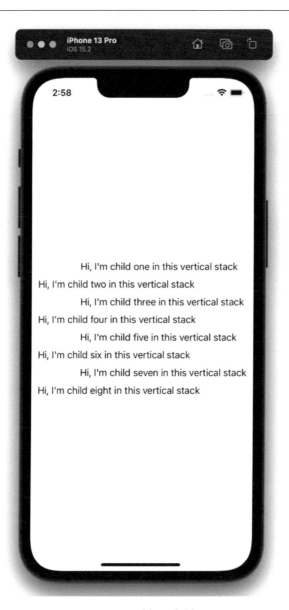

Figure 1.18: Padding children

Each child view now has its own padding, either `leading` or `trailing`, which alters its placement on the screen.

Let's finish up this chapter by looking at closures, which is essentially a function without a name, and then another container view that offers some more flexibility than the other stacks we previously looked at – the `GeometryReader` view.

Closures

Here is the easy definition of a **closure**: a closure is a function without a name. Remember a function is a block of code that runs whatever code statements are in its body when it is called.

But let's look at a more detailed definition of a closure: a closure is a self-contained block of code that can be passed around and executed at a later time.

Closures are not exactly functions, but they are similar, with some key differences:

- Closures can be stored as variables and passed as arguments to functions
- Closures can capture and store references to any variables or constants from the context in which they are defined, which allows them to maintain the state and preserve data between invocations
- Closures don't have a name as a function would

In SwiftUI, closures are often used as a way to respond to user input or other events. For example, you might use a closure as the action for a button, or to provide a block of code to be executed when a view appears or disappears.

Here's an example of a closure being used as the action for a button in SwiftUI:

```
Button(action: {
    // this block of code will be run when the button is
      clicked
    print("Button was clicked!")
}) {
    Text("Button")
}
```

In this example, the closure is defined using the { } syntax and is passed as the `action` parameter to the `Button` view. Yes, that's right, the `Button` action is a closure, and when the button is pressed, the code inside the closure will be executed.

Closures can also be used to provide custom behavior for views in SwiftUI. For example, you might use a closure to perform some custom animation when a view appears or disappears:

```
struct MyView: View {
    var body: some View {
        Text("Hello, SwiftUI!")
            .onAppear {
                // this block of code will run when the view
                  appears
                print("The view appeared!")
```

```
        }
      }
  }
```

In this example, the onAppear modifier is called on the Text view and is passed a closure that will be executed when the view appears on the screen.

We also have trailing closures. A trailing closure is a closure that is written after the function or method it is passed to. The closure is "trailing" because it comes after the function or method.

Here's an example of a function that takes a closure as an argument:

```
func doSomething(completion: () -> Void) {
    // Do some work!
    print("Work complete")
    completion()
}
```

Here's how you would call this function and pass a closure as an argument:

```
doSomething {
    // this block of code will run when the "completion"
      closure is called
    print("completion closure called!")
}
```

In this example, the closure is written after the doSomething function and is therefore a trailing closure. In SwiftUI, you can use trailing closures to provide custom behavior for views. For example, you might use a trailing closure to perform some custom animation when a view appears or disappears:

```
Text("Hello, World!")
    .onAppear {
        // this block of code will be executed when the view
          appears
        print("View appeared!")
    }
```

In this example, the onAppear method is called on the Text view and is passed a trailing closure that will be executed when the view appears on the screen.

Don't worry if you haven't quite grasped how closures work yet; they are not as complicated as they appear, and you will understand them better as we progress throughout the book. For now, let's move on to GeometryReader.

GeometryReader

The **GeometryReader view** is another container view that offers more flexibility than the other stacks we previously looked at. The closure (function) of `GeometryReader` will contain the position and size of the view we are working with, and we can then alter or place that view however we want with the values that are returned by `GeometryReader`'s proxy.

Using these values, we can make the child views dynamically update their position depending on the device size and position when the orientation changes to either landscape or portrait. This all will become clearer when we see an example.

Let's look at how to create `GeometryReader`. The following is the initializer used to create the `GeometryReader` view:

```
GeometryReader(content: _)
```

The `content` parameter is a closure that receives a geometry proxy value with the view's position and dimensions.

To retrieve those values, we use the following properties and method:

- The `size` property will return the width and height of the `GeometryReader` view
- The `safeAreaInsets` property will return an `EdgeInsets` value with the insets for the safe area
- The `frame(in: )` method returns the position and size of the `GeometryReader` view

Here is the code to create an empty `GeometryReader`:

```
struct ContentView: View {
    var body: some View {
        GeometryReader {_ in
          //empty geometry reader
        }.background(Color.yellow)
    }
}
```

This is what we see when we run the code. Notice how it pushes itself out to occupy all the space on the screen; the yellow background shows all the areas of this empty `GeometryReader`, which is the entire screen.

Figure 1.19: GeometryReader

The default behavior of `GeometryReader` is to align its children in the upper-left corner and place them on top of each other. In this next example, the code places three views inside `GeometryReader`:

```
struct ContentView: View {
    var body: some View {
        GeometryReader {_ in
            Image(systemName: "tornado")
```

```
            Image(systemName: "tornado")
            Image(systemName: "tornado")
              }.background(Color.yellow)
            .font(.largeTitle)
      }
  }
```

When we run this code, notice that only one tornado image is visible:

Figure 1.20: GeometryReader default child alignment

There are actually three tornado images in this example, but you can only see one because the default behavior is to place them on top of each other in the upper-left corner.

We obviously don't want all the child views stacked on one another, so we will explore the following concepts to really utilize `GeometryReader`:

- Sizing a view to accommodate rotating the device

- Positioning a view anywhere on the screen

- Reading a view's position in terms of its global and local space

We'll look at these now.

Sizing views

Let's first look at the property that is used to access the `GeometryReader`'s size... aptly named, the `size` property. This will return the width and height of the `GeometryReader` view.

Here is an example of adding an image inside the `GeometryReader` view, and seeing how it adapts its size when the device is rotated:

```
struct ContentView: View {
    var body: some View
  GeometryReader { geometryProxy in
            Image("swiftui_icon")
                .resizable()
                .scaledToFit()
                .frame(width: geometryProxy.size.width / 2,
                    height: geometryProxy.size.height / 4)
                .background(Color.gray)
        }
    }
}
```

The following figure shows the size of the image in portrait mode:

Figure 1.21: GeometryReader size property (portrait)

In portrait mode, the image is bigger, but when the device is rotated to landscape, the image scales down to adapt to the screen change, as shown here:

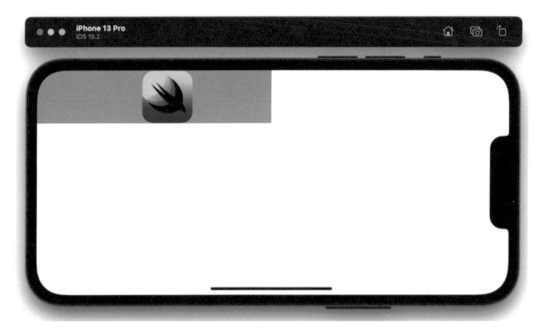

Figure 1.22: GeometryReader size property (landscape)

In this example, we added an `Image` view within a `GeometryReader` view. I defined the `Proxy` parameter as `geometryProxy`, but you can call it anything you want. `geometryProxy` holds the information about `GeometryReader`'s dimensions and position. Using this `Proxy` object, the size of the image is changed when we rotate the device. The image will be half the width of the container, and the height will be a quarter of the height of the container.

Using `geometryProxy.size` lets us access the height and width of `GeometryReader`. The `Image` view will adapt when the device is rotated. I'm also using the `scaledToFit` modifier so that we can keep the correct aspect ratio for the image.

I set the `Image` view's background to gray so that you can see the space that's available in both portrait and landscape modes. When it's in landscape mode, there's much more space available around the `Image` view because it scales down.

Also notice that the image is positioned in the top-left corner of the `GeometryReader` view. Again, that's the default location for its child views; they will simply stack up on each other in that area.

Next, we will look at positioning those child views anywhere we want within the `GeometryReader` container.

Positioning views

We've seen how GeometryReader can dynamically change the size of a view as it's rotated, but it can also position the views within it. The positioning information is returned by the geometryProxy closure, and we can pass that information into the x and y parameters of the position modifier via the size property. Here's an example:

```
struct ContentView: View {
    var body: some View {

GeometryReader { geometryProxy in
            //top right position
            VStack {
                Image(systemName: "tornado")
                .imageScale(.large)
            Text("Top Right")
                .font(.title)
            }.position(x: geometryProxy.size.width - 80, y:
              geometryProxy.size.height / 40)

            //bottom left position
            VStack {
                Image(systemName: "tornado")
                .imageScale(.large)

            Text("Bottom Left")
                .font(.title)
            }.position(x: geometryProxy.size.width - 300,y:
              geometryProxy.size.height - 40)
        }.background(Color.accentColor)
        .foregroundColor(.white)

    }
}
```

The code here has two VStacks within GeometryReader, and each VStack has the position modifier on its closing brace, so everything within the VStacks will be positioned according to the values in the position modifier's x and y parameters.

The result when running this code is the placement of the Image and Text views according to the size.width and size.height values, as shown in this figure:

Figure 1.23: GeometryReader positioning views

Let's continue with `GeometryReader` and see how we can read the values of its position.

Reading the position

If we need to get the position of the `GeometryReader` view in terms of its `coordinate` location, again, we can use the `geometryProxy` object and pass its information into the `frame()` method.

There are two coordinate spaces in SwiftUI:

- **Global space**: The coordinates of the entire screen
- **Local space**: The coordinates of individual views

When reading the values of the local coordinate space of the `GeometryReader` view, we will always see 0,0 for x and y. That's because `GeometryReader` always starts at that position, 0,0, the top-left corner of the screen.

So, to get the position of the views in relation to where they are on the screen, we need to use the global coordinates. Here is an example that gets and displays the local and global values for the `GeometryReader` view:

```
struct ContentView: View {
    var body: some View {
        GeometryReader { geometryProxy in
            VStack {
                Image("SwiftUIIcon")
                    .resizable()
                    .scaledToFit()
                Text("Global").font(.title)
                Text("X, Y \(geometryProxy.frame(in:
                    CoordinateSpace.global).origin.x, specifier:
                    "(%.f,") \(geometryProxy.frame(in: .global).
                    origin.y, specifier: "%.f)")")
                Text("Local").font(.title)
                Text("X, Y  \(geometryProxy.frame(in: .local).
                    origin.x, specifier: "(%.f") \(geometryProxy.
                    frame(in: .local).origin.y, specifier:
                    "%.f)")")
            }
        }.frame(height: 250)
    }
}
```

> **Note**
> Notice that the values are being formatted using a format specifier: %.f. This format specifier will truncate some of the decimal places so it displays fewer zeros.

Running the code will display the x and y coordinate values for both the global and local space for the views, when the device is in portrait mode, as shown here:

Figure 1.24: Reading the position (portrait)

Rotating the device into landscape mode changes the global values to reflect the new location of the Image and Text views, as shown here:

Figure 1.25: Reading the position (landscape)

The code in this example demonstrates the difference between the global and local coordinate spaces. The values for the local coordinate space always return 0, 0 because that is the starting position of `GeometryReader`, but the values for the global coordinate space are the origin of the `geometryProxy` frame within the entire screen. So, the global values change as the device is rotated because the view's position has changed. The local values do not change as they reflect the screen's upper-left corner, 0, 0.

SwiftUI also offers properties to get the minimum, middle, and maximum coordinate positions from within `GeometryReader`'s frame for both the global and local spaces:

```
Text("minX: \(geometryProxy.frame(in: .local).minX))")
Text("minX: \(geometryProxy.frame(in: .local).midX))")
Text("maxX: \(geometryProxy.frame(in: .local).maxX))")
Text("minX: \(geometryProxy.frame(in: .global).minY))")
Text("minX: \(geometryProxy.frame(in: .global).midY))")
Text("maxX: \(geometryProxy.frame(in: .global).maxY))")
```

We use these properties with dot syntax, right at the end of the `frame` method. Here is an example:

```
struct ContentView: View {
    var body: some View {
        GeometryReader { geometryProxy in
            VStack() {
                Spacer()
                Text("Local Values").font(.title2).bold()
                HStack() {
                    Text("minX: \(Int(geometryProxy.frame(in:
                        .local).minX))")
                    Spacer()
                    Text("midX: \(Int(geometryProxy.frame(in:
                        .local).midX))")
                    Spacer()
                    Text("maxX: \(Int(geometryProxy.frame(in:
                        .local).maxX))")
                }

                Divider().background(Color.black)

                Text("Global Values").font(.title2).bold()
                HStack() {
                    Text("minX: \(Int(geometryProxy.frame(in:
                        .global).minX))")
                    Spacer()
                    Text("midX: \(Int(geometryProxy.frame(in:
                        .global).midX))")
                    Spacer()
                    Text("maxX: \(Int(geometryProxy.frame(in:
                        .global).maxX))")
                }
                Spacer()

            }.padding(.horizontal)
        }
    }
}
```

This code will return the minimum, the middle, and the maximum x and y coordinates for `GeometryReader`'s frame and display them on the screen for both local and global spaces in portrait mode, as shown here:

Figure 1.26: Using the min, mid, and max properties (portrait)

When the device is rotated, those values will adjust to new values that reflect the change in the screen's orientation, as shown here:

Figure 1.27: Using the min, mid, and max properties (landscape)

The SwiftUI structures you have just learned about will be the building blocks for the programs we will write going forward. Rather than listing all the structures in one chapter, which can be a lot to take in, I will introduce new ones in different projects throughout the book.

Summary

To sum up what we learned in this chapter, we introduced SwiftUI and saw the difference between the two programming paradigms, imperative and declarative. After that, we explored the Xcode interface. Then, we covered the important function of the state, and finally looked at the building blocks of SwiftUI – these are fundamentals that you will use throughout this book and are an essential first step toward creating beautiful animations in SwiftUI.

In the next chapter, we will explore animations, how they work, and the kinds of properties that can be animated.

2

Understanding Animation with SwiftUI

In the first chapter, we covered many SwiftUI fundamentals we will see when we start building projects. In this chapter, we will look at how animations work, including timing curves and animatable properties, which will lay the foundation for the projects we build.

The following are the key topics we will explore:

- What is animation?
- Understanding timing curves
- Understanding animation types
- Triggering animations
- Exploring animatable properties

Technical requirements

You can find the code for this chapter on GitHub in the `Chapter 2` folder: `https://github.com/PacktPublishing/Animating-SwiftUI-Applications`.

What is animation?

Let's consider the book's definition of animation. **Animation** is a series of static images displayed in rapid succession to create the illusion of motion. The images, or frames, are usually displayed at a rate of 24 or 30 frames per second from the beginning to the end, which is fast enough to create the illusion of continuous motion. These can be created using a variety of techniques, including hand-drawn, computer-generated, and stop-motion animations.

Looking at this definition, we can see that there is a start point and an end point to animation, and the images in between are all slightly different; when played, our eyes cannot pick out the individual images, which means we perceive movement or animation.

In SwiftUI, we have to define the start point (where the animation begins) and the end point (where the animation ends). However, when we code, we don't actually put a bunch of still images between both end points (though we can); what we usually do is use a single image and then animate the properties of that image, such as its location on the screen, its opacity, or its color.

In addition to images, we can also animate RGB colors by changing their hue or the corner radius of shapes, and if we draw a shape, we can animate the individual lines (paths) or the strokes around it.

It works like this: if we want a rectangle to move from the bottom left to the top right of the iPhone or iPad screen, we declare it in code (that declarative syntax thing again) by using the `animation` modifier. Then SwiftUI does the magic for us, moving the object, or in SwiftUI speak, "transitioning" the object from a start point to an end point, filling in all the gaps along the way with whatever values we are working with (integers, colors, opacity, etc.). The process of going through all the values to create a smooth fluid motion is called **interpolation**.

SwiftUI fills in those gaps for us really well, but it cannot animate every property of every view. Only properties considered "animatable" can be animated; things such as a view's color, opacity, rotation, size, position, corner radius, and strokes. Nearly all properties that have a numerical value are animatable.

SwiftUI includes basic animations with default or custom easing or timing curves (a timing curve refers to the speed at the start and end of the animation), as well as spring animations. Spring animations have a bouncy effect to them and can be adjusted from a slight bounce to a very pronounced bounce, similar to a rubber ball bouncing on the floor.

You can also change many customization options, such as the speed of an animation, add a "wait" time before the animation starts, and have an animation repeat itself.

Let's continue by diving deeper into animation timing curves, seeing what they look like and how they affect an animation.

Understanding timing curves

Animations have what are called curves. A **curve**, or more specifically, a **timing curve**, refers to the speed at which the animation starts and how it should end.

SwiftUI provides several timing curves to choose from that we can use inside the `animation` modifier. It's called a timing curve because if you were to plot each point of the animation's movement from start to finish on a graph, and draw a line by connecting those points, most of them would create a curved line, as in this illustration:

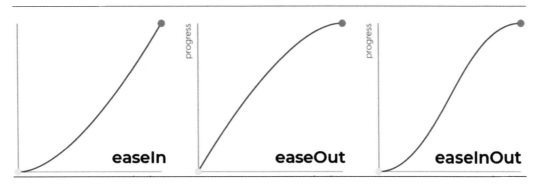

Figure 2.1: The ease timing curves

This graph shows three animation timing curves: **easeIn**, **easeOut**, and **easeInOut**. The beginning of the animation is at the bottom left, and the end is at the top right. In the `easeInOut` timing curve, the animation starts slow, speeds up, and then finally slows down before coming to a complete stop.

There is also a linear timing curve. An animation using this curve will have the same rate of speed at its beginning as it does at its end. If you were to plot it on a graph, it would be a straight line, like so:

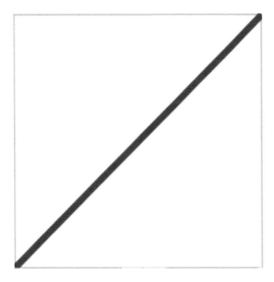

Figure 2.2: The linear timing curve

Timing curves are not complicated – we get to choose the ones we want based on how we want the animation to look and perform. If you don't specify a timing curve, you will get the default curve, the `easeInOut` one. We will use some of these SwiftUI-provided timing curves in our projects.

In the next section, I want to explain the two distinct types of animation in SWiftUI: implicit and explicit.

Understanding animation types

There are two types of animations in SwiftUI: implicit and explicit. Let's look at what these animation types do and the difference between the two.

An **implicit animation** is an animation that is automatically applied to a property when its value is changed. In SwiftUI, implicit animations are created using the .animation modifier. Here is an example:

```
struct ContentView: View {
    @State private var grow: CGFloat = 1
    var body: some View {
        Circle()
            .frame(width: 100, height: 100)
            .foregroundColor(.blue)
            .onTapGesture {
                self.grow += 0.5
            }
            .scaleEffect(grow)
            .animation(.default, value: grow)
    }
}
```

In this example, we use a tap gesture to scale up the size of a circle; when tapped, the circle will grow by half its size. The .animation modifier uses the default animation style, which will animate the circle using an easeInOut timing curve by default.

You can also use other animation styles. For example, here, I added a spring style instead of the default style:

```
var body: some View {
        Circle()
• • • • • • • •
                .scaleEffect(grow)
                .animation(.spring(dampingFraction:
0.3,blendDuration: 0.5),value: grow)
    }
```

This style will animate the circle and add a springy effect to it.

So implicit animations are a convenient way to add basic animations to your SwiftUI app without having to write any explicit animation code. The animations are applied using the `animation` modifier.

Sometimes though, you may want more from your animation, and implicit animations may not give you the degree of control that you are looking for. In this case, you can use explicit animations instead.

An **explicit animation** is an animation you create and add inside the code block using the `withAnimation` function. Here's an example:

```
struct ContentView: View {
    @State private var scaleUp: CGFloat = 1
    var body: some View {
        Button(action: {
            //Animate the scale of the view when the button is
                tapped
            withAnimation(.interpolatingSpring(stiffness: 60,
                damping: 2)) {
                scaleUp *= 1.4
            }
        }) {
            Text("Scale up")
                .scaleEffect(scaleUp)  // explicit animation
        }
    }
}
```

In this example, tapping the button will animate the scale of the text using a spring animation. The duration of the animation will be determined by the system's default animation settings, but the curve of the animation will be customized using the `interpolatingSpring` function.

Additionally, you can customize the duration of the animation by specifying a `duration` parameter in the `interpolatingSpring` function. The following is an example of this:

```
withAnimation(.interpolatingSpring(stiffness: 60, damping: 2,
duration: 2.5)) { scaleUp *= 1.5 }
```

This will cause the animation to last for 2.5 seconds.

So, the difference when using explicit animations versus implicit animations is that they can give you more control over the details of the animation, or when you want to animate multiple properties simultaneously; you can put as much code into the `withAnimation` block as needed. However, they can be more work to set up than implicit animations.

You can also have the animation repeat itself a pre-set number of times or indefinitely. Here's an example of repeating the previous animation forever and auto-reversing it:

```
withAnimation(.interpolatingSpring(stiffness: 60, damping:
2).repeatForever(autoreverses: true)) {
                    scaleUp *= 1.4
        }
```

In the previous example, I altered the code in the `withAnimation` function to include the `repeatForever` option and set the `autoreverses` parameter to `true`. When you run the code, the text will scale up with a springy effect, and when it's done bouncing (about 3 seconds or so), the animation will start over, repeating endlessly or until the app is stopped.

Those are the two types of animations; next is a list of ways to trigger animations.

Triggering animations

So, how do we trigger animations? There are several ways to do so in SwiftUI, including using the following SwiftUI modifiers, methods, and functions:

- The `.animation()` modifier: This modifier allows you to specify the type of animation used when a view appears or disappears or when its state changes.
- The `withAnimation()` function: This function allows you to wrap a block of code that changes the state of a view, and it will automatically animate the changes.
- A **gesture**: This is a way to interact with a view by performing actions such as tapping, dragging, or pinching. You can use a gesture to trigger an animation when a certain action is performed on a view.
- A **timer**: This allows you to specify an animation to be performed over a certain period of time. You can use a timer to animate the changes to a view's state over a specific duration.
- The `onAppear()` and `onDisappear()` modifiers: These modifiers allow you to specify code to be executed when a view appears or disappears. These modifiers can trigger an animation when a view appears or disappears.
- Button and other control views: A button, slider, picker, or other control type view in SwiftUI can be a trigger for an animation.

There are other ways to trigger animations, but these are the main ones that we will cover here. Whatever you choose will depend on the specific needs of your app and the behavior you want to produce. We will explore these different triggers when we start building our projects in the coming chapters.

Let's continue by looking at various properties that can be animated in SwiftUI.

Exploring animatable properties

In this section, we will explore some of the animatable properties. Here is a list of the ones that we will look at:

- Offset
- Hue rotation
- Opacity
- Scale
- Stroke
- Trim
- Corner radius

Let's take a look at them in more detail.

The offset property

The first property we will look at that is animatable is the **offset** property. This property is responsible for offsetting a view on the *x*- and *y*-axes, basically giving you control to place that view anywhere on the screen. The following is an example of animating the `offset` modifier that has been placed on a rectangle shape:

```
struct Offset_Example: View {
    @State private var moveRight = false
    var body: some View {
        //MARK: - ANIMATE OFFSET
        VStack {
            RoundedRectangle(cornerRadius: 20)
                .foregroundColor(.blue)
                .frame(width: 75, height: 75)
                .offset(x: moveRight ? 150 : 0, y: 350 )
                .animation(Animation.default, value: moveRight)
            Spacer()
            Button("Animate") {
                moveRight.toggle()
            }.font(.title2)
        }
    }
}
```

After you put that code into your `ContentView` file, your preview will look like *Figure 2.3*. When you press the **Animate** button, the blue rectangle will move to the right, and when you press it again, it will return to its original starting position.

Figure 2.3: Animating the offset

This is how the code works. When the **Animate** button is pressed, the `moveRight` variable has its value toggled or changed to `true`, and the `offset` modifier has a ternary operator in there for its x parameter.

A ternary operator is an operator that accepts a Boolean variable and checks to see whether it's `true` or `false`. If the variable is `true`, the value to the left of the colon is used, but if the variable is `false`, the value to the right of the colon is used. This makes it similar to an if statement but different because an `if` statement can check for multiple conditions.

So, if `moveRight` is `true`, then the rounded rectangle is placed `150` points to the right; otherwise, if `false`, it is left where it is (the `0` value means do nothing). The `animation` modifier also picks up on any change because it has the `moveRight` variable in there for the `value` parameter. This `value` parameter takes the variable that you are using for the animation. The `animation` modifier will then interpolate over the values from the start to the finish point and move the object smoothly, creating a nice, fluid animation.

Here's a way to really see how the `animation` modifier is working. If you comment out the `animation` statement in the code and press the button, you will see that the object still moves 150 points to the right, but it does so instantly; there is no gliding across the screen now; the object just appears at its new location 150 points to the right. To create smooth, fluid animations, we need that `animation` modifier and its behind-the-scenes interpolating magic. This is part of the reason why we use less code in SwiftUI versus coding animation in UIKit; much of the heavy lifting is already done for us in the background with SwiftUI.

This was an example of animating an object from one point to another by changing the numerical value for the x parameter in the `offset` modifier. Let's look at another property that's animatable: `HueRotation`.

Hue rotation

Hue rotation is a type of color effect that can be applied to views and other components. It's a modifier that allows you to adjust the hue of a color by adding or subtracting a fixed angle from its hue value. You can use hue rotation to create a range of related colors.

The modifier has an `angle` parameter that takes a value in radians or degrees. That value is based on a circle, which is 360 degrees and represents a wheel of all the colors that we can think of.

Let's look at an Xcode example:

```
struct Hue_Rotation_Example: View {
    @State private var hueRotate = false
        var body: some View {
        //MARK: - ANIMATE HUE ROTATION
        VStack(spacing: 20) {
            Text("ANIMATE HUE ").font(.title2).bold()
            // rotate the colors and stop halfway around the
                color wheel
            RoundedRectangle(cornerRadius: 25)
                .frame(width: 200, height: 200)
                .foregroundColor(.red)
                .hueRotation(Angle.degrees(hueRotate ? 180 :
                    0))
                .animation(.easeInOut(duration: 2), value:
                    hueRotate)
            // rotate the colors around the color wheel one
                full revolution (360 degrees)
            Divider().background(Color.black)
            Text("ANIMATE HUE WITH GRADIENT").font(.title2).
                bold()
```

```
AngularGradient(gradient: Gradient(colors: [Color.
    red, Color.blue]), center: .center)
    .hueRotation(Angle.degrees(hueRotate ? 360 :
        0))
    .animation(.easeInOut(duration: 2), value:
        hueRotate)
    .mask(Circle())
    .frame(width: 200, height: 200)
Button("Animate") {
    hueRotate.toggle()
}
    .font(.title)
        }
    }
}
```

When you add the code into Xcode, your previews will look like *Figure 2.4*:

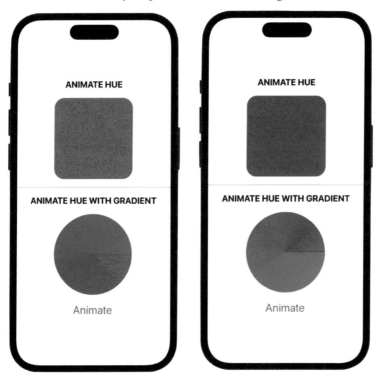

Figure 2.4: Animating the hue rotation

I created two objects in this example: a rounded rectangle and an angular gradient circle.

In the rounded rectangle, I used a ternary operator to check whether the `hueRotate` variable is `true`. When it becomes `true` via the **Animate** button being pressed, the value to the left of the colon inside the ternary operator is used, 180 degrees. Then the animation starts going through the color spectrum and stops halfway through to display that color.

Notice the use of the `duration` function just after the timing curve. This function allows us to set the duration of the animation; do we want it to happen fast, or do we want the animation to happen over a longer period? It has one parameter, and that is the amount of time we want the animation to take to complete; for that, we use an integer value. I set the value to 2, so it can slow things down a little, taking the animation 2 seconds to complete.

Looking at the angular gradient example, I'm using a value of 360 degrees. When we press the **Animate** button, the code animates through the entire color wheel and stops where it started (360 degrees is one revolution of a circle), thus displaying the original color.

Taking a look at the `hueRotate` variable inside the body of the button, we have two ways that we can start the animation. The first is by explicitly setting `hueRotate` to `true`, like this:

```
hueRotate = true
```

Or by using the `toggle` method like we're doing in the code:

```
hueRotate.toggle()
```

The difference between these two ways of starting the animation is that firstly, the animation starts and then finishes, but it never reverses itself with subsequent button presses. If you'd like the animation to start and finish, and on the next button press reverse itself, then use the `toggle` method.

What's also very interesting is that we can animate the colors of shapes and other objects, but also animate the colors that make up images, as we will see in the upcoming projects.

You can also use the `hueRotation()` modifier in combination with other modifiers, such as `brightness()` or `saturation()`, to create some complex and interesting color adjustments.

Let's continue looking at the different properties to animate and at a very common property, `opacity`.

Opacity

Opacity refers to the transparency of a view, whether you can see it clearly, whether it is partially visible, or maybe you can't see it at all. We can use the `opacity` modifier to make views appear and disappear. When we add animation to the opacity, the transition from shown to hidden is interpolated over, so it smoothly fades in and out.

Here's an example of adding opacity to an animation:

```swift
struct Opacity__Example: View {
    @State private var appear = true
    var body: some View {
//MARK: - ANIMATE OPACITY
        VStack{
            Text("Appear/Disappear")
                .font(.title).bold()
            Circle()
                .foregroundColor(.purple)
                .opacity(appear ? 1 : 0)
                .animation(.easeIn, value: appear)
                .frame(height: 175)
            Button("Animate") {
                appear.toggle()
            }.font(.title2)
//MARK: - OVERLAPPING OPACITY
            VStack{
                Text("Overlapping Opacity").bold()
                    .font(.title)
                Circle()
                    .foregroundColor(.yellow)
                    .frame(height: 100)
                    .opacity(0.5)
                Circle()
                    .foregroundColor(.red)
                    .frame(height: 100)
                    .opacity(0.5)
                    .padding(-60)
            }.padding(60)
        }
    }
}
```

The preceding code will produce the following results, as shown in *Figure 2.5*:

Figure 2.5: Animating the opacity

In our first example, the animation variable is called `appear`, and it's set to `true` as its default value, which shows the circle. When the **Animate** button is pressed, the variable gets toggled to `false`, and the circle animates itself until it completely disappears. And when the button is pressed again, the animation gets set to `true`, and the circle becomes visible again. Again, using the `animation` modifier initiates the interpolation over the start and end values, so the circle doesn't just appear or disappear instantly; there is a gradual change of state until the end of the animation is reached.

The second example of the two circles overlapping at the bottom of the screen demonstrates a unique component of opacity in SwiftUI. When we apply the `opacity` modifier to a view that already had its opacity transformed, the modifier will multiply the overall effect. For example, the yellow and red circles have their opacity set at 50%, overlapping each other. The top red circle allows some of the bottom yellow circle to show through, thus multiplying the opacity effect so that area is a little darker, and at the same time, mingling the two colors, creating orange.

Next, let's take a look at animating the size or scale of a view, which we can do with the `scaleEffect` modifier.

Scale

Every view has a specific size, and we can change that size by scaling it up or down with animation. We can do this with the `scaleEffect` modifier. Here's an example of how we can animate the scale of a view:

```
struct Scale_Example_One: View {
    @State private var scaleCircle = false
    var body: some View {
            //MARK: - ANIMATE THE SCALE OF A CIRCLE SHAPE
            VStack {
                Text("SCALE SHAPE").font(.title).bold()
                Circle()
                    .frame(width: 150)
                    .foregroundColor(.green)
                    .scaleEffect(scaleCircle ? 0.1 : 1)
                    .animation(.default, value: scaleCircle)
                Button("Scale Shape") {
                    scaleCircle.toggle()
                }
            }.font(.title2)
        }
}
```

The preceding code will produce the following results, as shown in *Figure 2.6*:

Figure 2.6: Scaling a shape

You should be starting to recognize much of the code that we're using; for example, we use a `VStack` to hold our views, so they get stacked vertically, and we can use the button control as a way to start the animation.

In the example, I'm creating a simple green circle and using the `scaleEffect` modifier, passing in our animating variable. When the state changes to `true`, the circle scales down to one-tenth of its size, and when `false`, it goes back to its original size.

We're using the `animation` modifier again with the default timing curve. The default curve is an easeInOut curve, which we discussed earlier in the chapter. An easeInOut curve will cause the animation to start slowly, then ramp up to its top speed, and then finish by easing out slowly again.

Let's look at another example of scaling up and down, but instead of scaling a shape that we created using the circle initializer, we're using a system image to show you that you can also scale images:

```
struct Scale_Example_Two: View {
    @State private var scaleBug = false
    var body: some View {
        //MARK: - ANIMATE THE SCALE OF A SYSTEM IMAGE
        VStack{
```

```
Text("SCALE IMAGE").font(.title).bold()
Image(systemName: "ladybug.fill")
    .renderingMode(.original) //allows multicolor
      for SF Symbols
    .resizable()
    .frame(width: 150, height: 150, alignment:
      .center)
    .scaleEffect(scaleBug ? 0.1 : 1)
    .animation(.default, value: scaleBug)
    .padding(10)
Button("Scale Image") {
    scaleBug.toggle()
}
}.font(.title2)
}
}
```

The preceding code will produce the following results, as shown in *Figure 2.7*:

Figure 2.7: Scaling an image

This particular image is a system image from the *SF Symbols* app. If you don't have this app yet, I highly recommend it. You can download it for free at the Apple Developer portal. In it, Apple has given us thousands of images we can use in our code. And what's new in the latest release is that now, many of the images can be rendered in multicolor: we have to set the rendering mode to `.original` so the image gets shown with colors, instead of just black or white.

> **Note**
>
> Not all images can be colored. Look in the SF Symbols app to see which ones can be colored.

Finally, in this third example of a scaling animation, we use the `anchor` method, which scales the view by the given amount in both the horizontal and vertical directions relative to an anchor point:

```
struct Scale_Example_Three: View {
    @State private var scaleFromAnchor = true
    var body: some View {
                VStack{
            Text("SCALE FROM ANCHOR ").font(.title).bold()
            Image(systemName: "heart.fill")
                .renderingMode(.original) //allows the use of
                    multicolor for SF Symbols
                .resizable()
                .frame(width: 150, height: 125, alignment:
                  .center)
                .scaleEffect(scaleFromAnchor ? 1 : 0.2, anchor:
                  .bottomTrailing)
                .animation(.default, value: scaleFromAnchor)
                .padding(10)
            Button("Scale from Anchor") {
                scaleFromAnchor.toggle()
            }
        }.font(.title2)
    }
}
```

The preceding code will produce the following results, as shown in *Figure 2.8*:

Figure 2.8: Scaling from an anchor point

All views have an anchor point, which is usually in the middle of the view. But we can change that anchor point, and have the animation scale the object based on where that anchor point is. In the code, I used the `.bottomTrailing` option as the anchor point, so when we press the button, the heart image scales down and toward the trailing edge (the right side of the screen), rather than scaling from the center of the object. However, SwiftUI also gives us the following anchor points to choose from:

- `bottomTrailing`
- `trailing`
- `bottom`
- `center`
- `top`
- `bottomLeading`

- `topLeading`
- `topTrailing`
- `leading`

In this final section, we will look at three more properties that can be animated: `stroke`, `trim`, and `cornerRadius`.

Stroke, trim, and corner radius

Let's now look at three more properties we can animate: the stroke of a line, the trim of a circle, and the corner radius of a rectangle.

The **stroke** of a shape is the outline or border of the shape. It has a particular color and width and can have various attributes such as line cap style or line join style. Let's animate the stroke of a rectangle, so it gets thicker or thinner with each button press:

```
struct Stroke_Example: View {
    @State private var animateStroke = false
    var body: some View {
        //MARK: - ANIMATE THE STROKE OF THE ROUNDED RECT
        VStack{
            Text("ANIMATE STROKE").font(.title).bold()
            RoundedRectangle(cornerRadius: 30)
                .stroke(Color.purple, style:
                    StrokeStyle(inewidth: animateStroke ? 25 :
                    1))
                .frame(width: 100, height: 100)
                .animation(.default, value: animateStroke)
            Button("Animate Stroke") {
                animateStroke.toggle()
            }
        }.font(.title2)
    }
}
```

Either a thick or thin stroke line is created around the rectangle, as shown in *Figure 2.9*:

Figure 2.9: Animating the stroke

The first thing we do is define our animation variable, setting its initial value to `false`. Looking inside the `stroke` modifier, I pass the `animateStroke` variable as an argument to the line `width` parameter, so when it does become `true`, it changes `stroke` to `25` points (otherwise, it will be `1` point). Again, we also use the default timing curve inside the `animation` modifier, and when we run this, `stroke` is smoothly modified from a thickness of `25` points, then back to `1` point when the button is pressed again.

Here is another example where we are using the `trim` modifier this time:

```
struct Trim_Example: View {
    @State private var animateTrim = false
    @State private var circleTrim: CGFloat = 1.0

    var body: some View {
        //MARK: - ANIMATE THE TRIM MODIFIER OF A CIRCLE
        VStack {
            Text("ANIMATE TRIM").font(.title).bold()
                .padding(.top, 10)
            Circle()
                .trim(from: 0, to: circleTrim)
                .stroke(Color.red, style: StrokeStyle(inewidth:
                    30, lineCap: CGLineCap.round))
                .frame(height: 150)
                .rotationEffect(.degrees(180))
                .animation(.default, value: animateTrim)
                .padding(.bottom, 20)
            Button("Animate Trim") {
                animateTrim.toggle()
                circleTrim = animateTrim ? 0.25 : 1
            }
        }.font(.title2)
    }
}
```

The `trim` modifier takes two parameters: `from` (meaning what part of the circle we want to start trimming from) and `to` (meaning where we want to end the trimming). The `from` parameter is set to `0`, which means there will be a complete circle on the screen as we are not trimming yet. The code produces the following results, a circle that has its line trimmed off and restored when the button is pressed, as shown in *Figure 2.10*:

Figure 2.10: Animating the trim

Also, notice we use two `@State` variables to work with the `trim` modifier, one called `animateTrim`, to trigger the animation, and one called `circleTrim`, which is a numerical value of the `CGFloat` type. This variable will hold the amount of circle we want to trim off. Initially, it gets set to `1`, so the whole circle is visible.

> **Note**
>
> A `CGFloat` type is a floating-point number. **CG** stands for **Core Graphics**, which is an older coding paradigm was used in Apple's graphic framework, but is still used in SwiftUI.

Looking inside the button code, then within the `circleTrim` variable, we're storing one of two values using the ternary operator: either `.25`, or `1`. This means that when `animateTrim` toggles to `true`, the code trims off 75% of the circle and leaves 25%; when `animateTrim` toggles to `false`, the value of `1` is used, which represents 100% of the circle. So, the values in the ternary operator represent how much of the circle to keep.

If we run the code, we see we have a nice trimming animation of this circle. The line of code called `CGLineCap.round` refers to the shape of the line that's drawn at the end points, and it can be `round`, `square`, or `butt line cap`.

And just to have a little fun here, if we go into the `trim` modifier and change the `from` parameter to `0.5` instead of `0`, we now start the drawing halfway through the circle. Run the code, and it looks like we're animating or painting a smile and then removing the smile when we press the button again.

> **Note**
>
> If this code seems a bit confusing, where you see the `trim` modifier being set for the circle, and the `circleTrim` variable being set in the button body, then think of the `trim` modifier as the "where" part of the trimming. This means where do we want to start and end the trimming? Then, think of the ternary operator inside the button as the "how much," meaning how much do we want to trim off the circle and how much of it do we want to keep?

Let's now move on to the final example. In this example, we will take a look at how you can animate the corner radius of a rectangle. The corner radius refers to how sharp you want to make the corners of a rectangle; you can go all the way from a 90° angle up to a much higher value to create a smooth, rounded corner.

All the code is similar to what we've used so far except for the use of the `cornerRadius` modifier. The following is an example of the code:

```
struct Corner_Radius_Example: View {
    @State private var animateCornerRadius = false

    var body: some View {
        //MARK: - ANIMATE THE CORNER RADIUS
        VStack{
            Text("ANIMATE CORNER RADIUS").font(.title).bold()
                .padding(.top, 30)
            Rectangle()
                .foregroundColor(.green)
                .frame(width: 150, height: 150)
            .cornerRadius(animateCornerRadius ? 0 : 75)
            .animation(.default, value: animateCornerRadius)
            .padding(.bottom, 20)
            Button("Animate Corner Radius") {
                animateCornerRadius.toggle()

            }
```

```
        }.font(.title2)
    }
}
```

This code produces the following results: a rectangle with its corner radius changed from a 90° angle all the way up to create a circle. So, we're changing a rectangle into a circle and back again when the button is pressed, as shown in *Figure 2.11*:

Figure 2.11: Animating the corner radius

In the code, the line that's doing most of the work is this one:

```
.cornerRadius(animateCornerRadius ? 0 : 75)
```

The `animateCornerRadius` variable gets passed into the `cornerRadius` modifier, which then gets checked for the `true` or `false` values; if it is `false`, it gets a value of `75` placed into it, which will make the size of this rectangle animate into a perfectly round circle. And when toggled back to `true`, the circle animates into a rectangle with 90-degree corners by having its corner radius changed to `0`.

Note that the reason why the code creates a perfect circle is that we set the frame of the rectangle's width and height to `150` points, thus creating a square, and anytime you set a corner radius to half the width or height of a square, you will always get a perfect circle.

SwiftUI gives us more ways to animate objects in addition to these, and we will explore them in the coming chapters when we start building projects.

Summary

In this chapter, we looked at how animations work, the two types of animation in SwiftUI, implicit and explicit, and many of the properties that can be animated. These include hue rotation, opacity, a view's position on the screen and size, stroke, trim, corner radius, and timing curves.

This was an important step needed to guide you along on your SwiftUI animations adventure. Remember, if a property is a numerical value, it almost always can have an animation applied to it.

In the next chapter, we will start working on some projects. For our first project, we will create an app similar to Apple's breathing app (very popular on Apple watches) and learn how to combine more than one animation in a view.

3

Creating a Breathing App

So far, we have looked at the SwiftUI fundamentals, some of the modifiers we can use to alter a view in a certain way, and many of the properties that can be animated. Now it's time to put that knowledge to work and build our first project.

In this chapter, we will build an animation that is similar to the breathing apps that are popular on Apple watches and iPhones. There will be three animations that we will combine to make six circle views move, recreating the slow, rhythmic motions of the Apple app.

There is not a lot of code needed to make this app work; however, as we move through the book, we will build upon this project and gradually ramp up the difficulty.

The steps needed to complete the project are as follows:

- Setting up the project with Xcode
- Adding the variables
- Implementing a background color
- Adding the circles
- Animating the circles

Technical requirements

You can download the completed project from GitHub in the Chapter 3 folder: https://
github.com/PacktPublishing/Animating-SwiftUI-Applications.

Setting up the project with Xcode

Let's start by opening Xcode. Then, choose either the **iOS** option to just build your project on an iPhone or choose **Multiplatform** if you want to build this project so it runs on an iPhone, iPad, or a Mac. After that, from the list of templates, choose the one called **App**, and click **Next**.

Now, give the project a name. I'm calling mine Animating Circles, but you can name it whatever you like. Then, fill out the rest of the details on this page. The two checkboxes can be left unchecked, as we are not using **Core Data** or **Tests**. Finally, select a location to save the project. I usually just save them on my desktop.

We are then taken to the Xcode interface; you'll notice that Xcode automatically imports the SwiftUI framework, so we can get right into our project.

Adding the variables

Our first task is to add some variables to keep track of the animations. There will be three animations, so in `ContentView`, we need three boolean variables for them. We need to give them an initial value of `false`, which will be changed to `true` when the app first starts up:

```
struct ContentView: View {
    //animation bools
    @State var scaleUpDown = false
    @State var rotateInOut = false
    @State var moveInOut = false
```

The variables are called `scaleUpDown`, `rotateInOut`, and `MoveInOut`. Usually, when you name your variables, you want to make them as descriptive as possible, so you don't have to guess what they are used for and can recognize them right away, as we did here.

All the variables are now in place, so let's move on to looking at the background of our animation.

Implementing a background color

For the background, we will go into the `body` computed property. This is where we add our views that will be seen on the screen by the user. The first thing we want to add is a `ZStack`; this is the main stack that's going to hold all of the views:

```
var body: some View {
    ZStack {
        }
    }
```

The reason we use the `ZStack` versus an `HStack` or a `VStack` is we want the views stacked on each other, so they appear as only one view, and later we will animate them separately with different modifiers.

Inside the `ZStack`, let's set a black background for the screen by using the `.foregroundColor` modifier, and specify the color to use; we will use black in this case:

```
Rectangle()
.foregroundColor(Color.black)
```

The following figure shows the result of that code:

Figure 3.1: Adding a black background

As you can see, when adding a background in SwiftUI, it will cover most of the iPhone screen, but there is an area on an iPhone that is known as the "safe area." This is the area reserved for the iPhone notch at the top (the earpiece area) and the very bottom of the phone where the colored background can't reach.

SwiftUI lets us hide the safe areas by using the `.edgesIgnoringSafeArea` modifier, then passing in the value `.all`, which extends the black color to the edges of the iPhone screen on all sides. To do this, add this line of code just underneath the `.fourgroundColor(Color.black)` line you previously added:

```
.edgesIgnoringSafeArea(.all)
```

This produces a completely covered iPhone screen with a black background, as shown here:

Figure 3.2: Using the .edgesIgnoringSafeArea modifier

There are also `.vertical`, `.horizontal`, `.leading`, and `.trailing` values that you can use to make the `.edgesIgnoringSafeArea` modifier more specific depending on what part of the device you want to be ignored.

So, we've set up the background of our animation. Now it's time to add the circles.

Adding the circles

Let's briefly review the goal of this project. We want to make six circles grow and shrink, and at the same time rotate them, and move them in and out. The six circles will be overlapping each other, which adds a nice look as they will be partially translucent.

To make this work, we need some more ZStacks, and then to place the circles, in pairs, into them. How the circles are aligned in relation to each other can be likened to the numbers on a clock. Going with this clock analogy, we need a `ZStack` to hold the three pairs:

- The first pair of circles will be placed in the 12 and 6 o'clock positions
- The second pair of circles will be placed in the 2 and 7 o'clock positions
- The third pair of circles will be placed in the 10 and 4 o'clock positions

Let's see how to add these three pairs of circles.

Adding the first pair of circles

The first pair of circles we will add will be placed in the 12 and 6 o'clock positions. The following is the code we need to accomplish that:

```
//MARK: - ZStack for the 12 and 6 O'clock circles
        ZStack {
            ZStack {
                Circle().fill(LinearGradient(gradient:
                    Gradient(colors: [.green, .white]),
                    startPoint: .top, endPoint: .bottom))
                    .frame(width: 120, height: 120)
                    .offset(y: moveInOut ? -60 : 0)

                Circle().fill(LinearGradient(gradient:
                    Gradient(colors: [.green, .white]),
                    startPoint: .bottom, endPoint: .top))
                    .frame(width: 120, height: 120,
                        alignment: .center)
                    .offset(y: moveInOut ? 60 : 0)
            }.opacity(0.5)
```

This code creates two circles using the circle shape initializer. Each circle gets a gradient color that makes them lighter toward the center of the screen, and darker in the opposite direction. The gradient works by filling the circles with a smooth transition between two colors. In this case, the gradient goes from green to white. The `LinearGradient` struct is used to create the gradient, and it takes a `gradient` parameter, which is an instance of the `Gradient` struct.

The `Gradient` struct takes a parameter called `colors`, which is an array of color values. In this case, the `colors` parameter is set to `[.green, .white]`, which means that the gradient will transition from green to white.

The `startPoint` and `endPoint` parameters of the `LinearGradient` struct determine the direction of the gradient. The `startPoint` parameter is set to `.top` and the `endPoint` parameter is set to `.bottom` for the first circle, which means that the gradient will start at the top of the circle and go toward the bottom. For the second circle, the `startPoint` parameter is set to `.bottom` and the `endPoint` parameter is set to `.top`, which means that the gradient will start at the bottom of the circle and go toward the top. The look we are going for is a whiter shade of green toward the part of the circles that are just touching each other, and a darker shade of green on the opposite parts of the circles.

All the circles will be of the same size to start out with, which is 120 points for the width and height, and that's accomplished using the `frame` modifier. Because we are in a `ZStack`, the two circles will be stacked on top of each other. If you would like to see both circles now, then change the `moveInOut` state property to `true`. The `moveInOut` property will be changed to true later when we add the `onAppear` modifier code, but for now, to see how the UI is shaping up, go ahead and change that property to `true`, and this is what you should see:

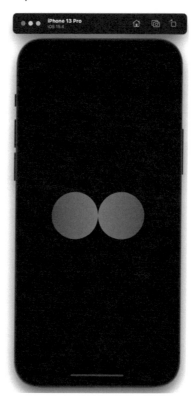

Figure 3.3: Twelve and six o'clock circles

Let's look at the move InOut variable now. Remember that I said the naming of our variables should be descriptive and should be related to what they do? Well, the move InOut variable is an example of that descriptive naming, because it will move the circles in and out of each other. It does this by controlling the vertical offset of the circles that are contained within the ZStack. The ternary operator is responsible for setting the move InOut value by choosing between two different numbers.

When move InOut is true, the first circle has a y offset of -60, which moves it upward by 60 points. The second circle has a y offset of 60, which moves it downward by 60 points. This results in the two circles moving toward the top and bottom of the ZStack respectively. When move InOut is false, the first circle has a y offset of 0, which keeps it in the center of the ZStack, and the second circle also has a y offset of 0, which keeps it in the center of the ZStack as well. This results in the two circles staying in the center, overlaying each other.

Next, by adding the opacity modifier at the end of the ZStack, both circles are set to a 50% opacity. This makes it easy to see through them and the other circles that we will add, as they overlap each other during the animation, and that also makes for a nice visual as the colors blend together and darken during the overlap.

Adding the second pair of circles

Now, for the next set of circles, we're doing almost the exact same thing... almost. Staying with our clock analogy, we need circles at the 2 and 7 o'clock marks. First, I will show you the code, then I will explain the parts that are new:

```
//MARK: - ZStack for the 2 and 7 o'clock circles
            ZStack {
                Circle().fill(LinearGradient(gradient:
                    Gradient(colors: [.green, .white]),
                    startPoint: .top, endPoint: .bottom))
                    .frame(width: 120, height: 120,
                        alignment: .center)
                    .offset(y: moveInOut ? -60 : 0)


                Circle().fill(LinearGradient(gradient:
                    Gradient(colors: [.green, .white]),
                    startPoint: .bottom, endPoint: .top))
                    .frame(width: 120, height: 120,
                        alignment: .center)
                    .offset(y: moveInOut ? 60 : 0)
            }.opacity(0.5)
                .rotationEffect(.degrees(60))
```

We're creating two circles with a gradient of green and white colors, which have the same width and height of 120 points, and they get offset by the animation variable, `moveInOut`. Again, depending on whether `moveInOut` is `true` or `false` will determine the placement of the circle. If it's `true`, the circles will separate, and if `false`, they will come to the middle with one circle placed over the second circle. Next, we set the opacity of these circles to 50%, as we did with the first set of circles, to make them slightly transparent, so we can see them overlap.

What's different for this set of circles is that we need to use the `rotationEffect` modifier on them. This modifier lets us rotate the placement of the circles by passing in a value for the amount of rotation we want.

Notice that this modifier is placed on the end of the `ZStack` that holds the two circles. This placement will make the entire `ZStack` and its children rotate, so it saves us some code as we don't need to place the modifier on both child circles individually.

I'm using a value of `60` for the `.degrees` parameter, which will rotate this `ZStack` 60 degrees from the previous pair of circles. The value of `60` for the rotation is half of 120, which is the width of each circle, so this rotation will cause the circles to overlap each other by half.

Again, if you want to see how the two pairs of circles look, change the `moveInOut` property to `true`, and this is the result:

Figure 3.4: Two and seven o'clock circles

Notice that we didn't have to rotate the first pair of circles using the `rotationEffect` modifier; that's because they're not overlapping any other circles as they are the first pair on the screen. If we don't use the `rotationEffect` modifier here, though, this second pair of circles will be placed exactly over the first pair of circles, and we won't see them.

Adding the third pair of circles

Finally, for the last pair of circles on our clock, they need to be placed at the 10 and 4 o'clock marks. Here is the code:

```
//MARK: - ZStack for the 10 and 4 o'clock circles
            ZStack {
                Circle().fill(LinearGradient(gradient:
                    Gradient(colors: [.green, .white]),
                    startPoint: .top, endPoint: .bottom))
                    .frame(width: 120, height: 120,
  alignment: .center)
                    .offset(y: moveInOut ? -60 : 0)
                Circle().fill(LinearGradient(gradient:
                    Gradient(colors: [.green, .white]),
                    startPoint: .bottom, endPoint: .top))
                    .frame(width: 120, height: 120,
                        alignment: .center)
                    .offset(y: moveInOut ? 60 : 0)
            }.opacity(0.5)
                .rotationEffect(.degrees(120))
```

Looking at this code, we can again see that very little is different from the other sets of circles. We're adding two circles with a gradient of green and white, and with a size of 120 points. They move in and out 60 points or -60 points on the y axis, as we have seen, but for this pair of circles, we're rotating them by 120 degrees, which places them at the 10 and 4 o'clock positions and completes the clock of circles. The result is shown here:

Figure 3.5: Ten and four o'clock circles – the complete design

Okay, so we've added all of the circles. Now it's time to add the fun part – the animation – and make them move.

Animating the circles

Now we have all our circle pairs in place, it's time to start animating them. I'm going to add the animation code. It may look a bit strange at first, but not to worry, I will explain it line by line:

```
//MARK: - Animations
.rotationEffect(.degrees(rotateInOut ? 90 : 0))
.scaleEffect(scaleUpDown ? 1 : 1/4)
```

```
        .animation(Animation.easeInOut.
          repeatForever(autoreverses: true).speed(1/8),
          value: scaleInOut)
        .onAppear() {
            rotateInOut.toggle()
            scaleUpDown.toggle()
            moveInOut.toggle()
        }
      }
    }
  }
```

The first line of code calls the rotationEffect modifier. For its .degrees parameter, I'm passing in the rotateInOut variable, which is then checked by a ternary operator. The ternary operator has one of two values to choose from, 90 or 0. If the rotateInOut variable is true, then the rotationEffect modifier will rotate the ZStack that contains all of the pairs of circles by 90 degrees. When rotateInOut is false, the rotationEffect modifier rotates the ZStack back to 0. So, all of the circles get rotated at once to either 90 degrees or back to zero, depending on the value that rotateInOut contains.

The next line of code is the scale effect animation. For the scaleEffect modifier, we pass in another ternary operator that has two values to set, either 1 or 1/4. When the scaleUpDown property is true, all the circles will be at full scale, which is reflected by the value 1; otherwise, when the scaleUpDown property is false, all the circles will scale down to one-fourth of their size.

The next line of code calls the .animation function. This is the magic function that applies the animation to any view we put it on. We are putting it on the end of the ZStack that contains all of the circles, so when any values change, for example, the variables change from true to false and vice versa, then the new values will be applied to the view, which is the ZStack and its children. Those new values don't get applied instantly; they are interpolated over, so the animation happens smoothly and fluidly.

I'm using the easeInEaseOut timing curve type and also adding the .repeatForever modifier, which will keep the animation going for as long as the app is running. And by passing the true value to the autoreverses parameter, the animation reverses itself when it completes its animations in one direction, so it can continue and animate in the opposite direction.

We can also set the speed of the animation. I'm using 1/8 as the value inside the .speed modifier, for a relatively slow animation. Since this project is similar to the familiar breathing app, I thought a slower animation rather than a faster one would be more appropriate, as the slow pace is helpful when focusing on breathing.

The `value` parameter requires one of our `@State` variables so it can monitor it for changes. All of the variables we are using are `@State`, and they will have their values changed at some point, so any one of them will work fine in this parameter for this code.

The final part of the project is to change the values in each of our variables so the animation can work. Remember we looked at different triggers for animations by using the `.onAppear` modifier. This will perform an action when the screen or view first appears and then trigger the animation. The action we want to perform as soon as the app starts up is to toggle each of the variables to their opposite states. We gave them initial values of `false`, but inside `onAppear`, they get toggled to `true`, which starts the animation.

> **Note**
>
> If you tested out the app earlier and changed the `moveInOut` variable to `true`, make sure to set it back to `false` again, so the animations will get triggered in the `onAppear` modifier.

And now we have three animations happening simultaneously:

- The circles are moving in and out from each other. When moving inward, the circles will overlap each other completely, and when moving out, they will separate until their edges are just touching. Again, this animation is monitored by the `moveInOut` state variable.

- The second animation is scaling the circles by using the `scaleEffect` modifier. It takes a single parameter, which is a value between `0` and `1` that represents the amount of scaling to be applied. In this case, the `scaleUpDown` variable is being used to control the value passed to the `scaleEffect` modifier.

- The final animation is rotating all of the circles by 90 degrees when `rotateInOut` is `true`, and rotating them back to 0 when `rotateInOut` is `false`.

Run the application and have a play around with it. The following figure shows the sequence the animation will take:

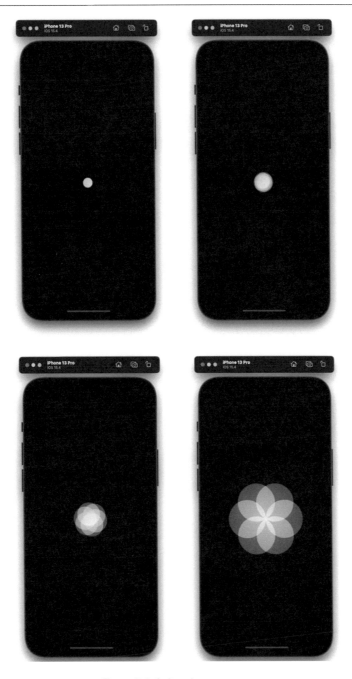

Figure 3.6: Animation sequence

The best way to understand how the different modifiers and functions work is to pass in different values and by experimenting. Always feel free to use your own creativity for everything – for the parameters, things such as the color of the gradients, the size of the circles, the speed, the location, the amount of rotation, and so on. Changing the parameter values to your liking will give you a better understanding of how each modifier acts on a view.

Later in the book, you will learn how to add sounds and music to a project, as well as how to add buttons and slider controls. When you know how to do that, you can come back to this project and tweak it to incorporate some music, and perhaps a slider to change the speed of the animations. For example, as this is a breathing app, and some people might want to relax by taking deep breaths and holding them for a second or more, you can alter the animation to pause for any amount of time to signify the holding of one's breath, all done through the use of various controls that you will learn about in upcoming projects.

Summary

Great job on the completion of this first project! By creating a breathing app, you've got to explore how to rotate, scale, and move a view to another location, all by using SwiftUI's intuitive modifiers and design tools. We also used a special modifier that does a lot of the work in the background for us, the `.animation` modifier, which interpolates over values after we define a start and end point, and creates a smooth seamless animation from those values.

In the next chapter, we will continue our journey into animation and build a record player. This project will look at how to animate a view around one of its anchor points, rather than from the center, as well as adding sound and a button to start the animation.

4

Building a Record Player

In this project, we will create a record player that will move an arm over the record, make the record spin, and play music when a button is pressed.

Sure, record players are a bit outdated now, but this project is a good way to learn new techniques about rotation – specifically, how to rotate objects around an anchor point. And you can always modify the design to look like a turntable, as many DJs still use vinyl, especially due to the vinyl resurgence in the last few years.

You might be thinking, *didn't we rotate circles in the first project?* Well, this project is different. In the last project, the rotation animation we applied was on SwiftUI-created shapes, (specifically, circles), but in this project, we will be applying a rotation animation onto a photo image, then controlling it with a button, and mixing in some sounds to add to the user experience.

Before we start, let's list our objectives for this project:

- Adding images to the Assets catalog
- Creating the record player elements
- Combining all the elements into one view
- Testing the project

Technical requirements

You can find the finished project in the `Chapter 4` folder on GitHub: `https://github.com/PacktPublishing/Animating-SwiftUI-Applications`.

Adding images to the Assets catalog

Okay, let's get started on the first objective: adding some images to the project. First, we need to create a new project in Xcode. I called mine `Record Player` (you can copy this name or choose something else if you like). Then, we need to fill out the other fields exactly as we did in the last chapter. Once this is done, we are ready to start.

When it comes to the images themselves, we need three: the record, the record player arm that will move over the record, and a wood grain image that we can use as the record player box. All of these images can be found on GitHub by clicking the link provided in the *Technical requirements* section.

There are three main methods to add images to the project.

The first method is using Xcode's special file folder called the **Assets catalog**. This is an organizational file structure that you'll see in the Project navigator that will hold all of your colors, app icons, and images. Simply click on the `Assets.xcassets` file in Xcode and you will be taken to the Assets catalog. The catalog is split into two sections: the section on the left is where your files are listed, and the section on the right is where you can actually see your files when you click on them in the left pane. To bring your images into the catalog, simply drag them into the left column:

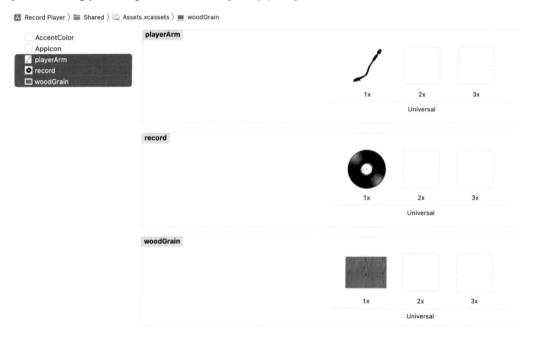

Figure 4.1: Adding files to the Assets catalog

These images will be accessible by referencing their name in the code we write (we will see how to do this shortly).

The second method to add image files to the project is just by dragging and dropping them into the Project navigator. However, this method includes the extra step of choosing how and where you want to copy the files into the project via the following pop-up window:

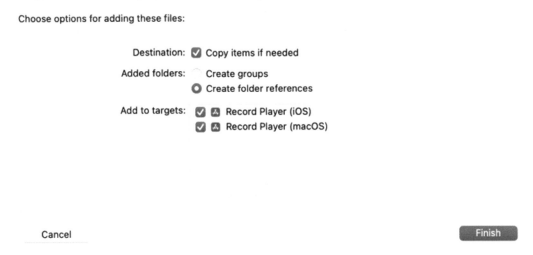

Figure 4.2: Adding files into the Project navigator

Here, you want to make sure that you tick the checkbox that says **Copy items if needed**. That's important because Xcode will copy your files into the project, so if they are no longer available on your computer, it won't matter, as they are part of your project now.

You also want to make sure that you check the boxes for the specific target you want to copy those resources to. For example, if you want to build the app on your Mac, then you want to check the **Record Player (macOS)** option in the **Add to targets** box. If you're just building it for the iPhone, then check the **Record Player (iOS)** option. You can also check both if you prefer.

The final method is opening the **File** menu and selecting the **Add Files to…** option:

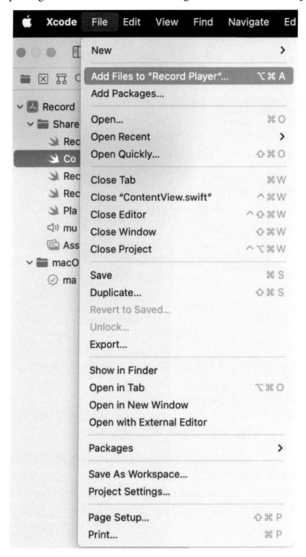

Figure 4.3: Adding files to the project via the File menu

Now that we have added all the images, the next objective is to create the record player.

Creating the record player elements

To create our record player, we will create three separate files, each in charge of performing specific tasks:

- The first file will hold the record player box
- The second file will hold the spinning record, the record player arm, and the button to control it
- The third file will hold the sound file that will play when the record player animation starts

Let's get started with the first file.

Creating the record player box

To create the file to hold the record player box, in Xcode, open the **File** menu, select **New**, then select **File**. You will notice that this brings up several template options:

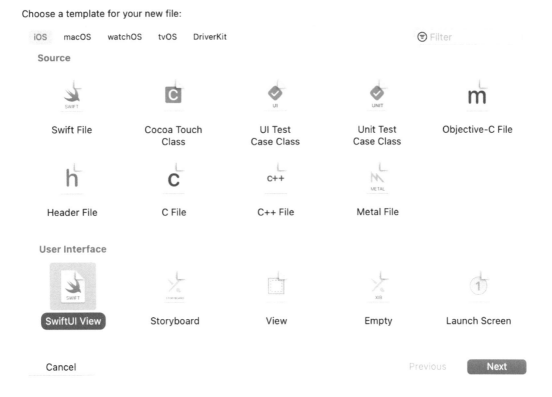

Figure 4.4: Creating a new SwiftUI file

Looking at the top of the window, the row of tabs lets you select which platform you want to write code for. We're only interested in iOS apps, so select the **iOS** tab. Then, under the **User Interface** heading, select **SwiftUI View**.

Click **Next**, and you will be asked to name the file. I'm calling it RecordPlayerBox. Make sure your targets are selected in the checkboxes so that the file and everything it contains will work correctly when you run the project. Once your targets have been set, click **Create**.

Now, we have our new file to write our code, and you'll notice it's the same as the ContentView file, except it's called RecordPlayerBox. Working in the body property, we will start with a ZStack; this will be our main stack to hold all of our views. Within the ZStack, we can build a rectangle using one of the images in the Assets catalog. Enter the following code, and then let's look at what it does:

```
ZStack {
        Rectangle()
            .frame(width: 345, height: 345)
            .cornerRadius(10)
        Image("woodGrain")
            .resizable().frame(width: 325, height: 325)
            .shadow(color: .white, radius: 3, x: 0, y: 0)
    }
```

First, we added a Rectangle view, and then, using the frame modifier, it gets a dimension of 345 points for the width and height, making a square.

Then, using the cornerRadius modifier, we rounded the corners of the rectangle by 10 points.

The next line of code is the Image initializer, which is a view that displays an image. We want to use the wood grain image that's in the Assets catalog, so we accessed it by typing the image's name within quotes to create a string inside the Image initializer. In our case, we typed "woodGrain".

Now we have our image, but we have to resize it. In order to do that, we need to use the resizable modifier, which is used to prepare an image or other view to be resized so it fits within its parent view. When it's applied to an Image view, the resizable modifier will determine how the image should be scaled to fit within the space available.

Then, the frame modifier resizes the wood image to a width and height of 325 points. This will make it a little smaller than the Rectangle dimensions; however, making it smaller will allow some of the rectangle edges to show through, creating a border. The reason why the border is black is that the default color for creating a rectangle shape is black, as it is with all shapes. We can change it to any color we want by using a color modifier, but I think I'll leave it black here.

The final line of code creates a shadow by using the `shadow` modifier. Again, all the modifiers we are adding are for the wood grain image, so each modifier placed on the wood grain has its own specific task of modifying the wood grain image in some way. Since this modifier is placed on the wood grain image and is using a white color, a white shadow will be radiating around the image. Setting the radius to a value of 3 means the shadow will extend out from the image by 3 points. We can also choose to put a value in for the x and y parameters, which will move the shadow on those axes either left, right, up, or down.

How much the shadow is moved depends on the size of the value you put in. For example, if you put a value of 10 in for the x parameter, the shadow will extend out from the right edge 10 points; if you put a value of 10 in for the y parameter, the shadow will extend out 10 points from the bottom edge of the box. I put in a value of 0 because I want the shadow directly over the wood grain image; it won't be shifted left or right or up and down.

Play with these numbers and with the color of the shadow so you can see how much the values that we've used affect the shadow location and intensity. Don't expect to see much of a difference with this `shadow` modifier yet though, because its color is white, and we're working over a white background. When we add a gradient to the whole background later, the shadow will become more prominent.

> **Note**
>
> You can easily see which modifiers you have on any given view by the way Xcode indents them. For example, look at the `Rectangle` view again. Its two modifiers, `frame` and `cornerRadius`, are indented to the right, which means they are acting on the rectangle only. The same goes for `Image("Woodgrain")`; its two modifiers are indented to the right as well.
>
> Here's a quick shortcut if your code starts to get messy and the indenting is not lined up: press *Command + A* to select everything in the file, and then press *Control + I*. Xcode then properly indents the whole file, every bit of code, in one go.

Now, look at **Preview** to see how your record player box looks. The following is what I have according to the code we have written:

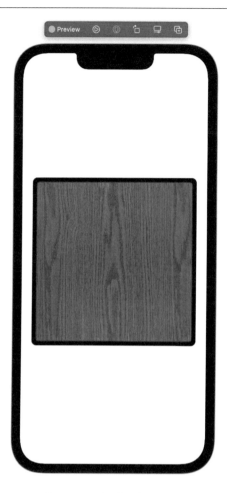

Figure 4.5: The finished box

Before we continue, I want to show you how you can alter the previews to display your creations in a size that fits the view or views on the screen. Notice in *Figure 4.5* that our box is much smaller than the iPhone **Preview** screen; sometimes, you might want to preview what you make in a screen size that fits the size of the view you just made – in our example, we made a box view. Here is how to shrink the **Preview** screen down to fit the box view.

At the bottom of every SwiftUI file is a struct that will have the same name as the struct we just used to write our code. This is a special struct that is used for development purposes, and it creates the **Preview** window that we need so we can see our work in real time.

Inside the preview struct, add this modifier right at the end of the `RecordPlayerBox()` code:

```
.previewLayout(.sizeThatFits).padding()
```

Using the `sizeThatFits` value will bring the **Preview** window size down to about the same size as our finished box. I don't want it exactly the same size, so I added a bit of padding around it. Here is the result:

Figure 4.6: The finished box fitting to the Preview screen

By using the `previewLayout` modifier, you can customize the **Preview** window to suit your needs.

And that's our finished box. Simple, right? Now, with the record player box done, we can move on to our next objective: creating the spinning record.

Creating the spinning record

As mentioned earlier, our second file is going to contain the record code. However, for simplicity's sake, we're actually going to make the record player arm and button in this file too. We could split those tasks up into separate files as we did with the box, so each part has its own file, but I think that for this small project, this one file will do the job for us.

Since we are creating three different views in this one file, let's give it a name that reflects each view the file will have, so `RecordButtonArmView`. Now, do you remember how to make a new SwiftUI file? If not, jump back to the *Creating the record player box* section for a refresher. There's also a shortcut to creating a new file: simply press *Command + N* and choose the file template you want to use; we want the **SwiftUI View** template from the options.

With the file made, let's work on making that spinning record. As we have done before, we will need properties to make everything work, so working at the top of the file, within the struct, add the following variables:

```
@State private var rotateRecord = false
@State private var moveArm = false
@State private var duration = 0.0

var animateForever: Animation {
    Animation.linear(duration: duration)
        .repeatForever(autoreverses: false)
}
```

One of these variables is a little different, so let me explain what we're doing.

The first three variables are `State` variables. The `rotateRecord` variable is going to keep track of the spinning record and will initiate the spinning animation when its value changes to `true`. The next `State` variable, `moveArm`, will keep track of the record player arm, and the third `State` variable, `duration`, is used to set the duration of the spinning record.

The final variable is a computed property. A computed property is a property that does not store a value but is, instead, computed every time it is accessed, meaning the code in its body will run every time the variable is used. The property we made is of the `Animation` type, which means we can use this in the `animation` modifiers.

By using `Animation.linear`, we initialize this variable with a linear timing curve for the animation. Remember we talked about timing curves in *Chapter 2* – a linear curve is a curve with no easing in or easing out; it's simply a steady, non-fluctuating animation from the beginning to the middle, and to the end.

Then, by keeping the `duration` parameter as `0`, this means the animation will have no duration and cannot start yet. This will change in order to start the animation later.

Then, we're using the `repeatForever` option because we want the spinning record to keep going until we stop it. And finally, the `autoReverses` parameter is set to `false`, as we don't want the record to spin backward.

Using a computed property in this way simplifies things, as now we only need to pass that property into the `animation` modifier, and four values will have been set with one computed property: `Animation.linear` curve, `duration`, `repeatForever`, and `autoReverses`. A computed property is also helpful if you are calling the animation modifier in several different places because rather than changing all the separate places to alter the animation, you could simply change the variable in one place. For example, if you want the auto-reverse feature in all of your other animations, all you have to do is change `autoreverses` in one place to `true`.

We now have all the variables we need to set up this file. Next, we will actually add the record. Let's first put everything in a main `ZStack`, which will hold all the views:

```
ZStack {
Image("record").resizable()
                .frame(width: 280, height: 280)
                .rotationEffect(Angle(degrees: rotateRecord ?
                   360.0 : 0.0))
                .animation(animateForever.delay(1.5), value:
                   rotateRecord)
   }
```

The first line of code accesses the `"record"` image in the Assets catalog to create the record on the screen by using the `Image` initializer (just as we did with the `"woodGrain"` image).

Next, by using the `resizable` modifier again to initiate the resizing, we can change the size of the record image by using the `frame` modifier. Passing in a value of `280` points for the width and height makes the image just right for the screen.

In the next line of code, we added the `rotationEffect` modifier to the record. This modifier will rotate (or spin) the image to any angle we want. For the `degrees` parameter, we're using the ternary operator and rotating the record `360` degrees, which is one full rotation. So, the record will spin one complete revolution, but it will only do so when the `rotateRecord` variable becomes `true`.

Next, we added the animation to the record, by using the `animation` modifier and passing in the `animateForever` computed property for its first parameter. Remember, this property is doing a few things for us already: it's setting a timing curve to linear, making the animation repeat forever, and stopping the animation from playing in reverse.

Notice the use of the `delay` modifier. This will add a 1.5-second delay to the start of the spinning record. This delay is added because old record players didn't start spinning until the arm swung over the record first. This will add a little realism to the animation.

Finally, the animation's `value` parameter gets passed in the `rotateRecord` variable, which supplies the animation to the record.

Before we move onto the record player arm, let's make **Preview** smaller so it reflects the size of the record, just like we did with the box:

```
struct RecordButtonArmView_Previews: PreviewProvider {
    static var previews: some View {
        RecordButtonArmView()
            .previewLayout(.sizeThatFits).padding()
    }
}
```

Now, the record is complete and ready to spin some tunes. Here's what it looks like:

Figure 4.7: Record disk

Nothing will happen yet because we have to add the other views and functionality, but we're making good progress. Next up, let's work on the record player arm.

Creating the record player arm

With the spinning record completed, the next objective is the record player's arm. Still working in the `RecordButtonArmView` file, here is the code I want you to add, just underneath the call to the `animation` modifier for the record:

```
//Arm
            Image("playerArm").resizable()
                .aspectRatio(contentMode: .fit)
                .frame(width: 150, height: 150)
                .shadow(color: .gray, radius: 2, x: 0, y: 0)
                .rotationEffect(Angle.degrees(-35), anchor:
                    .topTrailing)
                .rotationEffect(Angle.degrees(moveArm ? 8 : 0),
                    anchor: .topTrailing)
                .animation(Animation.linear(duration: 2),value:
                    moveArm)
                .offset(x: 75, y: -30)
```

Similar to the record image, we use the `Image` initializer to display the `"playerArm"` image that we imported earlier into the Assets catalog. It gets resizable behaviors using the `resizable` modifier, and the aspect ratio is set to `fit`, which will fit the image proportionally on the screen. Next, the image's width and height are set to `150` points, using the `frame` modifier, as we have seen before.

Continuing, the next line of code sets a shadow with a gray color and casts it around the arm with a 2-point radius. If you like, you can change the radius to whatever size you prefer, and experiment to see what works for you.

Then, the arm gets rotated by -35 degrees; this value lines it up perpendicular with the record on the left. Also, we set the anchor point here to `topTrailing`, so when the arm swings over the record, the `topTrailing` (or top-right) anchor point will not move but will serve as a pivot point for the whole arm to move.

The next line of code calls the `rotationEffect` modifier again – this time, passing in the `moveArm` variable. Once this becomes `true`, the arm will move 8 points to the left, and when it's `false`, it goes back to its original spot, using a value of `0`.

As we have seen, to have an animation, we need the `animation` modifier, which is the next line of code. This has a linear timing curve and sets the animation to 2 seconds to complete, meaning it should take the arm 2 seconds to move over the record.

Finally, we need to position the arm just right in relation to the spinning record, so using the `offset` modifier here, we can place it exactly where we want on the record player box. For our purposes, a record player's arm is usually placed to the right of the record, with an inch or two of spacing between the arm and the record.

Here's what the project should look like so far with the arm in place:

Figure 4.8: Record player arm

We're actually almost done with the project, but two more key components are needed.

The first of these is a button that will start and stop the animation. This will be a dynamic button, meaning that the title of the button will change depending on what it's doing. If the record player is not playing a record, we will keep the button color black, display the word **Play**, and show the triangular *play* symbol. If the record player is playing the record, then the button will be red, display the word **Stop**, and show the square *stop* symbol instead.

The second component is to add sound to the project. This involves importing an audio/video framework specifically made for sound and video files.

Let's tackle the button component first.

Adding a custom dynamic button

A button is a control that performs an action when triggered. It can be configured to display a text label, an image, or both. When the user taps it, an action is sent to its target, which can trigger a method to be executed. So, let's add one now.

Still working in the `RecordButtonArmView` file, as before, I will add the button code, and then explain how it works:

```
//Button
Button(action: {
    rotateRecord.toggle()
    if rotateRecord {
        duration = 0.8
        moveArm = true
    } else {
        duration = 0.0
        moveArm = false
    }
\
}) {
    HStack() {
        if !rotateRecord {
            Text("Play").bold().
                foregroundColor(Color.black)
            Image(systemName: "play.circle.
                fill").foregroundColor(Color.
                black)
        } else {
```

```
                              Text("Stop").bold().
                                 foregroundColor(Color.black)
                              Image(systemName: "stop.fill").
                                 foregroundColor(Color.red)
                       }
                    }
                    .padding(.horizontal, 10)
                    .padding(.vertical, 5)
                    .background(Capsule().strokeBorder(Color.
                       black, lineWidth: 2.00))
                 }.offset(x: -105, y: 135)
```

The Button control has an action parameter, and this is where we put the code that we want to be executed when the button is pressed. Inside this action closure, we toggled the rotateRecord variable before doing anything else. The reason for this is that we want the button to change the state of the variable because that's the one that controls the spinning record. So, by toggling it, we're changing the state right away.

Next, we checked to see what the state of rotateRecord is when using an if else statement. If it's true, we set the duration variable to 0.8 seconds, as that's how long we want it to take for the record to spin one revolution (this is a good speed for producing a spinning record effect). Next, we want to set the moveArm variable to true when the button is pressed, because setting that to true gets the arm to move over the record by 8 degrees.

All of that happens if rotateRecord is true, but if it's false, the code falls into the else block. In the else block, the duration is set to 0, which effectively stops the record from spinning, and moveArm is set to false, which will allow the arm to animate back to its original starting position: off the record, and to the right side.

Then, we move into the labeling part of the button. Within this initializer, I declared an HStack, and inside there, another if else statement. I'm using the not operator (!) in front of the rotateRecord variable too, which will read like this: if the rotateRecord variable is not true (this is another way of saying the variable is false), then the record is not playing, so set the text for the button to the word "Play", make it bold and black, and provide a system image for it (a triangular *play* button). But if the code falls into the else block here, it means the record is spinning; in this case, we want to make the text bold, change the foreground color to red, and provide a system image of a *stop* button.

To finish off the button, we added a little bit of padding on its horizontal and vertical sides, gave it a capsule shape, and used the strokeBorder modifier to put a 2-point black line around the button.

> **Note**
>
> You might be wondering, why use the not operator (`!`) when you can say `if false` instead? You can use the `if false` statement instead of `if !true`, but the `!` operator can help to make your code more readable. For example, consider the following code:
>
> ```
> if !fingerprintAccepted {
>
>     //access granted
>
> } else {
>
>     //access denied
>
> }
> ```
>
> The `!` operator negates the Boolean value, making the code more readable because it emphasizes the opposite of what is expected. In the example, if `fingerprintAccepted` is `false`, access will be granted. If `fingerprintAccepted` is `true`, access will be denied. The `!` operator makes it clear that the code is checking for the opposite of `fingerprintAccepted`.

With that code placed into your project, the current interface should look like this:

Figure 4.9: Adding the button control

Now, there's a **Play** button to control the record. Next up, we want our record player animation to actually play sound, so let's do that.

Creating a sound file to play audio

Now, we are going to add sound to the project so that it plays when the record spins. To do this, navigate back to the GitHub folder for this project and drag the .m4a file called music into the Project navigator. Make sure to check the **Copy files to project** box if that box is unchecked.

With our .m4a audio file, we need to create a separate Swift file for this sound. Press *Command +N* to create a new file, but instead of creating a SwiftUI View file, we will create a simple Swift file instead. Then, name it PlaySound.

> **Note**
>
> The main difference between a SwiftUI View file and Swift file is the purpose of the code contained in the file. A SwiftUI View file contains the code needed to define a view and its layout, while Swift file can contain a wide range of code that is not specifically related to defining views.

In this file, the first thing we need to do is import the AVFoundation framework:

```
import AVFoundation
```

The AVFoundation framework includes classes and methods that allow developers to manipulate and work with audio and video in their apps.

Next, let's instantiate (create) an audio player:

```
var audioPlayer: AVAudioPlayer?
```

Notice that this variable is an optional type, denoted by a question mark at the end. I made it optional because if for any reason the music file cannot be found within the project, it will stop the app from crashing. Instead, the app will still work but simply won't play the music.

Now, let's now create a function called playSound that will search through the project for the audio file, and load it if it finds it:

```
func playSound(sound: String, type: String) {
    if let path = Bundle.main.path(forResource: sound, ofType:
type) {
        do {
            audioPlayer = try AVAudioPlayer(contentsOf:
              URL(fileURLWithPath: path))
            audioPlayer?.play()
        } catch {
            print("Could not find and play the sound file")
        }
```

```
      }
   }
```

Here's how the function works. It has two parameters, both of which are strings: one is called `sound` and the other is called `type`.

The first thing we do is to create a `path` constant using what is called **optional binding** with an `if let` statement. Optional binding is a feature that lets us check the value of an optional, and if there is a value in it (meaning it's not nil), then bind that optional to a variable or constant.

This constant called `path` will be assigned a path from the app's bundle. The bundle is where the app and its resources are stored, and we need to get the path to the sound file that we added to the project, which is in the app's bundle. We can access the main bundle of the app by using the `Bundle.main` property. This property returns a `Bundle` object that represents the main bundle of the app, and we can use this object to access any of the resources in the app, such as images, sounds, or other files.

So, the `if let` statement reads as follows: the code searches the main bundle for a file with the given sound's name and type extension. If found, the file path is stored in the `path` constant and runs the code in the `do` block. Otherwise, if for whatever reason the path to the file can't be found, then the file we are looking for is missing or corrupt, and the flow of the program will proceed into the `catch` block and execute the code there.

Okay, let's assume the file path has found our sound file, then the code moves into the `do` block, in which the code will try to create an audio player using that `path` constant. If that is successful, then it will try to play that file. But again, if for any reason the file can't be played, the code will then fall into the `catch` block and print an error message to the console (`"Could not find and play the sound file"`). That error message won't be shown to the user, it's only for our debugging purposes, but the user's app won't crash with this code in place; the sound just won't play.

> **Note**
>
> Here, it would be helpful to show the user an alert if we fall into the `catch` block; however, we won't do that just yet. If you would like to do this, we will cover this in *Chapter 12*, where we create a word game.

Okay, we have everything in place to test the app, but before we can do that, we need to combine our three files – the `RecordPlayerBox`, `RecordButtonArmView`, and `PlaySound` files – into one unified view.

Combining all the elements into one view

To put all of our finished views together into one unified grouping to make the finished project, let's go back into the `ContentView` file and add the following code:

```
struct ContentView : View {
```

```
var body: some View {
    ZStack {
        //MARK: - ADD THE GRADIENT BACKGROUND
        RadialGradient(gradient: Gradient(colors: [.white,
          .black]), center: .center, startRadius: 20,
         endRadius: 600)
            .scaleEffect(1.2)
            //.ignoreSafeArea()
        //MARK: - ADD THE RECORD PLAYER BOX
        RecordPlayerBox()

        //MARK: - ADD THE RECORD, THE BUTTON, AND THE ARM
            RecordButtonArmView()
    }
  }
}
```

Again, we're using ZStack as the main view because we want to layer our other views on top of each other.

First, let's look at the RadialGradient view. This is a struct that takes an array of colors that are placed one by one between the open and closed brackets. Within those brackets, you can put as many colors as you want, separating each color by a comma (I'm using two colors: white and black).

The RadialGradient view works by using the first color in the array to color the center of the background, and subsequent colors will surround that center. Using startRadius and endRadius values of 20 and 600, respectively, will make the radial gradient expand to cover the entire screen; however, it doesn't include the safe areas of the iPhone (again, those are that little area by the notch at the top and a small area at the bottom of the phone). We can handle the safe areas in two ways: we can use the ignoreSafeArea modifier as we've done before, or we can use the scaleEffect modifier as we are doing here. By passing in 1.2 as a value for the scaleEffect modifier, the gradient scales up 1.2 times the size of the iPhone screen, covering all the edges. This is effectively doing the same thing as the ignoreSafeArea modifier would do.

The next line of code makes a call to the RecordPlayerBox view and places it over the gradient (remember that we are working in ZStack, so views get stacked up onto one another). The final line of code makes a call to RecordButtonArmView, placing it over the box, to complete the interface.

This is how our project will look (if you didn't make any modifications along the way, that is):

Figure 4.10: The finished interface

The final piece of the puzzle is to use the sound file that we created. This is easy to do, so as a challenge, try and think of where you would place the audio code to get the app to play music.

Did you figure it out? If you thought of putting code into the body of the button, then you are correct! The button is the view that controls the action: it gets the arm to swing over the record, and the record to spin, as well. So, inside the RecordButtonArmView file, and then inside the button's if statement, add the following code:

```
playSound(sound: "music", type: "m4a")
```

This line of code calls the function that we made in the PlaySound file, passing in the name of our music file, which is simply called music, and the file extension for the type parameter, which is m4a. When the button is pressed, it means the user wants to spin the record and play the music, and this code will grab the music file and play it.

When the button is pressed again, that means the user wants to stop the music, so we need to add the following code to the `else` block to do just that:

```
audioPlayer?.stop()
```

This line of code calls the audio player that we created and uses the `stop` function to stop the music. Notice the use of the question mark before calling the `stop` function. That's because the `audioPlayer` variable was created as an optional. When we create optional variables, we need to use the question mark or exclamation mark when using them too.

Testing the project

And with that, the project is done. Let's come back to `ContentView` and test everything out. If you hit the **Play** button in the **Preview** window or run it in the simulator, you should see that the record won't start spinning until the player's arm is directly over the record. As the record starts spinning, you should hear a golden oldy from the big band era of the 40s, complete with the scratchy intro sound that old records were notoriously famous for. You will also notice that the text on the button changes from **Play** to **Stop**, and the color of the button changes from black to red, as shown in this figure:

Figure 4.11: The spinning record

When you press **Stop**, the arm goes back to its original place, the record stops, and the **Play** button will reappear again.

After all of that, that completes our second project!

Summary

To recap what we covered in this project, we added images to the Assets catalog and accessed them in our code. Then, we created three separate files to hold the elements that we need – one to hold the record player box; one to hold the spinning record, the arm moved with an anchor point, and a dynamic button; and one in which we wrote code to access a sound file. Once we created these elements, we merged them into one view, to create a record and animated record player.

In the next chapter, we're going to continue working with Swift animations by exploring colors. We will create a simple project that displays various images and then, using `hueRotation`, change the color of the images to display a kaleidoscope effect. We will also look at how to pass data bidirectionally to another view, which gives up more flexibility than using the `@State` property wrapper.

5
Animating Colorful Kaleidoscope Effects

In this chapter, we will look at how we can animate colors with a modifier called `hueRotation`, where "hue" refers to the colors of the object, and "rotation" refers to the colors being rotated or animated. We will create a simple project that displays various images and then, using `hueRotation`, we can change or shift the colors of the images so that they will resemble somewhat of a kaleidoscope effect.

Along with `hueRotation`, there are some other important concepts we will explore in this project.

We will work with a Picker view for the first time, which is exactly what the name suggests; it lets the user pick from a variety of options, which can then be displayed on the screen.

Also, we will look at how to pass data bidirectionally to another view. If you remember the moving circle project in *Chapter 3*, it was built inside one file and then within one view, the `ContentView`. In *Chapter 4*, we built the record player using several files and then put those files together inside the `ContentView`. In both of those projects, we didn't pass any data from file to file or view to view; the views contained blocks of code that just needed to be called in the main `ContentView`. But in this project, we will see how to pass data from different views using a special property wrapper called `@Binding`.

So, let's lay out the objectives before we dive in:

- Adding the Binding variable and images
- Adding a Picker control and using a `ForEach` view
- Adding the variables and background color
- Adding the Image view and using the `hueRotation` modifier

Technical requirements

You can find the completed project and the images we will use in the `Chapter 5` folder over on GitHub at `https://github.com/PacktPublishing/Animating-SwiftUI-Applications`.

Adding the Binding variable and images

Okay, let's get started. So, create a new Xcode project, give it a name, and we will get underway.

We will start by adding a new SwiftUI file to the project, which I'll call **ImagePickerView** (you should be very familiar with the process of adding new files as you've done it several times now). Then within the struct, add a variable called `selectedImage`, and make it of the `String` type. We will prefix this variable with the **@Binding** wrapper, as shown here:

```
struct ImagePickerView: View {
    @Binding var selectedImage: String
    var body: some View {
        Text("Hello World")
    }
}
```

The `@Binding` property wrapper is used to create a two-way binding between a source of truth (for example, a state property in a parent view) and a view that depends on that state. This `ImagePickerView` is the source of truth as it's the parent view here. The `@Binding` wrapper allows a view to read and write to a value, but also makes sure that any changes made to the value are propagated back to the original source of truth. This is how views can be updated and re-rendered automatically whenever the source of truth changes, without having to manually pass down new values and refresh the view.

Let's now add some images that we need to the project. You can find them in the GitHub repository – just download the resources for this chapter. There are five images: `ornament`, `landscape`, `dog`, `dice`, and `cat`. Open the Assets catalog and drop the five images into the catalog (just like we did when creating the record player).

With the images in place, let's create an array of strings that can hold the names of the images. Here is the code, which gets placed under the `@Binding` property:

```
struct ImagePickerView: View {
    @Binding var selectedImage: String
    let images: [String] = ["ornament", "landscape", "dog",
        "dice", "cat"]

    var body: some View {
```

```
        Text("Hello World")
    }
}
```

To create the array, we first give it a name, `images`, then use the `String` keyword within square brackets, then another pair of square brackets in which we fill the `images` array with five `String` elements, which are the names of the images we want to use. Each string is separated by a comma.

Now the `images` array is ready to use. Let's add a Picker control and see how we can loop through this array using a `ForEach` view to store each string name in the picker.

Adding a Picker control and using a ForEach view

SwiftUI offers us a sufficient number of pre-built controls to help put together a user interface that is both nice to look at and very functional. One control that is useful for providing your user with a list of options is the **Picker view**, which can provide as few or as many values as you need to display for your app. A Picker view is a view that lets the user select an item from a list of options and is usually used together with a Binding variable, which will store the currently selected value.

We will be using a `forEach` view to iterate through the `images` array and populate the picker. Working in the body property, let's add the `PickerView` first, and a `ForEach` view inside the picker:

```
struct ImagePickerView: View {
    @Binding var selectedImage: String
    let images: [String] = ["ornament", "landscape", "dog",
      "dice", "cat"]
    var body: some View {
        Picker("", selection: $selectedImage) {
            ForEach(images, id: \.self) { value in
                Text(value)
                    .foregroundColor(.white)
            }
        }
```

Okay, there's a lot going on here, so let's break it down. Quick note though: don't worry about the preview struct below the `ImagePickerView` just yet; that's going to show an error, but we'll fix that in a moment.

For the Picker's first parameter, you'll notice there's an empty `String` value. The string will allow you to give the Picker a label if you think it needs one; however, we do not need it here so we're leaving the `String` parameter empty. Inside the next parameter, called `selection`, is where the `selectedImage` binding property will go, and this property will bind to a `State` property in the `ContentView` later. We haven't added any State properties in the `ContentView` yet, but we will soon.

Now the `selectedImage` property in this `ImagePickerView` file will be bidirectionally connected to a `State` property in the `ContentView`. That connection allows for the instant refreshing of views between those two structs when the value changes in either struct.

The syntax does require that we put the dollar sign ($) before the property in order to tell SwiftUI that this property is a binding property and can connect to the `ContentView` (the source of truth) and update the views.

The next line of code is the `ForEach` view. What we want to do is loop through the `images` array and display all those String labels of that array in the `Picker` view. In order to loop through the array of strings, they need to have some sort of ID that identifies each element in this array uniquely. And since they all have different names, why not use the names of each element, which already constitute unique IDs? To use each image's name as an ID for the loop, we used the `\.self` syntax, placed after the `images` array.

The `value` keyword in this code is the looping variable; it will store each element from the `images` array as the `ForEach` view loops through them. This looping variable can be named anything you like, but I called it `value` in this example as that makes the most sense (it temporarily holds the value of each element in the array, one at a time).

Now looking at the code in the `ForEach` view's body, we only need to add one `Text` view with the `value` variable inside it. That will display everything that is in the `images` array in the `PickerView`. Next, we change the color of the text to white using the `foregroundColor` modifier. We do this because when we go into the `ContentView` file, we will make the screen's background black; that way, we'll see the white letters over the black background.

That completes the `Picker` view functionality; let's now style the appearance of the `Picker` view by adding some modifiers to it after the view's closing bracket:

```
}.pickerStyle(WheelPickerStyle())
.frame(width: 300, height: 150)
.background(Color.red.colorMultiply(.blue))
.cornerRadius(20)
.shadow(color: .white, radius: 5, x: 0, y: 0 )
```

Let's look at each of the modifiers used:

- The first modifier I've added is `pickerStyle()`, which is used to change the appearance of the `Picker` view. There are four built-in styles we can select from to style the Picker using the `pickerStyle()` modifier. The following are the ones available:

- `DefaultPickerStyle()`: The default style that is chosen automatically by the system based on the platform and current context. This presents the choices to the user in a menu style.

- `PopUpButtonPickerStyle()`: This is a pop-up button-style picker, often used on macOS. This presents the choices in a button style to the user.

- `WheelPickerStyle()`: A wheel-style picker, often used on iOS. This presents the choices in a wheel style to the user.

- `SegmentedPickerStyle()`: A segmented control-style picker, commonly used on iOS, watchOS, and tvOS. This presents the choices in the style of a segmented button to the user.

We chose the `WheelPickerStyle` for this project.

- The second modifier is the `frame` modifier, which sets the dimensions of the picker control. Here, we set the dimensions as `300` points wide and `150` points tall.

- Next is the `background` modifier, which sets the background color of the picker to red. `colorMultiply` then modifies the red color instance by multiplying its RGB values with those of another color, blue in this case. The result is a dark shade of purple.

- After that, we used the `cornerRadius` modifier to round the corners of the picker by 20 points.

- We finish styling the picker using the `shadow` modifier. This will add a white shadow with a radius of 5 points and will be visible when we change the background to black.

Now, let's return to the error that our code is experiencing and see how we can make sure the app builds cleanly. The error says that we are missing an argument from the `ImagePickerView`'s call. And that's true, because we added a `Binding` property into the `ImagePickerView` struct called `selectedImage`, and since the `Preview` struct is referencing the `ImagePickerView`, it needs to use that `Binding` variable in itself too in order to build cleanly.

To fix this problem, we need to go into the `Previews` struct at the bottom of the file and change the first line of code to this:

```
ImagePickerView(selectedImage: .constant("ornament"))
```

By using the `constant` function, the error goes away. The `constant` function will accept any value we want as long as it's of the String type, because that's the data type of the `selectedImage` property. I'm using the `"ornament"` string from the `images` array, and that string will be shown in the picker.

Now that the code builds cleanly, the result should look like this:

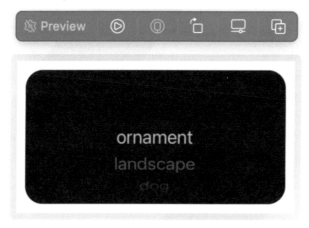

Figure 5.1: Picker View

Spin the wheel picker and you can see all of the string names from the `images` array.

Now that we are done with the `ImagePickerView` file, let's continue by setting up the `ContentView` file.

Adding the variables and background color

Moving into the `ContentView` file now, our first task here will be to add a couple of variables and a constant. Let's start with adding a variable that will bind to the `selectedImage` binding property in the `ImagePickerView` file.

To do that, we need to create a `State` variable, which needs to be the same data type as the `selectedImage` variable, a `String` type. We can give it the same name as the variable too, `selectedImage`, so that you know this variable is bidirectionally linked to the variable in the `ImagePickerView` file.

Add this code inside the `ContentView` struct, at the top:

```
@State private var selectedImage: String = "ornament"
@State private var shiftColors = false
let backgroundColor = Color(.black)
```

The `selectedImage` variable gets set to a String value called `ornament`. Next is a variable to track the animation called `shiftColors`, which is set to `false`. Finally, we have a constant to hold the background color, which will be black.

Moving into the `body` property, let's add a `VStack`, which will take care of vertically organizing three views that the user interface needs: a background, which will be black; an `Image` view, to display the image selected by the user; and a call to the `ImagePickerView` that we created in the `ImagePickerView` file, which allows the user to select an image.

To do all of this, first add a `VStack` into the `body` property of the `ContentView`:

```
var body: some View {
VStack {
        }
  }
```

Next, add the `ImagePickerView` into the `VStack` with the `frame` modifier on it, as shown here:

```
var body: some View {
    VStack {
        ImagePickerView(selectedImage: $selectedImage)
        .frame(width: 350, height: 200)
      }
```

To color the background, we need a `ZStack` so it can overlay the color onto the whole screen. Add this code inside the `VStack`:

```
  ZStack {
        backgroundColor
            .scaleEffect(1.4)
      }
  }
```

As we have seen before, this code will color the background black, and by using the `scaleEffect` modifier and passing in the value of `1.4`, the black background will stretch out so it covers the entire screen.

Now that the background is set, let's add an `Image` view to display the images, and then start animating some colors.

Adding the Image view and using the hueRotation modifier

With the background set up and all of the variables in place, let's add an `ImageView` to display the images, and add the `hueRotation` modifier to it.

Add the following code right after the `scaleEffect` modifier:

```
Image(selectedImage).resizable().padding(20).frame(width:
  400, height: 400)
    .hueRotation(.degrees(shiftColors ? 360 : 0))
    .animation(Animation.easeInOut(duration:
      2).delay(0.3).repeatForever(autoreverses: true),
      value: shiftColors)
    .onAppear() {
      shiftColors.toggle()
            }
          }
        ImagePickerView(selectedImage: $selectedImage)
            .frame(width: 350, height: 200)
      }.background(backgroundColor)
      .edgesIgnoringSafeArea(.bottom)
  }
}
```

Here we are using the Image view to display the images on the screen, resizing it and adding a little padding to it. Then we set the frame of the image view to a size of 400 by 400.

Next comes the `hueRotation` modifier. Hue rotation is an image-processing effect that adjusts the hue of an image by rotating the colors in the hue color wheel by a specified angle. It changes the overall color tone of an image by shifting the hue of each pixel.

The speed at which it does this is determined by the values that get passed into its parameter. And if you have an image with many different colors, then `hueRotation` will cycle through and rotate all of them, creating a sort of kaleidoscope color effect.

Looking at the `hueRotation` parameter, it needs a value to represent degrees, which is for the amount of rotation to apply to the colors in this view, and that is handled by the `degrees` function. Inside the `degrees` function is a ternary operator, which will select from two choices: either a value of 360 when the `shiftColors` variable is `true`, or 0 when it is `false`.

Next, the `animation` modifier is added to animate to the color-changing effect. It uses an `easeInOut` timing curve with a duration of 2 seconds to complete the animation and a delay of 0.3 seconds between animations.

Then we use the `onAppear` modifier, which runs the code within its body as soon as the view appears. This is a perfect place to trigger the animation by toggling the `shiftColors` variable to its opposite value.

After that, we set a frame width and height of `350` by `200` for the `ImagePickerView` and colored the background of the `VStack` by using our `background` variable. We also used `edgesIgnoringSafeArea` for the bottom edges, so the background color will go below the screen. We want the whole screen black with our views on top of it, and this code does just that.

Guess what? With all that finished, the project is done! Here's what it should look like:

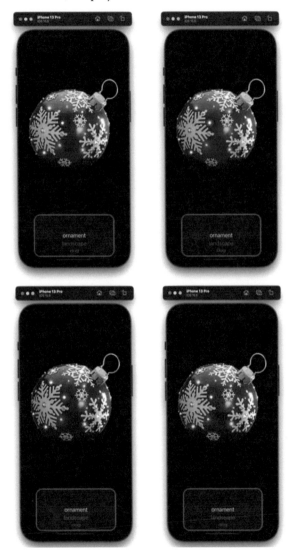

Figure 5.2: Finished project

Go ahead and run the project – you'll see that the colors from your selected image will all shift and rotate over the span of 2 seconds.

Summary

Good work on completing the project! As you worked through it, you got to see how to use a `Binding` property so data can be bound between views, the `Picker` view, a view with different styles that allows users to select an image or other data, and finally the `hueRotation` modifier, which rotates colors.

In the next chapter, we will explore the process of cutting up an image into different parts, then rotating those separate parts using the `rotationEffect` modifier, to create an animation of a girl on a swing.

6

Animating a Girl on a Swing

Welcome to the next project. In this one, we're going to animate parts of an image, specifically an image of a girl on a swing, and make those individual parts move with a natural motion.

To do this, we're going to take a look at an animating technique that uses any image or vector file of a subject and then cuts that image up into various parts in order to animate them separately. We will also take a look at a new modifier called `mask`, which is used for setting the opacity of a view.

Let's take a look at what we will learn in this project:

- Gathering and slicing images
- Adding animating variables
- Adding images to the scene
- Using the `mask` modifier

Technical requirements

You can download the resources and the finished project from the `Chapter 6` folder on GitHub: `https://github.com/PacktPublishing/Animating-SwiftUI-Applications`.

Gathering and slicing images

In this project, I will be using some simple graphics, including an image of a girl, a leafy background, and a branch. And, as I mentioned, we will be animating two parts of the scene: the swing and the girl's legs.

The first thing you need to do is download the images as explained in the *Technical requirements* section and then cut the images into various parts. To do this, I will simply use Mac's Preview app, which is a free app that's already installed on your Mac computer. Inside this app, there is an option called **Markup**, as shown here:

Figure 6.1: Accessing the Markup tools

Clicking on **Markup** will open up an array of helpful editing tools that we can use to transform an image in unique ways. One of the best tools for cutting images is the **Lasso Selection** tool, which lets us draw a selection box around some or all of the parts of the image, and either cut it out or copy it to another window. You can find the tool in the drop-down menu located here:

Figure 6.2: Accessing the Lasso Selection tool

To use it, click and drag your cursor around any object, and then connect the start and end points when you're done. We want to drag the lasso around the girl's lower legs, just above the knee joint, like so:

Figure 6.3: Using the Lasso Selection tool [Credit: <a href="https://www.freepik.com/vectors/clip-art">Clip art vector created by brgfx - www.freepik.com</a>]

With the legs selected using the **Lasso Selection** tool, copy the selection by pressing *Command + C*. Now they are saved to the Mac clipboard. To make that copy into a separate image, go to **File**, and select **New from Clipboard**. Save the PNG to your desktop and rename it `leg`. Your image will look something like this:

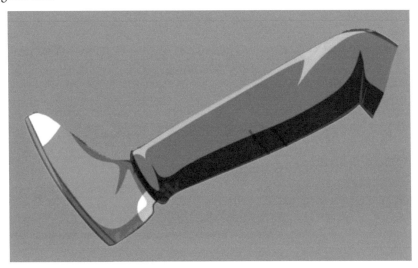

Figure 6.4: Separating the leg with the Lasso Selection tool

This image is okay, but there's a problem. The image contains a background that won't look good in the scene; we only want the leg without any background. The best way I have found to remove backgrounds is to use a helpful free online tool called **removebg**, which you can access here: `https://www.remove.bg/upload`. Simply drop the image onto that website, and it identifies the background and removes it.

At this point, we now have our image of a leg (though our animation includes two legs, one image will work just fine to represent both legs of the girl).

Next in our project, we also want a piece of rope, which we will use to tie the swing to the tree in our background image. However, if you look at *Figure 6.3*, the rope is a little too short for what we need. To get an extra piece of rope, I used the **Lasso Selection** tool around the rope, copied it, and made a new image, then removed the background with **removebg** (as we did with the leg). *Figure 6.5* is the result; this is what we will use in the scene to extend the existing rope:

Figure 6.5: Rope

Next, I looked for a suitable background, which was a tree with some grass and a sky. Here is the one we will use (it originally had a tire swing; however, I didn't want that kind of swing, so I removed it using some other software called Affinity Photo). Now we have a tree and we can tie a swing to its branch:

Figure 6.6: Our background image

[Credit: https://www.istockphoto.com/vector/tire-swing-in-autumn-gm165677003-10337433?phrase=tyre%20swing]

I also thought the tree was a little sparse, so I found some leaves that can be positioned onto the branch later, and they will also hide the top part of the rope:

Figure 6.7: Our leaves image

As you play around with slicing up images and making the individual parts to animate, you may find that you want something better than Mac's Preview app. You may also find that, even though **removebg** works in most cases, it may not work in every instance. If so, you can use professional software such as Photoshop; however, that can be expensive. Instead, you can try my favorite image editing software that I mentioned earlier, Affinity Designer and Affinity Photo. They are very reasonably priced and as robust as Photoshop, but they are much more user-friendly. Definitely take a look at them if you want to learn how to manipulate images that you can use in an iOS app without paying a yearly subscription, as you would for Photoshop.

Once we have all the parts we need for the girl in the swing scene, we can start assembling it in Xcode. So, create a new project – I have called mine `Girl On A Swing` – then open the Assets catalog and drop all the images inside as we have done before.

Now we can start coding in the `ContentView` file; this is the only file we need for this project as there is very little code required to make this project work.

Adding the animating variables

As we have done before, we start off by adding the properties needed to keep track of the different parts we want to animate. In our case, we need three properties:

- One property for the girl image, aptly called `girl`

- One for the left leg, called `leftLeg`

- One for the right leg, called `rightLeg`

Even though we are using one image for both the right and left legs, we still need two separate leg properties for the animation to work because the legs will be moving at different times and speeds.

All of these properties will be `State` properties, so they will update the view instantly as their values change. Put the following code into the `ContentView` file, just above the `body` property:

```
@State private var girl = false
@State private var leftLeg = false
@State private var rightLeg = false
```

As usual, all the properties are all set to `false` so the animation won't start until they are changed to `true`.

We're also going to add a fourth property, which I'm calling `fadeOutRope`. This isn't strictly necessary, but it gives me an opportunity to show you how to use the `mask` modifier, which masks a view by changing its opacity; if we pass in a gradient color, we can make the rope fade out as it reaches the tree branch. Here is the property I want you to add under the previous ones:

```
let fadeOutRope = Gradient(colors: [.clear, .black])
```

The `Gradient` function needs an array of colors to work, so I gave it two colors: a `clear` color (or non-color), and a `black` color. These two colors will be blended together into the rope image, making the top portion fade out. As I said, this is not strictly necessary; however, I think it's better to fade out the top of the rope because it's not tied to the branch of the tree in the image we are using, so we want to blend it in a little bit, giving the appearance that it is attached somewhere in the tree. Later, we will use the `mask` modifier, add an image of some leaves to help conceal the top of the rope, and make the scene look even more natural.

Adding the images to the scene

There are four images we need to add to our scene, which we will add in the following order:

- The background

- The right leg

- The girl
- The left leg

So, let's get started!

Adding the background

We'll add the background inside a `ZStack`, this will be the first view in the file, and so all subsequent views will be placed on top of this. Here is the code you need:

```
var body: some View {
        ZStack {
            Image("tree").resizable()
                .frame(width: 550, height: 900)
                }
            }
```

In `ZStack`, we call the `Image` initializer and pass in the `tree` string. Next, we use the `resizable` modifier to resize the tree, and then set the `frame` of the background to a width of `550` and a height of `900` so the background image can extend to the edges of an iPhone of any size.

Adding the right leg

When it comes to adding the `rightleg`, `leftleg`, and `girl` properties, we need another `ZStack` so we can layer all of the views on top of each other, then use the `offset` modifier to move them into place as needed.

To add the right leg to the scene, enter the following code:

```
ZStack {
    ///right leg
    Image("leg").resizable().aspectRatio(contentMode: .fit)
        .rotationEffect(.degrees(rightLeg ? -20 : 50),
          anchor: .topTrailing )
        .scaleEffect(0.12)
        .offset(x: -448, y: 92)
        .animation(Animation.easeInOut(duration:
          1).delay(0.09).repeatForever(autoreverses: true),
          value: rightLeg)
        .onAppear() {
```

```
                    rightLeg.toggle()
            }
        }
    }
```

First, the `Image` initializer gets passed into it the name of the image we want to display; here, it's `"leg"`. Remember, we are using this one image to represent the right and left legs (we can get away with using a single image because this is a 2D scene; we don't have a 3D view around the image, so we can't really see any variance in each leg).

Next, we will use the `resizable` modifier and set the aspect ratio to `fit`. Using the `fit` option resizes the image content to use all the available screen space, both vertically and horizontally.

The next line of code sets the `rotationEffect` on the leg. The right leg will be rotated by `-20` degrees when the `rightLeg` property is `true`, and it will rotate `50` degrees when it is `false`.

Notice the `anchor` parameter too? An anchor point is the point around which the image will rotate. When thinking about humans (and animals too), our anchor points are our joints. We bend and move from those joints, our pivot points. In our project, by using the `topTrailing` option, the leg will rotate about the knee joint.

> **Note**
>
> If you type a dot (`.`) into your code, you can see the other options Xcode offers for your anchor point.

After that, we need to scale the image down to a usable size. As it is, it's too big for the screen, so by using the `scaleEffect` modifier, we have scaled it down to 12 percent of its original size. For our scene, that's a nice fit.

The next line of code uses the `offset` modifier to place the right leg in the exact location we need. It needs to be placed at the knee joint of the girl image, which I worked out to be a value of -448 for the *x*-axis and 92 for the *y*-axis. Arriving at those coordinates is really just a matter of trial and error. For example, if you want to move the part up on the screen, add a smaller number for the *y* position, and if you want to move the image to right, add a larger number for the *x* position.

Finally, we get to the animation, most of which we have seen before. Here, the `animation` modifier does the work of moving the leg, with a `duration` of 1 second, which is the time it takes for the animation to finish. Also, using a slight `delay` of `.09` seconds will give a more random look to the animation as we will set the left leg to a different delay.

As well as this, we want the animation to repeat forever, or at least until the user stops the app, so that's why the `repeatForever` function is used. The `autoReverse` parameter has a value of `true` because we want the animation to go forward in one direction, finish, reverse itself, and continue in the opposite direction. Also, the `animation` modifier needs a property for its `value` parameter, and for that, we pass the `rightLeg` property into it.

The final part of this code is the onAppear modifier. This modifier is used to run code when the view appears on the screen, hence the name onAppear. In body, we toggle the rightLeg property to true to activate the animation.

Now, having a leg on the screen that is animating back and forth is not really the look we are going for, so let's add the girl now, followed by the left leg.

Adding the girl

To add the girl to the scene, enter the following code:

```
Image("Girl").resizable().aspectRatio(contentMode: .fit)
                .scaleEffect(0.25)
                .offset(x: -300, y: 0)
```

This is similar code to adding the leg: we used the Image initializer, passed in the Girl image, made it resizable, and set its aspectRatio to fit. Then we only needed two more modifiers to finish this image off: scaleEffect, which will scale the image down to fit in the scene, and offset to place the girl image in the correct position on the *x*-and *y*-axes (using values of -300 for x and 0 for y will place the girl in about the middle of the screen).

Adding the left leg

Finally, to complete the girl image, she needs a left leg:

```
///left leg
    Image("leg").resizable().aspectRatio(contentMode: .fit)
        .rotationEffect(.degrees(leftLeg ? -45 : 30),
          anchor: .topTrailing)
        .scaleEffect(0.12)
        .offset(x: -455, y: 90)
        .animation(Animation.easeInOut(duration:
          0.4).delay(1).repeatForever(autoreverses: true),
          value: leftLeg)
        .onAppear() {
            leftLeg.toggle()
        }
```

The code for this left leg is pretty much the same as for the right leg, but we used the leftLeg property and changed some values. For example, the duration property for this leg is 0.4 and the delay property is 1 second. As I mentioned earlier, by adding different durations and delays from the other images, we can randomize the swinging effect a little bit so that the legs don't both go up and down together. This will give the animation a more natural swinging motion.

Bringing the images together

With this code in place, we have finished piecing together the girl in the swing scene, but if you look at the preview, it only shows the background so far:

Figure 6.8: Our animation with just the background

Where are the two legs and the girl that we just coded? Well, it's all there, but it's just not positioned over the background yet; it's all off to the side of the screen. This is because we positioned the legs in relation to the girl, but we didn't position the completed image in relation to the background scene. To do that, let's come out of the second ZStack brace and add the following code:

```
.offset(x: 25, y: 0)
.rotationEffect(.degrees(girl ? -30 : -45), anchor:
   .top)
.animation(Animation.easeInOut(duration:
   1).delay(0.09).repeatForever(autoreverses: true),
   value: girl)
.onAppear() {
      girl.toggle()
}
```

This is what the code does:

- The first line offsets the completed Girl image a small amount so it's centered.

- The second line sets the rotation parameters for the completed image, meaning how far we want the girl to swing back and forth. If the girl property is true, the girl image will swing to the right (-30), and if it's false, the image will swing to the left (-45); this creates the swinging animation. The anchor point is placed above the girl image; this is where we want the image to pivot from.

- And the third line adds the animation to the completed image, with a duration value of 1 second and a slight delay of 0.09 seconds.

And with that code completed, you can now see the girl and the legs. However, there's still a problem: the image of the girl and her legs looks too small, and the legs are not connected to the girl:

Figure 6.9: Our animation with the image parts disconnected

To fix this, we need to add one line of code just after the closing brace of the very first ZStack:

```
.frame(width: 950, height: 900)
```

This code sets the frame's width and height of all the views inside the ZStack so it's in proportion to the background. Here is the result:

Figure 6.10: Our animation with the image parts (nearly) connected

Go ahead and run the application to see what it does. There are three animations happening here; the girl is swinging back and forth, and each leg is separately kicking up and down, as shown here:

Figure 6.11: The animation (with the parts nearly connected)

Everything is now animating... but look at the top of the swing in *Figure 6.11*. The rope ends in mid-air. Let's use the rope and leaf images in the Assets catalog to fix this.

Using the mask modifier

The rope is not attached to anything – how can we fix that? Well, it's easy: by adding two rope pieces and using a mask modifier to help them gradually fade out at the top.

Directly after the closing brace of the onAppear modifier for the left leg, add this code:

```
//MARK: - ROPE
///right side rope masked
Image("rope").resizable().aspectRatio(contentMode:
  .fit)
    .mask(LinearGradient(gradient: fadeOutRope,
      startPoint: .top, endPoint: .bottom))
    .frame(width: 57, height: 80)
    .offset(x: -189, y: -100)
```

```
///left side rope masked
Image("rope").resizable().aspectRatio(contentMode:
  .fit)
    .mask(LinearGradient(gradient: fadeOutRope,
      startPoint: .top, endPoint: .bottom))
    .frame(width: 57, height: 80)
    .offset(x: -228, y: -108)
```

We need two pieces of rope because the swing has two pieces, a right piece and a left piece. For this reason, I added two blocks of code, one for each piece.

The code to add the rope is nothing new; we're just using the Image initializer to pass in our rope image and setting the aspect ratio to fit. But what is new here is that we're using the mask modifier. The mask modifier applies a masking view to the view it's called on. The masking view defines the visible area of the view it is applied to, and any parts of the view that fall outside of the masking view's frame will not be visible.

The mask modifier takes a single parameter, which is the view that will be used as the mask. If we pass in gradient as we're doing here, we can gradually fade out the rope as it extends upward. This is where the LinearGradient function and our fadeOutRope property come into play; the latter contains an array of gradient colors (two colors actually, clear and black) that we pass into the LinearGradient function.

We also need to consider the startPoint (where you want to start blending in the next color) and the endPoint (where you want to end one color and start another color). In our code, the startPoint for the gradient is at the top of the rope image, and endPoint is at the bottom of the rope image. The reason why we want the start point at the top is so that it will have a clear color so we can fade out the rope as it moves upward.

In the final two lines of code, we set the size of the left and right rope images and offset them so they fit perfectly over the rope that's attached to the swing. This is the result of adding the two rope images with the mask modifier:

Figure 6.12: Our animation after adding the mask modifier

If you run the app now, you'll see that the rope extends up and fades away at the top. This looks much better because now the rope appears to be somewhere near the branch.

To improve this even further, we can partially cover up the end of the rope by adding the leaves image to the scene. To do this, add this final bit of code at the very end of the first ZStack:

```
Image("leaves").resizable().aspectRatio(contentMode: .fit)
        .frame(width: 460, height: 400)
```

```
        .rotationEffect(.degrees(-10), anchor: .trailing)
        .offset(x: -50, y: -180)
```

This is familiar code that we have used already, adding leaves to the scene, setting an appropriate `aspectRatio` and `frame` size, rotating it to the correct angle, which is perpendicular to the branch, and finally locating it on the x-and y-axis with the `offset` modifier.

Now the rope at the top is partially hidden by the leaves, giving the effect that it's tied off somewhere up in the branch:

Figure 6.13: Our completed animation

And with that, the project is complete. Run it and see what you think.

Summary

In this project, we learned how to take an image and cut out various parts at the joints, use those new images in code, and animate them in different and interesting ways. We also worked with modifiers that we have worked with before, including `rotation`, `scale`, and `offset`, but also a new modifier, `mask`.

There are ways to take this project further. If you're feeling curious, see whether you can cut the arms and head from the picture, and then give them some animation as well. Play around with the parameters so you can make each part move just enough to look natural. Maybe you can make the arms pivot at the elbow just slightly as the swing moves forward and backward. Add a button if you want so you can start and stop the animation that way. Mainly, just experiment and have fun!

In the next project, we will look at the three different axes of rotation, x, y, and z, and create an animation that will rotate a fan using gears and chains, similar to a bicycle chain that turns its gears.

7

Building a Series of Belts and Gears

In this project, we're going to explore rotation, and more specifically, how to use the `rotation3DEffect` modifier to rotate objects on the *x*-, *y*-, and *z*-axis. We will be doing this by animating a series of gears and belts that will eventually move a fan blade.

As we create this project, we will also explore how to use Groups and Pragma Marks to make your code more organized, and the `zIndex` property, which changes the depth of views.

In this chapter, we will cover the following topics:

- Animating our first circular gear

- Adding a worm gear using shadows

- Using a marching ants effect to create a gear belt

- Animating a gear shaft image

- Animating a fan image

- Bringing everything together in `ContentView`

Technical requirements

You can download the resources and finished project from the `Chapter 7` folder on GitHub: `https://github.com/PacktPublishing/Animating-SwiftUI-Applications`.

Animating our first circular gear

To begin with, let's create a new project, which I'm calling `Gears and Belts`. Then, add the images for the project (which you can find in the GitHub repository provided in the *Technical requirements* section) by dragging and dropping the images into Swift's asset catalog. The images we are using are `singleGear`, `doubleGear`, `wormGear`, `motor`, `shaft`, `fan`, and `goldBackground`.

In this section, we are going to start by animating a gear image around the *z*-axis, so let's make a SwiftUI file that will handle creating all the gears we need (as we have done in previous projects, we are going to work on each element for the project in separate files, and then piece them together in `ContentView` to create the finished animations).

To do this, go to **File** | **New** | **File**, and then choose the **SwiftUI View** template. Alternatively, you can use the Mac shortcut *Command + N* to get to the same place more quickly. Whichever method you choose, name this file `GearView` and press **Create**.

Now, we can fill this file by adding the variables needed to make and animate gears images. Let's start with a `State` variable that keeps track of the animation state, the state being whether the animation is in motion or not. Add this `@State` variable to the file:

```
@State private var rotateGear = false
```

This variable will help to keep track of whether the gear image is rotating or not, so I have called it `rotateGear`. It is also set to `false`, which means the animation will start inactive until this variable is changed to `true`.

The next variable will be of the `String` type, which we can use to set the name of the gear image:

```
var gearImage: String = ""
```

If you look back into the asset catalog, you will see that you placed three different types of gear in there: a single gear, a double gear, and a worm gear. So, when it comes time to use all these files in `ContentView`, this `gearImage` variable will help save time, as all we need to do is to type in the name of the gear we want to use.

Next, we need to be able to set the size of the gear; here's another variable to handle that:

```
var gearWidth: CGFloat = 0.0
```

You might be wondering why we are setting the width of the gear but not the height. Well, the gear images we are using are circles (except for the worm gear); as you may know, circles only need one dimension, the width or height, because circles have a diameter that is always the same, regardless of which dimension is measured.

Continuing with the variables needed for this file, let's add another variable that indicates the number of degrees our gear will turn:

```
var gearDegrees: Double = 0.0
```

This variable is called `gearDegrees`. A value of `360` will turn the gear image for one revolution, but right now, it is initialized as `0.0`.

We will also place gears all around the screen, so we'll need to set a couple of variables to handle the location of these gears. We will use two of them to set the X and Y location:

```
var offsetGearX: CGFloat = 0.0
var offsetGearY: CGFloat = 0.0
```

Next, we need to be able to rotate the gears, and later the belts, to different orientations in relation to their surroundings, so let's add a variable that will be in charge of setting that value:

```
var rotateDegrees: Double = 0.0
```

Then, we will add a variable to set the duration of the spinning gear, meaning how long it takes to finish one revolution:

```
var duration: Double = 0.0
```

The duration variable is set to `0`, but when it gets set to a value such as `7`, for example, that means it will take 7 seconds for the gear to turn one full revolution.

Finally, for this file, we need three more variables to set the *x*-, *y*-, and *z*-axis position of the gear:

```
var xAxis: CGFloat = 0.0
var yAxis: CGFloat = 0.0
var zAxis: CGFloat = 0.0
```

Each of these variables will control the axis that the gear rotates around. The axis is what allows us to rotate an object in three dimensions, which will help create perspective and the effect of depth in the scene. These variables are appropriately named `xAxis`, `yAxis`, and `zAxis`.

We have all the variables in place, so let's now add the code into the body of the struct and make our first gear. First, let's add a `ZStack` to hold all of the views we need:

```
ZStack {
        }
```

Now, inside the `ZStack`, we can use the `Image` initializer, which will place a gear image on the screen:

```
ZStack {
    Image(gearImage)
        }
```

Remember, we have initialized the preceding `gearImage` variable to an empty string; this is what we want because it allows us to pass in different string names that represent the gear images in the asset catalog.

Next, we need several modifiers to size and place the gear image, as well as the animation modifiers to make the gear image turn. Add the following code under `Image(gearImage)`:

```
ZStack {
            Image(gearImage)
                .resizable()
                .aspectRatio(contentMode: .fit)
                .frame(width: gearWidth)
                .rotationEffect(.degrees(rotateGear ?
                  gearDegrees : 0))
                .animation(Animation.linear(duration:
                  duration).repeatForever(autoreverses: false),
                  value: rotateGear)
                .rotation3DEffect(
                    .degrees(rotateDegrees),axis: (x: xAxis, y:
                      yAxis, z: zAxis))
                .offset(x: offsetGearX, y: offsetGearY)
        }
```

Let's look at the modifiers we are using here:

- Firstly, we know that we need to give the image the ability to resize, which is what the `resizable` modifier is for.

- Then, we want to constrain the gear image dimensions with the `fit` aspect ratio option; as we have seen before, this mode preserves the content's aspect ratio and indicates that the object should be scaled to fit within the available space while maintaining its aspect ratio. This means that the object will be scaled down if necessary so that it fits within the space it's being displayed in, without distorting its shape.

  The other option is `fill`; this means that the object will be scaled up or down to fill the space it is being displayed in without distorting its shape. Some parts of the object may be outside of the visible area, but the object will maintain its aspect ratio. We haven't used this here though.

- Next, the frame of the image is set with the `gearWidth` modifer, which has been initialized to `0`. By doing this, we can pass in whatever value we need to create any size gear.

- The next line calls the `rotationEffect` modifier, which will rotate `gearImage` by a value we pass in. This modifier will only rotate the gear image when the `rotateGear` variable becomes `true`; otherwise, a value of `0` gets used, meaning no rotation.

- After that, we add the animation modifier, which gets a linear animation. The duration of the animation will depend on the value that's held in the duration variable – here, we have set the duration to repeatForever and autoreverses to false. Then, we have the value parameter, which accepts into its parameter the variable we want to animate and then applies the animation to the view.

- The next modifier is an interesting one, it's called rotation3DEffect. This rotates a view in three dimensions around the given axis; the amount of rotation will be determined by the degrees modifier that is being used within it. To understand how the view will be rotated, it's important to know where the *x*-, *y*-, and *z*-axes exist on an iPhone screen. Look at the following illustration:

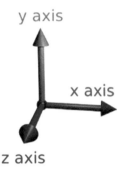

Figure 7.1: The three axes

The *x*-axis runs from left to right on the iPhone screen, the *y*-axis runs from top to bottom, and the *z*-axis runs from back to front. These axes are three different planes of dimensional space that hold views or objects, and when an object rotates, it does so on one, or all, of these axes. Looking at the rotation3DEffect modifier, if we pass a value in one of the axis parameters, the view will then rotate on that axis by the specified number of degrees.

- Back to the code, lastly, the gear image will need to be placed somewhere on the screen; for that placement, we can use the help of the offset modifier. This modifier has two parameters, x and y, and the values will be determined by the offsetGearX and offsetGearY variables.

With the modifiers all in place, we only need to start the animation, so let's add the following code at the end of ZStack's closing brace:

```
.onAppear() {
            rotateGear.toggle()
        }.shadow(color: .black, radius: 1, x: 0, y: 0)
```

The onAppear modifier, as we have seen before, will run the code in its body when the scene first appears. In the code, we want to toggle the rotateGear variable to true to start the animation. I'm also adding a little bit of black shadow to the gear image, which gives it a nicer look around its border.

Now, with everything we coded so far though, we still don't see any images in the previews! Let's fix that and add some values into the `Previews` struct in order to create a gear. In this example, we'll use the double gear image, and give it a size. Place the following code in `GearView_Previews` so we can see the animation work:

```
GearView(gearImage: "doubleGear", gearWidth: 100, gearDegrees:
    360, offsetGearX: 0, offsetGearY: 0, duration: 5)
            .previewLayout(.fixed(width: 200, height: 200))
```

This code fills out the `GearView` struct with some values. The first parameter uses the `doubleGear` image from the asset catalog as the gear to display. Next, the `gearWidth` and `gearDegrees` parameters receive values to set the width and turning degree. Then, for the `offset` parameters, by setting them to zero, the gear will just stay in the middle of the screen. Finally, adding a duration of 5 seconds means it'll take 5 seconds for the gear to turn for one complete revolution.

With all that in place, now, we can run the previews and check what we have done so far:

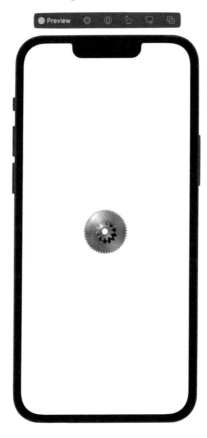

Figure 7.2: Adding our first gear

The gear now turns, again, at a rate of one revolution in 5 seconds.

Also, notice that I'm setting a fixed width and height for the preview window, as we don't need a full-size screen to display a small gear; 200 x 200 is more than enough room.

Now, with our gear in place and this file complete, anytime we need to make a gear anywhere in the project, all we have to do is call the `gearView` struct and pass in some values to create a gear of any size, wherever needed on the screen.

However, despite all that work, there is one gear that we won't be able to turn in any meaningful way, because it's not a circular shape, and that's the worm gear image in the asset catalog. In the next section, I'll explain what a worm gear is, and how to make it turn, or at least make it look like it's turning.

Animating a worm gear using shadows

Worm gears look like big screws with spiral threads, but without a screw head on the top. They're used in equipment and machines where strength is an important factor because they are very durable and can handle a lot of torque. Here is a typical worm gear:

Figure 7.3: A worm gear

If we add a worm gear image to the project and animate it as we did with the round gear, it wouldn't work very well, simply because the worm gear image is not a round shape. So, how can we make an irregularly shaped image appear like it's turning as it would in the real world?

What we can do is place small, shaded rectangles over the shiny parts of the worm gear image and animate those rectangles instead, which will create the illusion that the image is turning or spinning. Clever, right?

First, create a new file, choose the **SwiftUI View** template, and name it `WormGearView`. Inside this file, within the `WormGear` struct, we will start off by adding four `State` properties, one for each rectangle we need:

```
@State private var rect1 = false
@State private var rect2 = false
```

```
    @State private var rect3 = false
    @State private var rect4 = false
```

Now in our main `ZStack`, let's add another `ZStack` within to display the worm gear image:

```
ZStack {
    ZStack {
            Image("wormGear").resizable().frame(width: 100,
               height: 75)
        }
    }
```

The `Image` initializer declares the image and resizes it to a width and height that we can use.

Next, we will create the first rectangle that we need to place over the shiny part of the worm gear. To do so, add the following code:

```
HStack {
              Rectangle()
                  .frame(width: 4, height: 40)
                  .foregroundColor(.black)
                  .cornerRadius(5)
                  .opacity(rect1 ? 0 : 0.3)
                  .offset(x: 2, y: rect1 ? 14 : -8)
                  .animation(Animation.easeInOut
                     (duration: 0.5).repeatForever
                     (autoreverses: true), value: rect1)
                  .rotationEffect(.degrees(-4), anchor:
                     .top)
                  .onAppear() {
                      rect1.toggle()
                  }
        }
```

The rectangles will be placed in an `HStack` because we want to put them side by side, going from left to right across the gear. We're also using familiar modifiers that we've used before. We've made the rectangles black and given them a slight corner radius. The opacity of the rectangle will depend on whether the animating variable called `rect1` is `true` or not: if the `rect1` property becomes `true`, then we will give the rectangle a bit of visibility using an `opacity` of `0.3`; when the `rect1` property is `false`, we'll remove all opacity and hide it.

The next line of code uses the `offset` modifier to place this rectangle directly over the first shiny part of this worm gear on the left side. This `offset` modifier is also responsible for moving the small rectangle up and down on the *y*-axis, either up `14` points when `rect1` is `true`, or it will move the rectangle down to `-8` points when it becomes `false`. The effect we're going for here is to animate these tiny rectangles up and down and at the same time, fade them in and out over the shiny part of the worm gear image, creating the illusion that the part is turning.

Now for the `animation` modifier: this uses an `easeInOut` timing curve, has a duration of half a second, and is set to `repeatForever`, with `autoreverses` set to `true`.

After that, the `rotationEffect` modifier is used to rotate this small rectangle exactly where we want it on the worm gear. The rectangle will rotate around the anchor point, which we have set to the top part of the rectangle.

And finally, in the `onAppear` modifier, we toggled `rect1` so the animation starts when the view appears.

Now, go ahead and run the project; you can see the results in the preview:

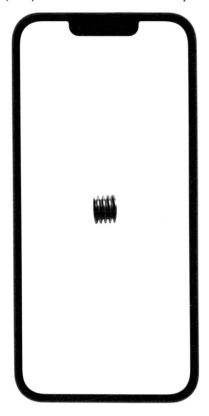

Figure 7.4: A worm gear in our animation

Looking at the figure, it's a bit hard to see the rectangle, but it's definitely there, a faint thin rectangle just after the third tooth. If you want to see the rectangle better, remove the worm gear by misspelling `wormGear` in the `Image` initializer, which will remove the worm gear from the previews (they hate when we misspell something!). When you run the project again, this is what you'll see:

Figure 7.5: The rectangle that overlays the worm gear

You should see the rectangle moving up and down, as well as fading in and out.

For the placement of this rectangle, ideally, we want it to be on the left, over the first tooth; however, that will happen when we add the other rectangles into this `HStack`. Remember, an `HStack` lines everything up from left to right, but since we only have one rectangle in the `HStack`, the `HStack` places it in the middle for now.

So, let's now add a second rectangle into the `HStack`, just under the first one:

```
Rectangle()
    .frame(width: 4, height: 40)
    .foregroundColor(.black)
    .cornerRadius(5)
    .opacity(rect2 ? 0 : 0.3)
    .offset(x: 7, y: rect2 ? -15 : -8)
    .animation(Animation.easeInOut
       (duration: 0.5).repeatForever
       (autoreverses: true), value: rect2)
    .rotationEffect(.degrees(-8))
    .onAppear() {
        rect2.toggle()
    }
```

This code is almost identical to what we've just added for the first rectangle. The difference here is we are offsetting the rectangle to a different location over the gear image, and the rotation is slightly different so it can be lined up over the next shiny part of the gear.

Run the code and you'll see two animating rectangles. They're not quite centered over the first and second shiny teeth of the gears yet, because we have two more rectangles to add, and then the HStack will center each animating rectangle perfectly for us.

Before we continue and add the third and fourth rectangles though, take a look at the first three modifiers of these two rectangles that we just added. They both have identical values in them, so we are repeating the code here, which is what we try to avoid when programming. Since the values don't change in these modifiers and we will use them in all four rectangles, instead, we can make a custom modifier into which we can put these three modifiers and shorten our code a little bit.

To create a custom modifier, we need to create a struct that conforms to the ViewModifier protocol. This protocol has one requirement, which is to implement a method called body content that will accept our content and then must return a view.

We can create a custom modifier at the bottom of the WormGear file. Moving outside of the WormGear struct completely and coming to the bottom of this file, add the following struct:

```
struct RectModifiers: ViewModifier {
    func body(content: Content) -> some View {
        content
            .frame(width: 4, height: 40)
            .foregroundColor(.black)
            .cornerRadius(5)
    }
}
```

This is a custom modifier struct, which I called RectModifiers; as you can see, we are implementing the body content method inside it, which is the requirement needed to satisfy the ViewModifier protocol. Then, I added the three modifiers that we were repeating in our code (i.e., the ones that weren't changing in value: frame, foregroundColor, and cornerRadius).

Now, all we have to do is go back to the first rectangle that we created, just after the worm gear creation, remove those three modifiers, and instead, call our custom modifier:

```
.modifier(RectModifiers())
```

To use it, we pass into it the name of the custom struct we just made, RectModifiers. This new modifier struct can hold as many modifiers as we want to put in there, so modifiers that don't change in value are probably a good idea to use here; this reduces the amount of code we need to write, especially if we have many views (for example, if we were to add 30 or 40 rectangles in this file).

Now, we can proceed to add the final two rectangles to help with the illusion that this gear is turning. Here's what the code looks like:

```
Rectangle().modifier(RectModifiers())
    .opacity(rect3 ? 0 : 0.3)
    .offset(x: 5, y: rect3 ? -5 : -10)
    .animation(Animation.easeInOut
        (duration: 0.5).repeatForever
        (autoreverses: true), value: rect3)
    .rotationEffect(.degrees(-8), anchor:
        .top)
    .onAppear() {
        rect3.toggle()
    }
Rectangle().modifier(RectModifiers())
    .opacity(rect4 ? 0 : 0.3)
    .offset(x: 4, y: rect4 ? -10 : -10)
    .animation(Animation.easeInOut
        (duration: 0.5).repeatForever
        (autoreverses: true), value: rect4)
    .rotationEffect(.degrees(-7), anchor:
        .top)
    .onAppear() {
        rect4.toggle()
    }
```

Before we try it out, let's add some shadow to these moving rectangles to help make them a little more pronounced. Add this code at the end of the closing brace of the first ZStack:

```
.shadow(color: .black, radius: 0.4, x: 0.0, y: 1)
```

By using the shadow modifier, and passing in a black shadow to go over each rectangle, I have given this shadow 4 points of radius, and the shadow will be shown on the *y*-axis with a value of 1. Using a positive number value will move the shadow along the *y*-axis, while using a negative number will move the shadow along the *y*-axis in the opposite direction. Play around with these numbers so you can see how they affect the shadow's prominence and location.

And with that code, this file is now complete. Run the project and see what you think:

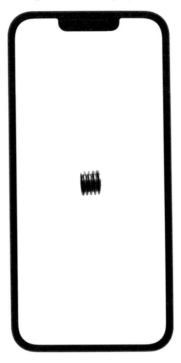

Figure 7.6: The finished worm gear

We have a worm gear that actually looks like it's turning. Notice that each rectangle has lined up completely over the teeth of the worm gear, starting from the left and moving to the right. The shiny parts are being covered up and exposed over and over again, at a nice even pace, which is actually about how fast many worm gears work.

Now we have finished animating the worm gears, we're going to create a marching ants effect that we can use to simulate a moving gear chain. We can accomplish that using the `dashPhase` initializer.

Using a marching ants effect to create a gear belt

Now that we have animated our circular and worm gears, next, we need to make some belts that can be used to wrap around those gears and connect them.

What we are actually doing is creating a marching ants effect. You probably have used this effect before, but without knowing what it was called – anytime you used your mouse or trackpad and outlined a view or created a bounding box around objects to select them, you were using the marching ants effect. You may remember that in *Chapter 6* when we used the **Lasso Selection** tool in Mac's Previews app, the little dashes that outlined the portion of the image selected were an example of this effect.

So, to create our gear belt, let's start this section by adding another new file, which we'll call `BeltView`. Then, as we usually do, we'll add the variables that make everything work first, inside the `BeltView` struct:

```
@State var animateBelt: Bool = false
    var beltWidth: CGFloat = 0.0
    var beltHeight: CGFloat = 0.0
    var offsetBeltX: CGFloat = 0.0
    var offsetBeltY: CGFloat = 0.0
    var dashPhaseValue: CGFloat = 45
    var rotateDegrees: Double = 0.0
    var xAxis: CGFloat = 0.0
    var yAxis: CGFloat = 0.0
    var zAxis: CGFloat = 0.0
```

Each one of these variables is in charge of a specific task:

- `animateBelt` keeps track of the animation for the belt.
- `beltWidth` and `beltHeight` set the width and height of the belt.
- `offsetBeltX` and `offsetBeltY` locate the belt in specific areas on the screen.
- `dashPhaseValue` is in charge of designing the belt – for example, how far we want to space the belt segments apart from each other, how thick they should be, and so on.
- `rotateDegrees` is used after we position the belt to rotate it either horizontally or vertically by passing in a degree number.
- `xAxis`, `yAxis`, and `zAxis` orient the belt on the *x*-, *y*-, and *z*-axes, respectively. You will see these three variables come into play when we start piecing together all these separate files into `ContentView`.

With the variables in place, we can move into the body of the struct and start adding the code to create the belt. There's not a lot of code to make a belt. First, start by adding a `ZStack` to hold our views:

```
ZStack {
        }
```

Next, we want to create the shape of the belt. If you look at most belts or chains that are gear-driven, they have a shape similar to a capsule, and luckily, SwiftUI gives us a capsule shape that we can use. Add the following code, including its modifiers, inside of the `ZStack`:

```
Capsule()
    .stroke(Color.black, style: StrokeStyle
        (lineWidth: 7, lineJoin: .round, dash:
```

```
        [5, 1.4], dashPhase: animateBelt ?
        dashPhaseValue : 0))
    .frame(width: beltWidth, height: beltHeight)
    .animation(Animation.linear(duration:
        3).repeatForever(autoreverses: false).
        speed(3), value: animateBelt)
```

This is only about five lines of code, but it does a lot of work here. First, we declare the capsule shape that we need and then use the `stroke` modifier on it. The `stroke` modifier does quite a bit and is also responsible for designing the belt: its first parameter will give the belt a color (we have chosen black), and the second parameter is the `strokeStyle` parameter, where we pass in a `StrokeStyle` struct.

This `StrokeStyle` struct has some parameters of its own that help style the belt:

- The first one is the `lineWidth` parameter. This one is fairly self-explanatory; it just means how wide we want to make the belt, which we have set to 7 points.

- There's also a `lineJoin` parameter. This is a value that determines how the segments of the belt will join together. There are three options we could use, `round`, `bevel`, and `miter`; I thought the line segments would look best using the `round` option, however feel free to experiment with all these values and numbers to get the best look for you.

- The next parameter is called `dash`, which is responsible for the length of the segments that's used to create the belt, and the gap between those segments. The first value of this parameter will determine the length of the segment (a larger number makes the segments bigger, while a smaller number makes the segments smaller); I'm using 5 points for this value. The second value determines the gap size between the segments (a larger number creates a larger gap, while a smaller number creates a smaller gap); for this value, a `1.4` point value creates gap that looks really good.

After the `strokeStyle` struct, the next modifier is the `frame`, which sets the width and height of the whole belt. Then we added an `animation` modifier, with a `linear` animation and a duration of three seconds to complete one revolution, and `autoreverses` set to `false` (as we just want the belt to turn in one direction only).

Now we need to add the `onAppear` modifier so we can start the animation when the app loads up. To do that, add the following code right under the existing code:

```
.onAppear {
        animateBelt.toggle()
    }
```

This code toggles the `animateBelt` property to `true`, kicking off the belt animation.

There's only one last bit of code we need to add to finish off the styling of the belt, and that is to rotate the belt to the proper angle for the gears. Coming out of ZStack, just after its closing brace, add the following code:

```
.shadow(color: .black, radius: 10, x: 1, y: 0)
.rotationEffect(.degrees(rotateDegrees), anchor:
  .center)
.offset(x: offsetBeltX, y: offsetBeltY)
```

This code will act on everything that is in the ZStack because it's been put after its closing brace. Here, I added a shadow modifier, setting the color to black and a radius of 10 to make the belt more pronounced, and placed the shadow on the *x*-axis. You can play around with the colors and these numbers for the shadow: by increasing the radius, you will make the shadow bigger, and by increasing the numbers for the x and y parameters, you can move the shadow up, down, left, and right. Remember, you can use negative numbers to move the shadow in the opposite direction.

The next modifier we are placing on the entire ZStack is rotationEffect. This will rotate the completed belt to the angle we specify; when we call these various methods later in ContentView, we'll pass in different values that'll orient the belt and size it just the way we want.

Finally, we added the offset modifier, which allows us to place the belt anywhere on the screen using the *x*- and *y*-coordinates.

If you try to test out what we've done, you won't see anything in the previews yet because we've just added a bunch of different variables into the BeltView struct. However, we're not using those variables in the Previews struct. To fix this, let's update the Previews struct to the following:

```
struct BeltView_Previews: PreviewProvider {
    static var previews: some View {
        BeltView(animateBelt: true, beltWidth: 380, beltHeight:
          48, offsetBeltX: 0, offsetBeltY: 0, rotateDegrees:
          90)
            .previewLayout(.fixed(width: 100, height: 400))
    }
}
```

When you run `Previews` now, you'll see the belt in action:

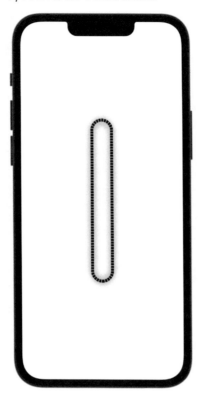

Figure 7.7: The finished belt with the marching ants effect

It's turning clockwise, has a nice style and spacing to fit our gears later, and the shadow makes it really come off the screen a bit.

> **Note**
>
> If you notice that the belt is not animating smoothly, meaning it's rotating but pauses slightly every few seconds or so, what you can do is play around with the `dashPhase` value, which is used to specify the starting point of the dashes in a dashed or dotted line. I set it to an initial value of `45` and that removed the pause for me, but if it does not remove it for your project, simply increase or decrease that value by 1, check the animation, and then tweak the value again by 1 until you find the sweet spot.

And that's another file under our belt (sorry, couldn't help myself!). Let's continue on to the next section, where we'll add a gear shaft to the mix. This object will turn a belt, which, in turn, will spin a fan.

Animating a gear shaft image

Continuing on to the next component, we need a gear shaft. A gear shaft is a cylindrical rod that has round gears at each end and is used to attach other gears or belts together, ultimately producing some form of output or work. For example, within the motor in your car, there is a gear shaft that turns due to the gasoline combusting. The output or work produced by that process moves the car forward. Our gear shaft won't move a car, but instead, will turn a fan. After creating this, as with the worm gear, we will animate the gear shaft by using animating rectangles. Again, this is because the image we are using is not round, so we cannot rotate it on the *z*-axis like the other gear images.

Let's start off by creating a new SwiftUI View file, which we'll call `GearShaftView`. Next, let's add the variables we need for this file; we only need one variable, and that's to track the animation:

```
@State var animateRect: Bool = false
```

After the variable, we just need to add the code for the gear shaft image and animate it. Add the following code inside the `body` property:

```
var body: some View
      ZStack {
          ZStack {
              Image("shaft").resizable().frame(width: 160,
                  height: 40)
              Rectangle().frame(width: 140, height: 8)
                  .foregroundColor(.black)
                  .cornerRadius(5)
                  .opacity(animateRect ? 0 : 0.5)
                  .animation(Animation.easeInOut(duration:
                      0.5).repeatForever(autoreverses: true),
                      value: animateRect)
                  .onAppear() {
                      animateRect.toggle()
                  }.offset(x: 0, y: -7)
          }
      }
  }
```

We start by bringing the gear shaft image into the scene and setting the width and height dimensions for it. After that, we add a rectangle, which will be the animating shadow moving up and down over the shaft. The color of the shadow is black, with a little bit of a corner radius added on. The opacity will animate from 0, which is invisible, to 0.5, which is 50% visible. This will produce a nice shadowy rectangle that appears and disappears at the same cadence that the gears and shafts are turning.

In the next line of code, the animation is added, with a duration of one-half a second to complete one revolution. It has `autoreverses` set to `true` because if we set `autoreverses` to `false`, then the animation would look too abrupt (it needs `autoreverses` in order to slide the rectangle back down).

Then, we start the animation in the `onAppear` method and offset the rectangle so it's neatly placed exactly where we want it, over the shaft image, using the `offset` modifier set to 0 for x and −7 for y.

We are getting close to putting all these files together, but next up, we're going to animate the fan image.

Animating a fan image

There are actually two components left to create, the fan and the motor. However, we will add the motor when we start piecing all of the files together inside `ContentView`. For that reason, let's focus on creating the fan now.

Like always, create a new file, select the **SwiftUI View** template, and call it `FanView`. In this file, we only need two variables – one for the state of the animation and one to hold the degrees of rotation for the fan; here they are:

```
@State private var rotateFan = false
var degrees: Double = 360 * 4
```

This file is quite short, so just add the following code to complete it:

```
var body: some View {
    ZStack {
    Image("fan").resizable().aspectRatio(contentMode:
      .fit).frame(width: 200)
        .rotationEffect(.degrees(rotateFan ? degrees : 0),
          anchor: .center)
        .animation(Animation.linear(duration: 4)
          .repeatForever(autoreverses: false),
          value: rotateFan)
    }.onAppear() {
        rotateFan.toggle()
    }.shadow(color: .black, radius: 15)
    }
```

Let's review this code. Inside the ZStack, we added the image of the fan and resized it. Then we used the rotationEffect modifier on it to make it turn. We want the fan to spin around its center, so we set the anchor to center, and then add the animation with a duration of 4, which means it will spin 4 revolutions in 4 seconds. After that, set the animation to repeatForever and set autoreverses to false (reverse because we want the fan to spin only in one direction).

Then, let's start the animation using the onAppear modifier and add a nice heavy shadow around the fan with a 15-point radius.

And that completes the fan. Now, let's now head over to ContentView to create the final component – the motor – and start bringing all the files together in one view.

Bringing everything together in ContentView

Okay – we have accomplished a lot, including creating files for single and double gears, a worm gear, a gearshift, and a fan. Now, let's create the final file for the motor and organize all these files together in ContentView.

We're going to use a Swift feature called **Pragma Marks**; this is a special syntax that labels and delineates blocks of code with a very thin line between them and makes those labels appear in one drop-down menu for easy searching and navigation. That's very helpful when you have very large files with hundreds or thousands of lines of code.

We will also use a SwiftUI feature called **Groups**; this can help us further organize all the code in the ContentView file by grouping multiple objects together, such as views, scenes, or even commands, into a single unit. We will organize much of the code into groups based on whether it is animated on the x-, y-, or z-axis.

And then we will use the **ZIndex** modifier. This modifier works with views that are overlapping each other, so it can be used to force a view either to the front or the back of other views. This is important because sometimes we need a view to be more prominent in the scene and another view to be hidden behind the scene, with only parts of it visible. You'll see how this works soon.

To help you complete this project, I have also labeled all the views to help you identify their location on the screen, and how they are oriented:

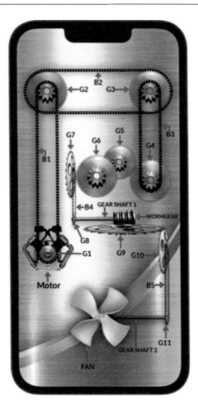

Figure 7.8: Our project with the views labeled

G annotations refer to the gears and **B** annotations refer to the belts. I numbered each gear and belt according to how it will appear in the code. We will be writing this code sequentially by the numbers – so, **G1**, then **G2**, then **G3**, and so on. The diagram shows the placement of all the parts.

As always, we have the ContentView file already created for us when we started the project, so we don't need to create any more new files. The first thing we are going to do here in ContentView is to add the motor.

Adding the motor

To add the motor, move into the body property of ContentView and then add a main ZStack to hold everything. Then, inside that, place another ZStack:

```
ZStack {
    ZStack {
        }
    }
```

Inside the second `ZStack`, let's add our first organizational structure, the Pragma Mark. To make a Pragma Mark, the syntax requires two forward slashes and `MARK` written in capital letters, followed by a colon. That will create a thin line moving across the file. You can write whatever you want after that for the title.

So, to create a Pragma Mark for the motor, enter the following code:

```
//MARK: - MOTOR
```

Now, notice the very thin line that the Pragma Mark creates from one end of the code file to the other within the editor:

```
8                    ZStack {                                    ▼
9                        //MARK: - MOTOR
```

Figure 7.9: Our first Pragma Mark

The Pragma Mark also does something very useful behind the scenes too. If you look at the top left of your Xcode menu bar, where all the tabs appear, you'll see a **MOTOR** tab:

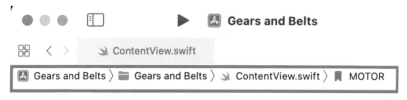

Figure 7.10: The Pragma Mark tab

If you click on the tab, a drop-down menu will open up, containing all the Pragma Marks that you created; clicking on any one of them will take you immediately to the code in that part of the file. You'll see the usefulness of this when you have dozens or even hundreds of different blocks of code in one file, eliminating the need to scroll through a lengthy file.

Now, let's add the code that creates the motor in the scene:

```
Group {
        Image("motor").resizable().aspectRatio(contentMode:
          .fit).frame(width: 140, height: 120)
            .offset(x: -120, y: 90)
                }
```

This is our first time using the `Group` syntax. Looking at the code inside the group, it contains everything that we've been doing all along: creating the motor using the image that's in the Assets catalog, resizing it, setting the aspect ratio so the motor fits on the screen as we want, giving it a frame size, and offsetting on the *x*- and *y*-axis.

If we run the code, this is what we should have in the previews so far:

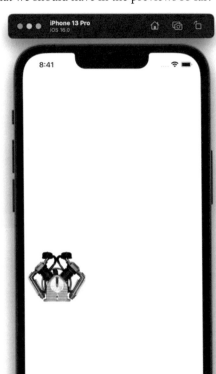

Figure 7.11: The motor

There's only one object in that group, the motor, but that's perfectly fine – we'll be adding more objects into further groups as we make them. For now, let's now add some gears to the scene.

Adding the gears along the x-, y-, and z-axes

In this section, we will use the GearView struct to add the gears. Remember, we already designed and animated the gears in the GearView file, so all we need to do is call the GearView struct here in ContentView and pass in some values.

This is where we will also be rotating the gears and belts on the x-, y-, and z-axes, so to recap how each axis operates on the screen (shown back in *Figure 7.1*):

- The y-axis runs from top to bottom and bottom to top.
- The x-axis runs from left to right and right to left.

- The *z*-axis moves from back to front or front to back. Holding an object in your hand and moving closer to your eyes is an example of moving that object along the *z*-axis.

With that understanding, let's start adding components. Put the following code in right after the closing brace of the motor group:

```
//MARK: - GEARS ANIMATING ON THE Z AXIS
Group {
    ///Gear 1
    GearView(gearImage: "doubleGear",
        gearWidth: 40, gearDegrees: 360,
        offsetGearX: -124, offsetGearY: 102,
        duration: 5)
    ///Gear 2
    GearView(gearImage: "doubleGear",
        gearWidth: 100, gearDegrees: 360,
        offsetGearX: -124, offsetGearY: -280,
        duration: 7)
    ///Gear 3
    GearView(gearImage: "doubleGear",
        gearWidth: 100, gearDegrees: 360,
        offsetGearX: 124, offsetGearY: -280,
        duration: 7)
    ///Gear 4
    GearView(gearImage: "doubleGear",
        gearWidth: 100, gearDegrees: 360,
        offsetGearX: 124, offsetGearY: -70,
        duration: 7)
    ///Gear 5
    GearView(gearImage: "doubleGear",
        gearWidth: 80, gearDegrees: -360,
        offsetGearX: 49, offsetGearY: -113,
        duration: 5)
    ///Gear 6
    GearView(gearImage: "doubleGear",
        gearWidth: 100, gearDegrees: 360,
        offsetGearX: -6, offsetGearY: -80,
        duration: 7)

}
```

I titled this group GEARS ANIMATING ON THE Z AXIS. Here, I'm calling the GearView struct six times, which creates six gears that are turning on the *z*-axis. Let's just look at Gear 1, as they are pretty similar, just with different values.

So, in Gear 1, I set the gear's width to 40 points, which makes a small gear, and positioned it directly over the front of the motor using the offsetGearX and offsetGearY parameters. The amount of degrees passed into the gearDegrees parameter is 360; that's one revolution of a circle, as we want these gears to turn for a full revolution.

Since these are 2D images and not 3D images of gears, the depth is not really perceivable, and the gears will lie flat and be animated clockwise. The duration parameter controls the amount of time it takes the gear to turn one full revolution; I'm using a value of 7 for the larger gears, and a value of 5 for the smaller ones. The small and larger gears are made using the gearWidth parameter.

Looking at the gearDegrees parameter, the values I'm using are all set to 360 (a positive number) to move them clockwise. Well, that is except for Gear 5, which is set to -360 (a negative), as that gear will move counterclockwise.

This is what the previous code we just wrote should look like:

Figure 7.12: The gears rotating on the z-axis

If you run this in the simulator, all of those gears will now be turning because we set the animation up already in the `GearView` file.

Let's continue and add another group of gears that animate on the *y*-axis this time. Add the following code right under the closing brace of the previous group:

```
//MARK: - GEARS ANIMATING ON THE Y AXIS
Group {
    ///Gear 7
    GearView(gearImage: "singleGear",
      gearWidth: 100, gearDegrees: -360,
      offsetGearX: -62, offsetGearY: -85,
      rotateDegrees: 76, duration: 7, xAxis: 0,
      yAxis: 1, zAxis: 0)
    ///Gear 8
    GearView(gearImage: "singleGear",
      gearWidth: 25, gearDegrees: -360,
      offsetGearX: -59, offsetGearY: 19,
      rotateDegrees: 76, duration: 7, xAxis: 0,
      yAxis: 1, zAxis: 0)
    ///Gear 10
    GearView(gearImage: "singleGear",
      gearWidth: 100, gearDegrees: -360,
      offsetGearX: 160, offsetGearY: 94,
      rotateDegrees: 76, duration: 7, xAxis: 0,
      yAxis: 1, zAxis: 0)
    ///Gear 11
    GearView(gearImage: "singleGear",
      gearWidth: 25, gearDegrees: -360,
      offsetGearX: 163, offsetGearY: 252,
      rotateDegrees: 76, duration: 7, xAxis: 0,
      yAxis: 1, zAxis: 0)
}
```

Again, we start off this group of code by adding our organizational Pragma Mark called GEARS ANIMATING ON THE Y AXIS. Here, we call the `GearView` struct four times, creating four gears that will rotate on the *y*-axis.

Looking at Gear 7 as an example, this has a width of 100 points, and `gearDegrees` is set to -360 (which means the gear rotates counterclockwise). Next, the code repositions the gears using the `offsetGearX` and `offsetGearY` parameters. And by using the `rotateDegrees` parameter, and passing in a value of 76, we can rotate this gear on the *y*-axis.

The other three gears are almost exactly the same, except their size and offset locations vary, but they will all turn on the *y*-axis.

After adding this group of code, this is what your previews should look like:

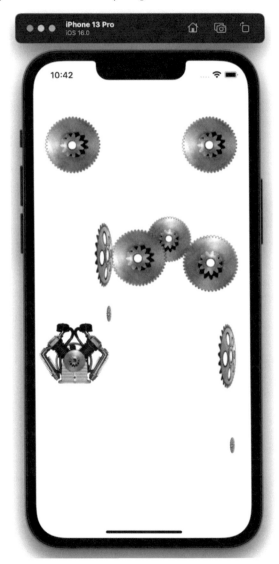

Figure 7.13: The gears rotating on the y-axis

Now, when you run the simulator, all these gears will be turning on their set axis.

Let's continue and add another group that will make a gear animate on the *x*-axis. Add the following code right after the closing brace of the previous group:

```
//MARK: - GEAR ANIMATING ON THE X AXIS
Group {
                ///Gear 9
                GearView(gearImage: "singleGear",
                    gearWidth: 175, gearDegrees: 360,
                    offsetGearX: 60, offsetGearY: 39,
                    rotateDegrees: 84, duration: 7,  xAxis:
                    1, yAxis: 0, zAxis: 0)
    }
```

The GEAR ANIMATING ON THE X AXIS group just has one gear here and it's the biggest gear so far, with a width of 175 points. This gear will mesh up with two other gears – the gear to its right in the scene and the worm gear.

This is similar to the code we've already placed for the other gears in that we use the GearView initializer to create it and use the same parameters to size and locate it in the scene, but the difference here is that we're using the xAxis parameter, and passing in a value of 1. The xAxis parameter will rotate this gear on the *x*-axis, a completely different angle than for the *y*-axis or *z*-axis. The amount of rotation is 84 degrees.

Before we run this and check things out, let's add the worm gear to see how everything fits together.

Adding the worm gear

To add the worm gear to our ContentView, add the following code:

```
//MARK: - WORM GEAR
                Group {
                    WormGearView().offset(x: 60, y: 30).
                        zIndex(-1)
                }
```

This grouping is labeled WORM GEAR and is placed using the offset modifier. Something new here though is the zIndex modifier. The zIndex modifier places a view in front of or behind other views, which allows us to position our views from front to back or vice versa.

I've talked about the *z*-axis already, which relates to depth and objects moving closer to and farther away from us. Why would we want to move a view closer or further away from our perspective? Well, let's look at an example of what happens if we don't use the zIndex modifier in our code:

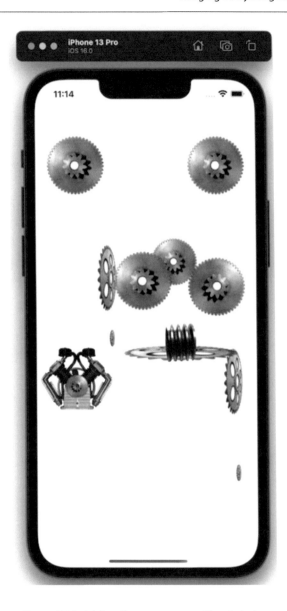

Figure 7.14: Adding the worm gear without zIndex

From the illustration, you can see that the worm gear has now moved to the front, which is not the placement that I want. I want the worm gear to mesh up from behind Gear 9.

Let's now add the `zIndex` modifier back into our code and look at the results:

Figure 7.15: Adding the worm gear with zIndex

All views in SwiftUI have a default `zIndex` of 0, so when I passed in a negative number, the worm gear was placed behind `Gear 9`. As you can see, this can be an important modifier when trying to organize your views regarding how close or far away you want them to be.

And with that, we have finished all the gears, so now we can move on to adding the belts into the scene.

Adding the belts

Continuing with the building out of our scene, let's add the belts. Add the following grouping, which contains three belts that move on the *z*-axis:

```
//MARK: - BELTS ON THE Z AXIS
                Group {
                    ///Belt 1
                    BeltView(animateBelt: true, beltWidth:
                        425, beltHeight: 48, offsetBeltX: -124,
                        offsetBeltY: -90, rotateDegrees: 90)
                    ///Belt 2
                    BeltView(animateBelt: true, beltWidth:
                        352, beltHeight: 100, offsetBeltX: 0,
                        offsetBeltY: -280, rotateDegrees: 0)
                    ///Belt 3
                    BeltView(animateBelt: true, beltWidth:
                        258, beltHeight: 48, offsetBeltX: 124,
                        offsetBeltY: -175, rotateDegrees: 90)
                }
```

Here, we called the `BeltView` struct, set the `animateBelt` properties to `true`, and then gave each belt an appropriate width and height so it could connect to its corresponding gears using the `beltWidth` and `beltHeight` parameters. After that, we place the belts where they need to be using the `offsetBelt` parameters. Finally, we rotated the belts either by 90 degrees, which places the belt vertically, or by 0 degrees, which places the other belt horizontally. Here's what they look like in relation to the gears they mesh with:

Figure 7.16: The belts on the z-axis

Now, let's take a look at rotating belts on the *y*-axis. As before, add the following code after the closing brace of the previous group:

```
//MARK: - BELTS ON THE Y AXIS
        Group {
            ///Belt 4
            BeltView( beltWidth: 32, beltHeight: 125)
                .rotation3DEffect(.degrees(75), axis:
                    (x: 0, y: 1, z: 0))
                .offset(x: -60, y: -33)
            ///Belt 5
            BeltView(beltWidth: 28, beltHeight: 180,
                offsetBeltY: -10)
```

```
        .rotation3DEffect(.degrees(75), axis:
          (x: 0, y: 1, z: 0))
        .offset(x: 162, y: 185)
    }
```

Calling the `BeltView` struct again, we have set these two belts to a width and height appropriate for the gear they will be meshed with. Then, we used the `rotation3DEffect` modifier and rotated these belts on the *y*-axis. The rotation happens when we pass a value of `1` into the `y` parameter, and they will rotate by `75` degrees. As with the other belts, we offset them so that they line up with their corresponding gears using the `offset` modifier.

Now, your previews should look like this:

Figure 7.17: The belts on the y-axis

All those belts and gears will be fully animated if you run the project in the simulator. That leaves us with only two more groups to go – the gear shaft and fan, and a background.

Adding the gear shafts

To bring the shafts into the scene, add the following code next:

```
//MARK: - GEAR SHAFTS
                Group{
            ///Shaft 1
            GearShaftView().offset(x: 5, y: 28).
                zIndex(-1)
            ///Shaft 2
            GearShaftView().offset(x: 95, y: 260).
                zIndex(-1)

        }
```

This is our GEAR SHAFT group. Here, I'm calling the GearShaftView struct twice, to create two gear shafts. Then, all we have to do is simply offset them to the proper locations, and call zIndex on them, passing in a negative value. This will position them behind the other views, creating the illusion that the shaft is actually part of the worm gear. Here's what the previous code produced:

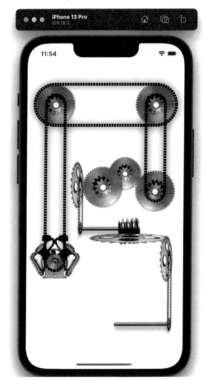

Figure 7.18: The gear shafts

The worm gear and the gear shaft are the two objects that we could not animate with conventional methods because that would not look good, and it wouldn't be an accurate representation of how they turn in the physical world. So, we created our shadow boxes and placed them strategically over these two shafts. When you run this in the simulator, you'll notice these rectangles appear to make the worm gear and two shafts turn.

Remember, these are just images that are sitting on the screen doing nothing, but because of a little trickery, they actually appear like they're turning!

Now, let's add the final group – the fan.

Adding the fan

It would be nice if all of these gears and belts would produce some sort of output, so in this project, that output will be to spin a fan. Let's now add the final grouping of code right under the existing group:

```
//MARK: - FAN
                Group {
                    ///Fan
                    FanView().offset(x: 0, y: 250).frame(width:
140, height: 140)
                }
```

All we have done is called the `FanView` struct, offset it to the bottom of the scene, and set a width for it (since it's round, we don't need to set a height).

Nearly there, just one last task: adding a background.

Adding the background

I have a nice gold background that'll look great with all the objects against it, so let's come out of the main `ZStack`, and after its closing brace, add the following code:

```
//MARK: - BACKGROUND
.background(Image("goldBackground").resizable().
aspectRatio(contentMode: .fill)
            .frame(width: 400, height: 1000))
```

This sets the gold background to a frame width and height of 400 x 1000, sitting nicely on an iPhone.

Finally, run that in the simulator and see what you think:

Figure 7.19: The completed project

Feel free to play around with all the parameters and settings, changing the colors of the belts or objects, changing the angles of rotation, and so on. This will allow you to really understand what these parameters and functions all do, and how they synergistically work together!

Also, notice that we continued to use Pragma Marks throughout the project. Let's see how handy they are; so, come back up to the menu bar and click on the last tab (this tab doesn't have a name, but you can *always* find the Pragma Marks in the last tab of the menu bar):

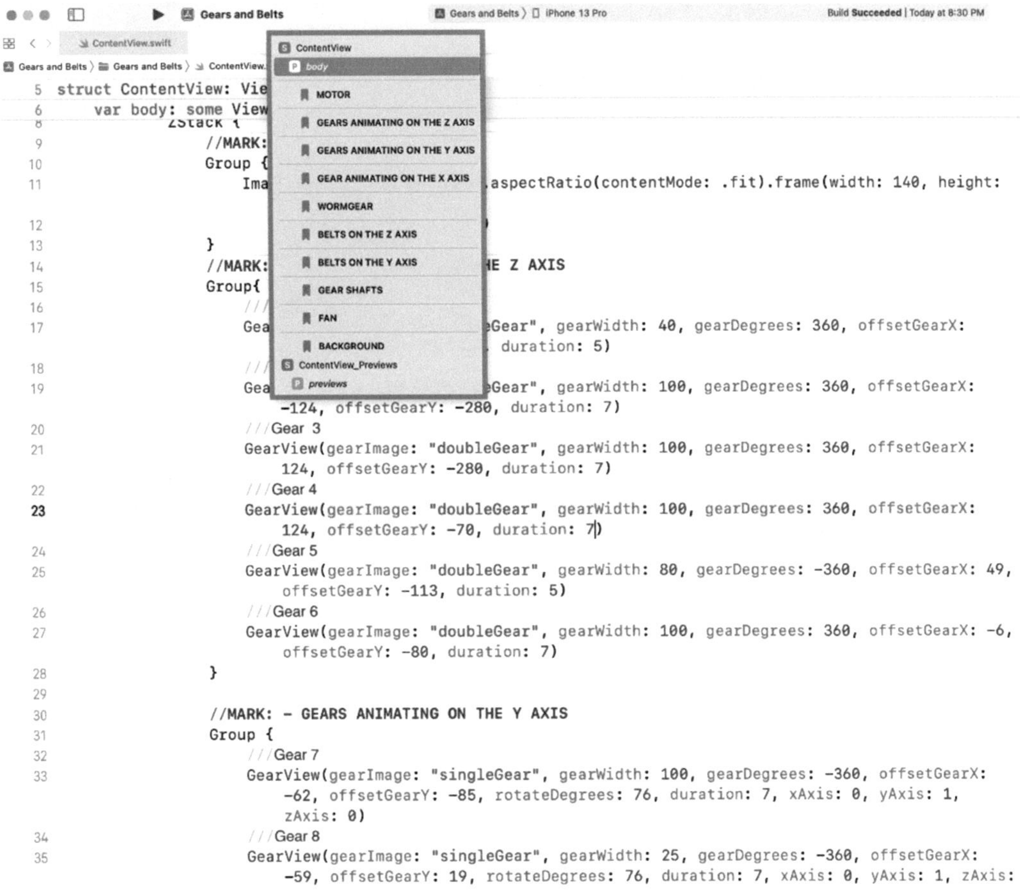

Figure 7.20: Viewing the Pragma Marks of the project

Every Pragma Mark indicates a different area of code based on the title we gave it, which makes it very easy to jump to in an instant, regardless of how big the file is.

Summary

In summary, through creating this project, we've accomplished quite a bit. As before, you saw how to create separate files – in this case, gears and chains – how to make a marching ants effect, how to combine everything into `ContentView`, and how to organize the code neatly using Pragma Marks and Groups. You also learned how to animate objects on all three axes, *x*-, *y*-, and *z*-, and saw how to use `zIndex` to place views more dynamically, from back to front, and vice versa.

In the next project, we will look at animating a flower and its petals so that it appears to be breathing, and creating some snow in the background.

8

Animating a Bouquet of Flowers

Welcome to the next project. Here, we will create a bouquet of flowers, animate the flower petals so they open and close, and then add a smoke/vapor effect to make it look like the flower is breathing by using the `blur` modifier.

Behind the flowers, we will place a winter backdrop, and make it snow too by using the `CAEmitter` class. The `CAEmitter` class is a UIKit class that was built for animation, but to be able to access it, we will need to use a SwiftUI bridging protocol called `UIViewRepresentable`. The `UIViewRepresentable` protocol will let us bridge the two frameworks, UIKit and SwiftUI.

Accompanying this, we will include two labels – **Breathe In** and **Breathe Out** – so that you can breathe along with the flowers, similar to a meditation app.

So, in this chapter, we will cover the following topics:

- Adding the variables and a winter background
- Animating the text labels
- Using the `blur` modifier to create a vapor effect
- Animating the flower petals in an arc
- Adding the flower bouquet and the animated breath
- Creating falling snow in the scene

Technical requirements

You can download the resources and finished project from the Chapter 8 folder on GitHub: `https://github.com/PacktPublishing/Animating-SwiftUI-Applications`.

Adding the variables and a winter background

Let's get started and create a new SwiftUI project – I have called it `Breathing Flower`.

Next, go ahead and download the assets for this project. The images are `bouquet`, `petal`, `smoke`, `snow`, and `winterNight`. After you download them, drop the images into the Assets catalog.

We now have the pictures we need loaded into the project. So, let's start in `ContentView` and add the variables we need to make this flower come alive:

```
import SwiftUI
struct ContentView: View {
    @State private var petal = false
    @State private var breatheInLabel = true
    @State private var breatheOutLabel = false
    @State private var offsetBreath = false
    @State private var diffuseBreath = false
    @State private var breatheTheBouquet = false
```

You should be familiar with the process of creating animating variables by now. Here, we made a variety of variables, including the following:

- `Petal`: To track the petal's movements
- `breatheInLabel` and `breatheOutLabel`: To track the **Breathe In** and **Breathe Out** labels
- `offsetBreath`: To move the breath from inside the flower to outside the flower
- `diffuseBreath`: To track the transformation of the smoke from a still image to an animation
- `breatheTheBouquet`: To keep track of the bouquet animation

Before we put these variables to use, let's head into the `body` property and add a winter image to the scene. First, create a `ZStack` in order to hold all of the views that we will be adding:

```
var body: some View {
    ZStack {
        //MARK: - ADD A WINTER BACKGROUND - AND THE SNOW
        Image("winterNight").resizable()
          .aspectRatio(contentMode: .fill)
                         .frame(width: 400, height: 900)
    }
}
```

This is familiar code to us now. Here, we are using the `Image` initializer and passing in the background image called `winterNight`, which is in the assets catalog. Then, we are resizing the image and using the `aspectRatio` option of `fill` to take up the whole screen, before finally giving it some dimensions with the `frame` modifier. This is what the scene looks like:

Figure 8.1: The winterNight background

Now that we have added the background to the scene, our next goal is to add some labels: **Breathe In** and **Breathe Out**. What we want to achieve here is to make the two labels grow and shrink at the same time as the flower petals open and close, so these labels will have the same duration and delay as the flower petals in the project, perfectly in sync.

Animating the text labels

Now, let's add two labels that can act as a guide for the user to watch their breath. Still working in the `ZStack` and moving directly underneath the previous line of code, add another `ZStack`, and fill it with the following:

```
//MARK: - ANIMATE TEXT LABELS SO THEY GROW AND SHRINK
```

```
//a ZStack so we can offset the entire scene vertically
ZStack {
  Group {
    Text("Breathe In")
        .font(Font.custom("papyrus", size: 35))
        .foregroundColor(Color(UIColor.green))
        .opacity(breatheInLabel ? 0 : 1)
        .scaleEffect(breatheInLabel ? 0 : 1)
        .offset(y: -160)
        .animation(Animation.easeInOut(duration:
          2).delay(2).repeatForever(autoreverses:
          true), value: breatheInLabel)
            Text("Breathe Out")
        .font(Font.custom("papyrus", size: 35))
        .foregroundColor(Color(UIColor.orange))
        .opacity(breatheOutLabel ? 0 : 1)
        .scaleEffect(breatheOutLabel ? 0 : 1)
        .offset(y: -160)
        .animation(Animation.easeInOut(duration:
          2).delay(2).repeatForever(autoreverses:
          true),value: breatheOutLabel)
  }
}
```

Let's dissect this code a little bit and see what we're doing. First, we're adding a second ZStack, then a group, to help keep the code organized.

Next, we use the Text initializer and type in whatever text we'd like to appear on the screen. In our case, we are typing in Breathe In and Breathe Out, and just like that, we have text on the screen. Then, using the font modifier, you can change the font to one of your choosing. Xcode comes with many built-in fonts, and I am using one called papyrus.

> **Note**
> If you'd like to know the names of the fonts that you can use for iOS, you can go to the following website: https://developer.apple.com/fonts/system-fonts/.

As well as choosing the specific font type, we set the font `size` parameter to `35`, and use the `foregroundColor` modifier to make the **Breathe In** label green and the **Breathe Out** label orange.

Next, the opacity of the text labels is animated here by using the `breatheIn` and `breatheOut` variables. When those variables are `true`, their opacity will be set to `0`, which makes the label text invisible. But when the `breatheIn` and `breatheOut` variables are `false`, the text will be set to `1`, and they will become visible again.

After that, we set the size of the two text labels by using the `scaleEffect` modifier. We're using a ternary operator, which checks whether the `breatheIn` and `breatheOut` variables are `true` or not; if so, then we will scale the labels down to `0`; otherwise, when the `breatheIn` and `breatheOut` variables are `true`, we will scale the text labels back up to full size, which is `35` points.

The next line of code positions the label on the screen for the `y` axis, using the `offset` modifier. Remember, the *y* axis position views vertically.

Lastly, we add the `animation` modifier. The animation will start as it usually does when the `breatheIn` and `breatheOut` variables become `true`. The animation will have a duration of 2 seconds, which means it will take 2 seconds to complete, and then it will have a delay of 2 seconds before starting again.

And that completes the animation of the **Breathe In** and **Breathe Out** labels. To see this in action, let's add the `onAppear` modifier right after the closing brace of the first `ZStack`:

```
.onAppear {
            breatheInLabel.toggle()
            breatheOutLabel.toggle()
    }
```

As we've seen, `onAppear` will run the code in its body when the view first appears – that is, when the user taps on the app to open it. The code we want to run is the `breatheIn` and `breatheOut` variables; we want to toggle them to their opposite Boolean value to start the animation.

When you run this code in the previews or the simulator, you'll see two labels, each with its own color, scaling up and scaling down, and at the same time, fading in and out:

Figure 8.2: The Breathe In and Breathe Out labels added

That completes the labels. Now, let's focus our attention on making an image that looks like vapor to represent breath.

Using the blur modifier to create a vapor effect

In this part of the project, we will be using the `blur` modifier, which will apply a Gaussian blur to an image using a radius value that we specify. If you're not familiar with what a Gaussian blur is, this is a technique that is widely used in image editing software (such as Photoshop) and works by reducing the noise and detail of an image to create a smooth blurring visual effect.

We will use an image of smoke, called `breath` (which is in the Assets catalog), and apply the `blur` modifier to it, which will create a vapor effect and make our flower look like it's breathing.

There is very little code needed to achieve this effect. Coming out of the previous group we made, let's make a new group and add the following code:

```
//MARK: - TAKE AN IMAGE AND CONVERT IT TO VAPOR (BREATH)
   USING THE BLUR MODIFIER
      Group {
          Image("breath").resizable().frame(width: 35,
            height: 125)
             .offset(y: offsetBreath ? 90 : 0)
             .animation(Animation.easeInOut(duration:
               2).delay(2).repeatForever(autoreverses:
               true),value: offsetBreath)
             .blur(radius: diffuseBreath ? 1 : 60)
             .offset(x: 0, y: diffuseBreath ? -50 : -100)
             .animation(Animation.easeInOut(duration:
               2).delay(2).repeatForever(autoreverses:
               true), value: showBreath)
      }.shadow(radius: showBreath ? 20 : 0)
```

In the group, we use the `Image` initializer and pass in the image we want to use, `breath`. Then, we give it some dimensions, with a width of 35 and a height of 125.

After that, the code offsets the image vertically on the *y* axis. Then, when the `offsetBreath` variable becomes `true`, the image moves 90 points up, so it's coming out of the flower, and when `offsetBreath` is `false`, the image moves back down and is set back to 0.

Next, we add the animation to the image and to the `offset` modifier (yes, we can animate an `offset` modifier too!). We are using the same `duration` and `delay` values as the text labels (2 seconds, respectively) so that the labels and vapor animate in sync.

The next line is the `blur` modifier – this is what creates the magic of turning the image into a puff of vapor. This modifier has a parameter called `radius`, which accepts any integer number; the smaller the number, the less Gaussian blur is applied to the image, whereas the larger the number, the more blurred the image becomes. The ternary operator oversees the setting of the `radius` value to either 1 or 60, so depending on whether the `diffuseBreath` variable is `true` or `false`, we can control the amount of Gaussian blur on the image. When `diffuseBreath` becomes `true`, the image gets blurred by only 1 point, but when `diffuseBreath` becomes `false`, the code will add 60 points of Gaussian blur to the image.

Let's look at the next line of code – this is the `offset` modifier and is responsible for positioning the blur. We want to offset the smoke so it moves from inside the flower to outside the flower. This is accomplished by checking the `diffuseBreath` variable; when it's `true`, the vapor moves 50 points up, and when it's `false`, the vapor moves 100 points down.

After that, the `animation` modifier will interpolate through all the Gaussian blur values, from 1 to 60. In this interpolation (or looping, if you will), these values will act on the image very quickly, so fast that the non-moving still image of smoke will be transformed into an actual animation of smoke that will move up and disperse, as real smoke does.

> **Note**
>
> You may also have noticed that we are using two `animation` modifiers here. The reason for this is that the first one is placed right after the `offset` modifier, so it is being used to animate the offset of the image up and down; any code we add *after* that `animation` modifier will not be animated, hence the use of the second `animation` modifier. The second one is used to animate the `blur` modifier to make smoke and to animate the offset that moves the smoke. So remember, the `animation` modifiers act on the views above them, but if we need to add more of them, we can just add them as needed to animate any subsequent views, as we have done here.

Lastly, we add the `shadow` modifier, which will add a subtle shadow of 20 points around the moving breath when it exits the flower.

Now, to see the smoke transformation, add the `offsetBreath` and `diffuseBreath` variables to the `onAppear` modifier, like this:

```
.onAppear {
            breatheInLabel.toggle()
            breatheOutLabel.toggle()
            offsetBreath.toggle()
            diffuseBreath.toggle()
        }
```

This is what we can see:

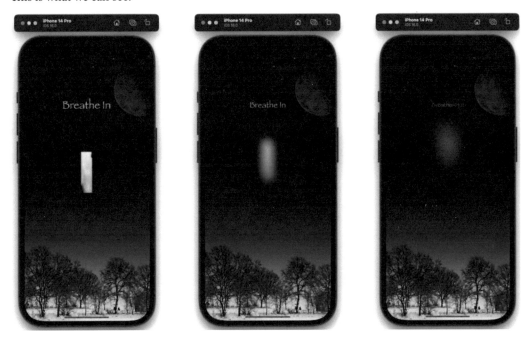

Figure 8.3: The smoke in our animation

As the animation starts out, the image of smoke is only being blurred by 1 point, but as the `offset` modifier moves the image upward, the blurring increases all the way to 60 points. At 60 points, the once still image has now been transformed into smoke, mimicking a breath.

As an aside, something interesting to check out later is that if you want to see the process of the smoke image turning into moving vapor at any time, then add this line of code beneath the `shadow` modifier:

```
.zIndex(1)
```

This will move the smoke image to the front of the scene, and you will see it being transformed into moving vapor.

With the vapor effect added, we can move on to the next step, which is adding the bouquet of flowers to the image.

Animating flower petals in an arc

We have a background, text labels, and an inhaling and exhaling breath effect; now let's add the petals to the scene. We can add the petal code in a separate file, so press *Command + N* to bring up the **New File** window, and create a new SwiftUIView file called `PetalView`.

The goal here is to make five petals move in an arc, so they open and close. We only need two variables for this, so this will be a very small file: we need one Boolean (`Bool`) variable to track the animation, and another variable to hold the number of rotations we want for each petal. Let's add them now:

```
@Binding var petal: Bool
var degrees: Double = 0.0
```

The `Binding` variable called `petal` will handle the animation. We are using the `Binding` wrapper because we are in a new struct, and we will need to use this variable in another struct, `ContentView`. When we prefix a variable with the `Binding` wrapper, we can then use it (bind it) to another struct or view.

Let's now move into the body property and create a petal. Add the following code:

```
struct PetalView: View {
    var body: some View {
        Image("petal").resizable().frame(width: 75, height:
          125)
            .rotationEffect(.degrees(petal ? degrees :
              degrees), anchor: .bottom)
            .animation(Animation.easeInOut(duration:
              2).delay(2).repeatForever(autoreverses: true),
              value: petal)
    }
}
```

There are only three lines of code to look at:

- First, we add the petal image from the Assets Catalog to the scene and appropriately size it.

- Next, we use the `rotationEffect` modifier to open and close the petal by choosing between two `degree` values: one value for the petal opening and one for its closing. We also anchor the rotation point to the bottom of the petal, so the petals will open and close in an arc.

- Then, we simply call the `animation` modifier to add the animation. Again, we continue to keep `duration` and `delay` at 2 seconds and set `autoreverses` to `true`.

To see the petal image in the previews, let's modify the `previews` struct to look like this:

```
struct PetalView_Previews: PreviewProvider {
    static var previews: some View {
        PetalView(petal: .constant(true))
    }
}
```

The only change in the `PetalView_Previews` struct is that we use the `petal` parameter and pass in the value of `.constant(true)`. This turns the `petal` variable to `true`, enabling the previews to display the contents of the `PetalsView` struct.

Let's now move back into `ContentView`, and call this new `PetalView` struct five times to display all five petals:

```
//MARK: - ANIMATE FLOWER PETALS IN AN ARC
    Group {
        PetalView(petal: $petal, degrees: petal ? -25 : -5)
        ///middle petal does not move
        Image("petal").resizable().frame(width: 75, height:
          125)
        PetalView(petal: $petal, degrees: petal ? 25 : 5)
        PetalView(petal: $petal, degrees: petal ? -50 :
          -10)
        PetalView(petal: $petal, degrees: petal ? 50 : 10)
    }
```

The code calls `PetalView` four times to add four petals to the UI, and then the fifth petal (the middle one) is added by a call to the `Image` initializer, as this petal will not be animated. The result is shown here:

Figure 8.4: The petals

Notice the dollar sign syntax ($) for the petal parameter: that is how we use the Binding variable in another struct. In the degrees parameter, we have two values: again, one for when the petal is open, and one for when it is closed. When the binding $petal property is true, the degrees value on the left is used, and when the $petal property is false, the degrees value on the right will be used.

Again, the middle petal will not be animated, so we only need to call the Image initializer and then set its size. The remaining petals use the same code; the only changes are the values for the degrees parameters.

And that completes the petals. Let's see how they animate by toggling the petal variable in the onAppear method, as we have done with the other variables:

```
.onAppear {
        petal.toggle()
        breatheInLabel.toggle()
        breatheOutLabel.toggle()
        offsetBreath.toggle()
        diffuseBreath.toggle()
    }
```

The petals open and close as we have set them up – to a specific point, rotating in an arc, and then closing again:

Figure 8.5: The petals animated

There are three components left to add to our project:

- A bouquet of flowers positioned directly over the petals
- The moving breath surrounding the flowers
- Snow falling in the background

In the next section, we will implement the first two points: adding the bouquet and the moving breath.

Adding the flower bouquet and the animated breath

Adding the first component, the bouquet, is relatively easy, as it is stuff we have already done; however, the second component, the moving breath, is a little tricky (but not to worry, we will go slow and everything will be explained).

So, first up, the bouquet. In `ContentView`, after the petal group's closing brace, add the following code:

```
//MARK: - ADD A BOUQUET OF FLOWERS AND MAKE THEM EXPAND
    AND CONTRACT SO THEY APPEAR TO BE BREATHING
```

```
Group {
  Image("bouquet").resizable()
  .aspectRatio(contentMode: .fit)
        .frame(width: 300, height: 400)
        .rotationEffect(.degrees(37))
        .offset(x: -25, y: 90)
    ///breathe the bottom bouquet 1
        .scaleEffect(breathTheBouquet ? 1.04 : 1,
          anchor: .center)
        .hueRotation(Angle(degrees: breatheTheBouquet ?
          50 : 360))
        .animation(Animation.easeInOut(duration:
          2).delay(2).repeatForever(autoreverses:
          true), value: breatheTheBouquet)

  Image("bouquet").resizable()
    .aspectRatio(contentMode: .fit)
        .frame(width: 300, height: 400)
        .rotationEffect(.degrees(32))
        .offset(x: -20, y: 95)
        .rotation3DEffect(.degrees(180), axis: (x: 0,
          y: 1, z: 0))
    ///breathe the bottom bouquet 2
        .scaleEffect(breatheTheBouquet ? 1.02 : 1,
          anchor: .center)
        .hueRotation(Angle(degrees: breatheTheBouquet ?
          -50 : 300))
        .animation(Animation.easeInOut(duration:
          2).delay(2).repeatForever(autoreverses:
          true), value: breatheTheBouquet)
}
```

This looks like a lot of code, but really, we are creating two bouquets using very similar code. The reason why I'm using two bouquets and overlapping them is to create the illusion of a full bunch of flowers.

Let's now look at the code. We start with the grouping organizational feature, and inside the group, we add the image for both bouquets. I'm setting the aspect ratio to fit, so the bouquet image keeps its proportional size, and framing the image with a value of 300 x 400.

Next, we call the `rotation` modifier on each bouquet, so we can rotate them to the proper angle we want in the scene; a 37-degree rotation for the first bouquet looks good, whereas 32 degrees for the second bouquet works better for that one. Then, each bouquet gets offset a little bit on the x and y axes, so they're neatly positioned directly over the breath. This location will help hide the breath, as we don't want to see that until it animates up from the bouquet.

The next line scales the bouquets up a little. The reason for this is that we want to create the effect that the bouquets are breathing as well, along with the petals. The top bouquet gets scaled up to 1.04, and the bottom bouquet gets scaled to 1.02. Notice the top bouquet gets scaled up slightly more than the bottom bouquet: this is because we wanted to stagger the two bouquets a little.

Then, `anchor` is set to `center`, so the two bouquets will expand and contract from that point.

The next line adds some hue rotation to the color of the bouquets so that they will change color along with the animation. We previously used the `hueRotation` modifier in *Chapter 5*, so that's nothing new here, but we are using different values for `hueRotation` to help make the bouquets more varied in appearance.

Also notice that we use the `rotation3DEffect` modifier only on the bottom bouquet. This is because the bouquet image for the top and bottom are identical; they are simply one image that we're using in two places, so by using the `rotation3DEffect` modifier here and passing in a value of 1 for the y parameter, this will flip the bouquet image on the *y* axis to the bouquet's opposite side. This helps give the overall look a more symmetrical appearance.

Finally, we add the animation for both bouquets; this is the same animation as we've done for the previous views, with a 2-second duration and a 2-second delay, so all the animations are in sync.

Now, in order to see this animation in action, once again, we need to add the animating variable in charge of the bouquet to the `onAppear` modifier. So, add the following code to the `onAppear` modifier:

```
}.onAppear {
            breatheInLabel.toggle()
            breatheOutLabel.toggle()
            offsetBreath.toggle()
            diffuseBreath.toggle()
            petal.toggle()
            breatheTheBouquet.toggle()
    }
```

Now, if we run the app, we will see the two bouquets expanding and contracting slightly, along with the petals moving too. You will also see the bouquets' colors changing, which is due to the `hueRotation` modifier we used.

Figure 8.6: The bouquet moving

The bouquet expanding and contracting is a subtle look (it's not pronounced like the petals opening and closing), which is the look we're going for here; we just want to create a slight expanding effect.

With that done and our app already looking really good, we just need to add one more component to the project: snow.

Creating falling snow in the scene

Making snow fall within your app really makes it come alive: it gives a rather magical look to it and sets the right mood for our winter scene. To do this, we need to utilize the power of UIKit and the UIViewRepresentable protocol, along with the CAEmitter class.

> **Note**
>
> As you continue through the rest of this chapter, don't worry if some of the UIKit classes and methods look different or unfamiliar to you as compared to the SwiftUI classes and methods we've been using. That's because they *are* different, and that's for a whole different book if you'd like to learn about UIKit. However, moving forward in this chapter, I will explain the different UIKit properties and methods used to make the snow for our animation, so you can get familiar with the process.

Adding the UIViewRepresentable protocol

The `UIViewRepresentable` protocol is what's called a **wrapper** for UIKit. It allows SwiftUI to work with UIKit and use UIKits classes and methods. If you've ever coded with UIKit, you'll know it's quite different compared to SwiftUI. For one thing, it uses something called **Storyboards**, which are a different way to design your layout and organize your views by way of dragging and dropping objects from an object library, such as buttons and sliders and text, and connecting them together on a big storyboard in Xcode. The positioning of all those objects is completely different as well and uses a system called **Auto Layout**, which is a system of methods and rules to keep your objects spaced apart and located on the screen, but it was very complicated and had a big learning curve.

SwiftUI eliminates Storyboards and Auto Layout and is a complete departure from UIKit in how you design and build apps. It's simpler and uses much less code to achieve the same results (as you probably already know). But, occasionally, we need to access some of the methods and classes that UIKit offers in order to do different things in our apps – for example, here, to make snow. That's why we need the `UIViewRepresentable` protocol.

The `UIViewRepresentable` protocol acts as a bridge between these two different frameworks, UIKit and SwiftUI, and lets us access the classes and methods we need.

So, let's create a new file to contain the snow code. Press *Command + N* and create a SwiftUIView file called `SnowView`. Then, at the top of the struct, we will modify its heading to make it conform to the `UIViewRepresentable` protocol. So, change the struct's heading to this:

```
//MARK: - CREATE SNOW FALLING ON THE SCENE
struct SnowView: UIViewRepresentable {
        }
```

When we add the `UIViewRepresentable` protocol to the struct's heading (right after the colon), this tells the system that we are now allowed to use the classes and methods from the UIKit framework. It also means we have to implement the required methods for this protocol. Some protocols only need you to declare them into a struct heading, as we have just done, but others also need you to implement some methods in order to satisfy the protocol requirements.

Dealing with methods and errors

`UIViewRepresentable` requires that we add two methods to the struct: `makeUIView` and `updateView`. But because we haven't added those methods yet, the change we just made will break our code and display an error: **SnowView does not conform to protocol UIViewRepresentable**. That is true because, as mentioned, we need to implement two methods to satisfy this protocol.

So, let's add the first method now, makeUIView, by adding the following code to the SnowView struct:

```
func makeUIView(context: Context) -> some UIView {
    }
```

The makeUIView method returns UIView, which will contain the snow, so we can use it in the ContentView later.

The second method we need to add is called updateView, which we can do directly under the previous method:

```
func updateUIView(_ uiView: UIViewType, context: Context) {
    }
```

This method is used when we want to update the view with new data. Since we don't need to do any updating when the snow is made, we can leave this method empty. However, it's a required method so it does have to be here in the SnowView struct; otherwise, the code won't work.

Now that we have the two required methods, the protocol should be satisfied. However, we still get an error: **Function declares an opaque return type, but has no return statements in its body from which to infer an underlying type**. This error refers to the makeUIView method and the fact that it has no return code in its body. The makeUIView method needs to return UIView (or simply, a view) in order for the error to go away. So, let's fill out the makeUIView method with the code that will return a view, which will, in turn, make our snow.

First, we need to set up the size of the view to fit the screen correctly. Remember, we are making a new view using UIKit's classes and methods, so we have to tell it how big the screen dimensions should be for this view. Add the following code to the makeUIView method:

```
func makeUIView(context: Context) -> some UIView {
//configure the screen
        let screen = UIScreen.main.bounds
        let view = UIView(frame: CGRect(x: 0, y: 0,
          width: screen.width, height: screen.height))
        view.layer.masksToBounds = true
    }
```

The first line of code creates a constant that will hold the bounds of the screen – that's the rectangle of the screen from top to bottom and left to right.

The second line of code creates the view that we will need to return when we finish writing this method out. We're setting the view to the size of the screen's width and height so that when we make the snow, we're using the entire boundaries of the iPhone screen, not just a little portion of it.

The next line of code uses the `masksToBounds` Boolean property and sets it to `true`. The `masksToBounds` property indicates to the system whether sublayers are clipped to the layer's bounds.

Sublayers are layers or views that will be added later in the code. Everything in code is made up of layers, code placed upon more code, placed upon even more code. You have seen that, when working with a `ZStack`, each view you place inside it gets stacked upon the previous view.

So with all this stacking up of views, there may be parts of a view that you may not want to show, and other parts of that same view you do want to show. The `maskToBounds` property will clip any subviews to the bounds of the screen, which is helpful because we only want the snow to fall within the size of the screen; we don't want any snow in any surrounding areas off the screen, only within the bounds of the screen, so we set this property to `true` to clip off any excess.

Now, we need to return a view in order to silence this error. Remember, the `makeUIView` method has a `return` statement in its declaration, so add the following code at the end of our previous code:

```
func makeUIView(context: Context) -> some UIView {
    //configure the screen
            let screen = UIScreen.main.bounds
            let view = UIView(frame: CGRect(x: 0, y: 0,
               width: screen.width, height: screen.height))
            view.layer.masksToBounds = true


    return view
}
```

Now, we have our screen size set up, we are returning a view, and we are error-free! The next task is to create the snow, which we can do by using UIKit's `CAEmitter` class.

Adding the CAEmitter class

CAEmitter (which stands for **Core Animation Emitter**) is a class that has methods and properties that let us emit, animate, and render particle systems.

So what's a particle system? A particle system is just what it sounds like: a system that can produce hundreds or thousands of little particles on the iPhone screen, in any size that we want, moving at any speed that we set, and in any shape that we design.

The particle shape that we want has already been designed because we will be using the `snowflake` image that we will drop into the assets catalog. However, we have to design how many snowflakes to make, how fast to make them move, how long to keep them on the screen, and the location on the screen from which they are made.

So, let's go ahead and create an `emitter` instance, using the `CAEmitter` class. Add the following code just underneath the `masksToBounds` line of code:

```
//configure the emitter
let emitter = CAEmitterLayer()
emitter.frame = CGRect(x: 200, y: -100, width:
  view.frame.width, height: view.frame.height)
```

The first line creates the `emitter` instance using the `CAEmitter` class.

The next line sets the location and size of the emitter. Here, we are locating the emitter 200 points along the x axis, which is about the middle of the iPhone screen, and -100 points along the y axis. This puts the emitter 100 points up and off from the iPhone screen. We put the emitter above the visible portion of the screen because we don't want to see the snowflakes being created, we just want to see them falling.

As for the size of the emitter, we're making it the exact size as the iPhone screen, which means using the `frame.width` and `frame.height` values.

Now that we've designed our emitter, let's design the cell. To explain the difference between these two terms, think of the **emitter** as a box that holds thousands of confetti particles, and each of those confetti particles is a **cell**. In our case, our cell will be a snowflake.

To add our cell and make it move on screen, add the following code just under the emitter code:

```
//configure the cell
let cell = CAEmitterCell()
cell.birthRate = 40
cell.lifetime = 25
cell.velocity = 60
cell.scale = 0.025
cell.emissionRange = CGFloat.pi
cell.contents = UIImage(named: "snow")?.cgImage
emitter.emitterCells = [cell]
view.layer.addSublayer(emitter)
```

Here, we created the `cell` instance using the `CAEmitterCell` class and loaded it up with different properties. The following is a list of what these properties do:

- `birthRate`: How fast each cell or particle will be made. Using a value of 40 mimics a gentle snowfall.

- `lifetime`: How long to keep the cell on the screen before it's removed. Using a value of 25 ensures that each snowflake stays on the screen long enough to make it to the bottom of the screen.

- `velocity`: How fast we want the cell to move on the screen. We're using a value of 60, which is a speed that's not too fast or too slow for the snowflake.

- `scale`: How big we want to make each cell. A value of .025 is a nice size for the snowflake, as it's not too big or too small for an iPhone.

- `emissionRange`: How far we want to spread out the cells as they are being emitted. For this value, we are using a mathematical expression called Pi (often shown as the symbol π), which is defined as the circumference of a circle divided by the diameter of the same circle. Without getting too mathematical here, the `CGFloat.pi` value equals 180 degrees – imagine a horizontal line drawn from the left to the right side of the phone screen; the value sets the snow to fall evenly from all areas of that line.

- `contents`: Sets the contents of the cell to an image of our choice, which was set as the `snow` image (make sure that you've added the image into the Assets Catalog so it can be accessed with this line of code).

- `emitterCells`: The cell particles that will become the snow.

- `addSublayer`: Adds a new layer to the scene. Remember that in SwiftUI, a layer is very similar to a view, and everything is a view in SwiftUI (buttons, text, colors, and more). In the UIKit world, a layer can also be thought of as a view – when the `addSublayer` function is called, it will add whatever layer is in its parameter to the scene.

As always, these cell configuration values are completely arbitrary, so go ahead and experiment and make the snowflakes as big as you want, design them how you want, and make them move on the screen according to what you want them to do. There are no hard and fast rules when adding values into a cell; it's all about experimenting and having fun.

And with that, we have completed the snow file. If you want to test the result, you can click **Play**; however, as the default background of the preview is white, you won't see our white snow. You can change this by swapping the background color, like so:

```
struct SnowView_Previews: PreviewProvider {
    static var previews: some View {
        SnowView()
            .background(Color.black)
    }
}
```

That will change the background color to black so you can see the snow; however, as we know, we will be using a winter background for the final animation.

So, to finish things off, we need to call this `SnowView` file inside `ContentView`. To do that, head back to `ContentView` and add this final line of code right under the background code:

```
//MARK: - ADD A WINTER BACKGROUND - AND THE SNOW
   Image("winterNight").resizable().aspectRatio(contentMode:
     .fill).frame(width: 400, height: 900)
   SnowView()
```

And that completes the project. You can now go ahead and run it:

Figure 8.7: The finished project

The project has a breathing label animation, a breathing petal animation, a breathing bouquet animation, and a snow animation.

Summary

In this project, we created the illusion of a bouquet of flowers breathing by using a collection of coding modifiers: we used `blur` to create the illusion of smoke, and `scale` and `rotationEffect` to make the flowers expand and contract in an arc, and we also added labels on the screen. On top of this, we used the `UIViewRepresentable` protocol and the `CAEmitter` class, and incorporated particle systems to create falling snow.

Here are some extra thoughts on how to take this app further, or just practice adding some more features, to help stretch your skills with SwiftUI animations. How about adding some sound to the project? We did that in *Chapter 4* with the Record Player project, and it's very easy to do – you could add some guided voice narration that simply says "breathe in, breathe out" or some meditative music.

Or how about adding a button or slider that will change the speed of the animation? Maybe you want to increase the petal opening and closing speed. If you're not sure how to do that, keep following along in the book because, later, we will build a color game with a UI that uses buttons and sliders.

Let's continue to the next chapter, where we will see how to animate a `stroke` modifier so it creates a moving line around any shape.

9

Animating Strokes around Shapes

In this project, we will take three images, create outlines around them, and then animate strokes along those outlines. A stroke is a line that follows the outline (or contours) of a shape, which we can give any color and thickness and animate to move around the image.

To do this, you'll learn how to convert bitmap images into vector images using the Inkscape software, and then take those vectors and convert them into Swift code using Sketch and Kite. We will then insert this code back into Xcode so that we can start animating our project.

The following are the objectives for this project:

- Converting images into Swift code
- Animating images with the `stroke` modifier

Technical requirements

You can download the resources and finished project from the `Chapter 9` folder on GitHub: `https://github.com/PacktPublishing/Animating-SwiftUI-Applications`.

You will also need the following:

- The Remove Background software, which is a free online tool you can access here: `https://www.remove.bg/upload`
- Inkscape, which is free and you can install here: `https://inkscape.org/release/inkscape-1.2.1/`
- Sketch, which you can install here: `https://www.sketch.com/switch-to-sketch/`
- Kite, which you can install here: `https://kiteapp.co`

Converting images into Swift code

In order to create the three outlines that we need, we first have to convert images into vectors and then convert those vectors into Swift code. Why do we have to convert an image into Swift code?

Well, in order to place an animating stroke around an image, we need a path for the animation to follow. When the image has been translated into code, it will then be easy to use Swift to follow the image outline.

However, there's a problem: bitmaps. A **bitmap**, also called a **raster image**, is a graphic that is created from different colored pixels, which together form an image. Bitmaps can be very simple, just made up of two colors (those would be black and white), or they can have many thousands or millions of colors that produce photograph-quality images. Some examples of bitmap formats that you will see use the file extensions PNG, JPEG, and TIFF. With a bitmap image, there is no defined outline for any code to follow, and thus it cannot have an animating stroke around it.

Vector images, on the other hand, are images created from code that have sharply defined edges and never get blurry like a bitmap when you zoom in on them. Since they are created with code, we can animate strokes around those images.

If you want to animate a stroke around a bitmap image, there are three main steps that you need to undertake:

- Removing the background of the image you want to use
- Vectorizing the image into an SVG file
- Translating the SVG file into Swift code

So, let's go through those steps now.

Removing the image backgrounds

Many images have a white or colored background, and in many cases, the background is not needed. It's easier to convert images into vectors if they are against a transparent background.

In our project, the images that we will be using are an image of the word "WE," an image of a heart, and an image of the SwiftUI logo. We will combine them in Swift so that they say, "We Love SwiftUI," like so:

Figure 9.1: The images we will use in our project

You can download these from the GitHub repository, where you will notice that the backgrounds have already been removed. However, if you are going to use your own images, you will need to do this yourself.

We already explored how to remove backgrounds in *Chapter 6* when we animated the girl on the swing. You can refer back to that chapter; however, to recap, you can use an online tool called Remove Background: `https://www.remove.bg/upload`. You just have to click **Upload Image** and choose the one you want to use. And that's it – in about 20 seconds, the website's algorithms will find the background and remove it, leaving only your subject. Then, all you have to do is download the new image file and you're good to go.

Alternatively, you can use Mac's Preview app to remove the background, or you can use paid software such as Affinity Designer. How you decide to remove the background is up to you; experiment and try to see what works best for the image you are using.

Also, although it's not strictly necessary, it's a good idea to crop your image, as we only want to work with the image and not any surrounding space. You can do this in pretty much any graphics editing program, including the Preview app.

Now you can proceed to the next step, which is vectorizing the image.

Vectorizing the images

The second step will be to create vectors from the bitmap image. To do this, we will need software with the proper algorithms to detect pixels, remove them, and replace them with code that will draw the shapes instead. The resulting code file will be a **scalable vector graphics** (`.svg`) file. One of the best software options on the market is called Vector Magic. This software is easy to use and automates the vectorization process with a click of a button to start the process, but the downside is it costs around $300.

Alternatively, we can use Inkscape, which is free software that does a really good job of tracing out a bitmap image and converting all its parts into vectors. This is what we will use, and you can download the latest version (at the time of writing) from the following link: `https://inkscape.org/release/inkscape-1.2.1/`.

> **Tip**
>
> Even though Inkscape can work with color images, it's usually better to have your images in black and white; the algorithms work better with these two colors. If you have color images, though, that's not a problem – you can still convert them into black and white by using a graphics program such as Affinity Designer.
>
> If you look at the images we are using for this project, two of them are in color, but that's okay because they have a limited number of colors and are simple shapes. If you have more complicated shapes, for instance, such as a portrait photograph with many colors in it, then it's better to convert them into black and white first.

Once you have Inkscape installed, you can get started. Grab one of your images (in my case, I am choosing the "WE" image), right-click on it, and open it in Inkscape. You will see this pop-up window:

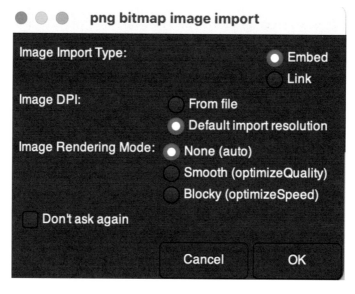

Figure 9.2: Importing an image into Inkscape

Set **Image Import Type** to **Embed**, **Image DPI** to **Default import resolution**, and **Image Rendering Mode** to **None (auto)**. Then, click **OK**. You will then see this screen:

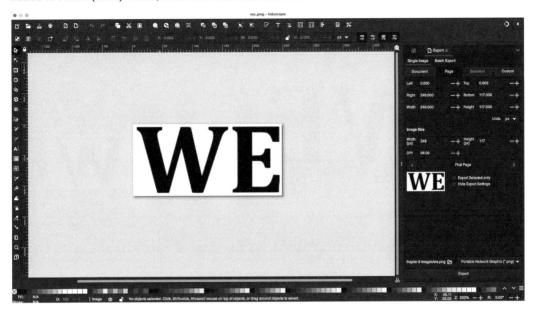

Figure 9.3: The Inkscape editor with our image

Before continuing with the conversion, I want to show you how a bitmap looks close up. On your Mac trackpad, pinch and zoom in very close to the image; you will see pixelization and blurriness appear. This is one way you can tell whether the image is a bitmap and not a vector. (Of course, the file extension will also let you know whether it's a bitmap or vector as well!)

Next, select your image on the Inkscape canvas (you will know it's been selected if you see black arrows around it), then go to the **Path** menu at the top of the screen, and choose **Trace Bitmap**. This will open up the **Preview** option on the right-hand side of Inkscape:

Figure 9.4: Inkscape Preview

In the **Preview** window, Inkscape shows us what the **Trace Bitmap** function will be able to trace, and what the image will look like as a vector graphic. Since the preview looks nearly identical to the "WE" image on the canvas, there will be a complete outline around the image.

You can't see the vector lines and points just yet in the preview, but you will shortly.

Since we are using a black and white image, Inscape has selected the **Single scan** option from the top of the **Preview** window (which you can see in *Figure 9.5*).

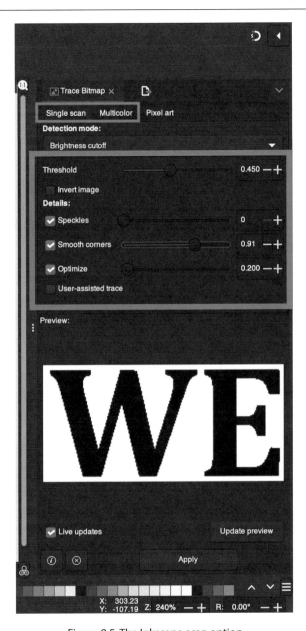

Figure 9.5: The Inkscape scan option

The **Single scan** option is used for black and white images, but if we use a multicolored image, then we need to select the **Multicolor** option. The **Multicolor** option will scan your image, looking at the many colors it contains, and do its best to trace an outline around each of those colors. This is why I said earlier that it's usually better to have a black-and-white image, as there are fewer colors to scan and thus less chance of not getting a good trace.

As highlighted in *Figure 9.5*, you can also adjust the **Threshold** and **Details** sliders to get the best possible image in the previews. These sliders are useful if Inkscape is having difficulty getting a good scan. By moving the sliders, you can fine-tune the parts of the image that Inkscape can see.

Let's look at the **Details** sliders:

- The **Speckles** slider will ignore the small spots in the vector – when set to maximum, it will ignore more speckles, and when set to minimum, it will ignore fewer speckles.

- The **Smooth corners** slider will smooth out any sharp corners that are in the trace.

- The **Optimize** slider will try to optimize paths by joining adjacent Bezier curve segments together; this means that the **Optimize** slider will try its best to remove as many vector nodes as it can. When you have fewer nodes in a vector image, there tends to be better tracing and fewer jagged edges.

We will see the **Threshold** slider later when creating a stroke around the heart.

What we want to see in the preview is an image that is as close to the one in the center canvas as possible. When we do see this, it means that Inkscape can trace all around the shape on the canvas correctly and capture all the vector lines. If you don't see an image that's close to the original, then try and adjust some of the sliders I just mentioned to fine-tune the output.

Once you have finished adjusting the image so it looks close to the original, click **Update Preview**, and then **Apply**. Inkscape places its newly created vectors directly over the original image. To see the result, click on the "WE" image in the editor and drag the new vectors to the side:

Figure 9.6: Creating the vectors

You can now delete the original image, as it is no longer needed.

Let's have a look at what Inkscape has done for us – it has traced the original image and created a new image that is now made of vector paths. To see the difference, pinch and zoom on your Mac trackpad on the new vector image as you did with the bitmap image. Do you see the difference? There is no pixelation or blurriness at all, as the image is created with code rather than pixels; the image can be blown up to any size and it will still remain sharp and crisp along its edges and curves:

Figure 9.7: Vector resolution

Now, remember that I mentioned that you will be able to see the vectors that Inkscape has created? Well, they are there, it's just that we need to select the right editing tool to see them. Select the image in the center of the canvas, go to the left toolbar, and select the **Node Editing** tool. When you click on that tool, you will be able to see all the vector lines that Inkscape created:

Figure 9.8: The vectors

Each of those small squares is a point (or node) that links lines, curves, and corners to make this new shape – and these points can now be edited by clicking on them and dragging them to any location to reshape the vector image.

With the new vectors created, we can export them. To do this, open **File** at the top menu and choose **Export**. Then, you can choose the export options at the bottom right of the software. Choose the file type that you want to export to – we want a **Plain SVG (*.svg)** file. Then, click on the **Export** button:

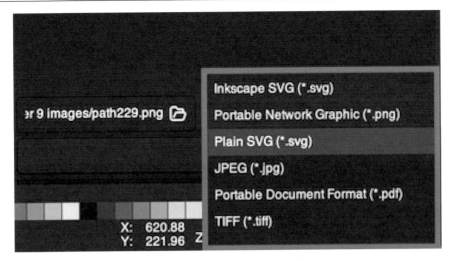

Figure 9.9: Exporting to an SVG file

Now, we have an SVG file stored on our computer, ready to be translated into Swift code. Do the same process for any of the other images that you want to use in this project – whether you are using your own images or following along with the book's project images – and then you can proceed to the next step.

Translating the SVG file into Swift code

Let's continue. We have an SVG file ready for the next step. An **SVG** file is a file written in XML, and **XML** is a markup language used for storing and transferring digital information. The XML code in an SVG file creates all of the shapes, colors, and text that comprise the image. We will be turning that XML code into Swift code shortly, but first, we need to edit the images' dimensions and we can do that in Sketch.

So, first, open the SVG "WE" image in Sketch. Then, in the **Utilities** area on the right, we can size the image however we like; in my case, I have set the width to **250**. To set this, make sure that the little lock icon in between the width and height fields is selected so that it's locked – this will keep the correct proportions for the image – and hit *Enter*:

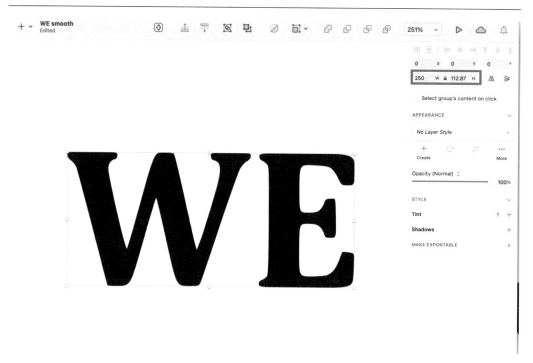

Figure 9.10: Sizing the image

And that's all we need to do in Sketch. Now, minimize your Sketch document (but don't close it!).

Next, we need a program that can turn XML code into Swift code. One option is Paint Code – although it is a great program, it costs around $200 per year for a subscription. Instead, we will use Kite – although this is currently $99 to buy outright with no subscription, you can always use the free trial to follow along with this project.

So, open up Kite. Then, click on **File** | **Import** | **From Sketch…**:

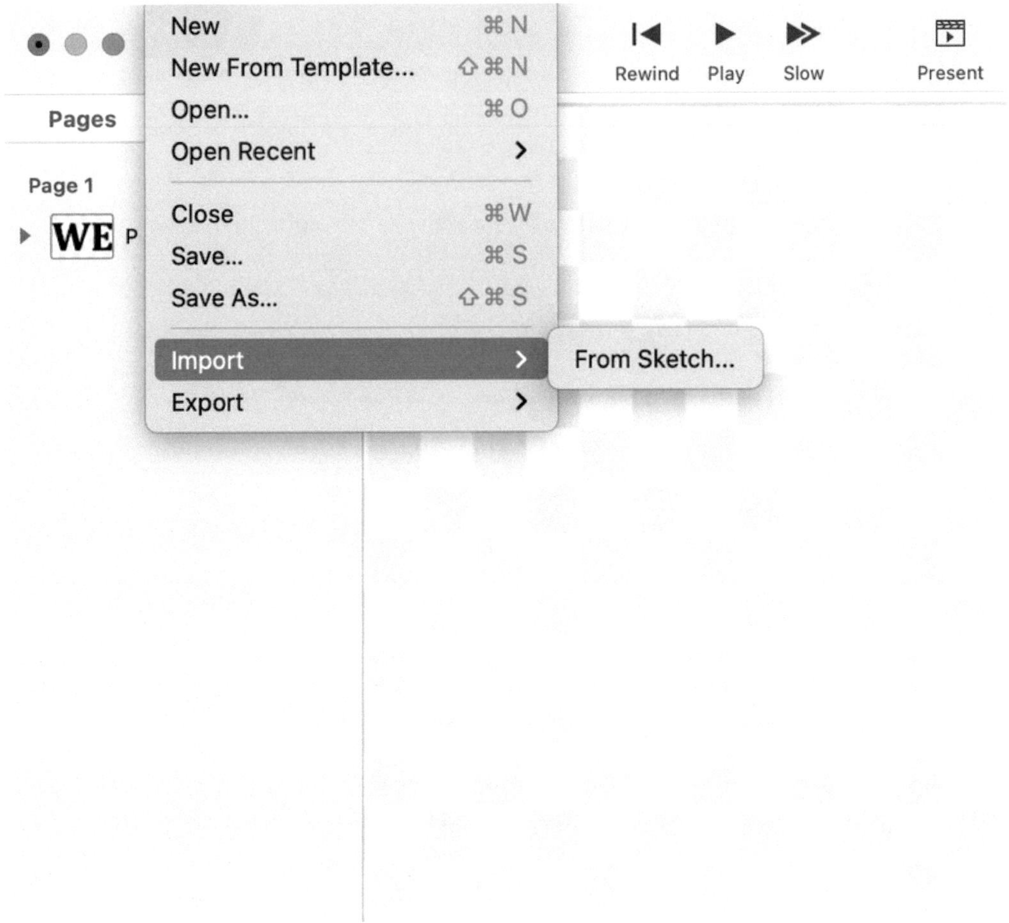

Figure 9.11: Importing from Sketch into Kite

You will then see a pop-up window asking how you would like to import the layers. Leave the default settings as they are, but make sure that **Import text layers as** is set to **Image Layers** and that **Import images at** is set to a scale of **1x**:

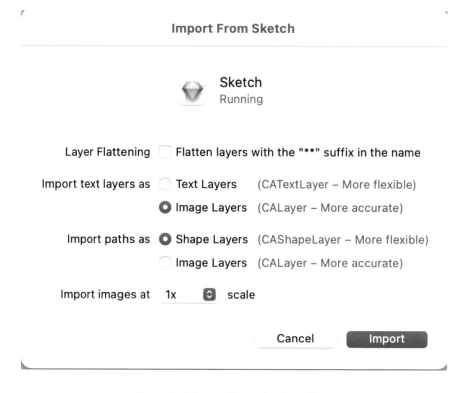

Figure 9.12: Import From Sketch settings

Then, click on **Import**. You now have your image in Kite and are ready to turn it into Swift code, and that process is as simple as clicking one button, the **Code** button, at the top of the screen:

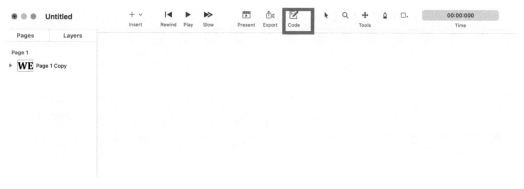

Figure 9.13: Converting the file into Swift code

The Swift code that is generated shows up in the bottom console, which you can resize like the Xcode console by dragging it upwards. Here is what the code console looks like for the "WE" image, containing all the Swift code that makes up its length, thickness, colors, position, and more:

Figure 9.14: The generated Swift code in Kite

That looks like a lot of code just to create an image with two letters, doesn't it? Well, yes, but there are a lot of things the code is doing – it's mapping out all the paths needed to create the lines and curves that form the shape.

Let's now get this code into Xcode. First, create a new Xcode project if you haven't done so already – I've called it **Animating Strokes**. Then, all we have to do is copy a small segment of it from Kite. You should copy the code starting from here:

```
let pathPath = CGMutablePath()
```

And continue all the way down the file until you reach these two lines:

```
pathPath.closeSubpath()
pathPath.move(to: CGPoint(x: 159, y: 104.854378))
```

So, we just want to copy all the code that starts with `pathPath`; everything else we don't need.

Now, before we enter Xcode, let's summarize what we have done so far. We have taken a bitmap image, removed its background and cropped it, opened it with Inkscape and turned it into a vector image, and then finally imported that vector into Kite, where we turned it into Swift code. This process will get faster with more practice.

Let's now proceed to Xcode and start making all this code work.

Animating images with the stroke modifier

In the following sections, we will be working in Xcode and refactoring the "WE" code somewhat in order to make it work in our project. We will use the Shape protocol that lets us draw a 2D shape using its `path()` function, and then use the `stroke` modifier to add a moving line around the path of our shapes. We will also get started on animating our heart and SwiftUI logo images.

Creating a stroke animation on the "WE" image

To start animating the "WE" image, we need to create a file inside the project. Press *Command + N*, choose a **SwiftUI View** file type, and name it – I'm calling it `WeView`.

Then, create a struct at the bottom of the file; this will be the struct that conforms to the shape protocol, allowing us to create 2D shapes by using the `path` function:

```
struct WeTextShape: Shape {
    func path(in rect: CGRect) -> Path {
    }
}
```

Now, we can paste in the code that we copied from the Kite program and place it right into that `path` function. This code is quite repetitive and long, as it is drawing a shape and must repeat itself for every line, curve, and corner. So, for the sake of brevity and to not take up too much space, I will just provide the beginning and end of the code (however, you can find the complete code in the GitHub repo):

```
struct WeTextShape: Shape {
  func path(in rect: CGRect) -> Path {
    let pathPath = CGMutablePath()
      pathPath.move(to: CGPoint(x: 33.544579, y:
        105.919167))
      pathPath.addCurve(to: CGPoint(x: 20.994799, y:
        60.169167), control1: CGPoint(x: 32.057159, y:
        101.184097), control2: CGPoint(x: 29.932928, y:
        93.440262))
      pathPath.addCurve(to: CGPoint(x: 3.45976, y:
```

```
        7.26897), control1: CGPoint(x: 8.184458, y:
        12.4843), control2: CGPoint(x: 7.749718, y:
        11.17275))
    pathPath.addLine(to: CGPoint(x: 0, y: 0.16917))
    .............................................................
    pathPath.addCurve(to: CGPoint(x: 236.485107, y:
        93.6082), control1: CGPoint(x: 237.051361, y:
        79.890518), control2: CGPoint(x: 236.884613, y:
        86.149673))
    pathPath.addLine(to: CGPoint(x: 235.758789, y:
        107.169159))
    pathPath.addLine(to: CGPoint(x: 197.379395, y:
        107.169159))
    pathPath.addLine(to: CGPoint(x: 159, y: 107.169159))
    pathPath.addLine(to: CGPoint(x: 159, y: 104.854378))
    pathPath.closeSubpath()
    pathPath.move(to: CGPoint(x: 159, y: 104.854378))
    }
}
```

When you paste the code into Xcode, you will get some errors – don't worry about these, as the code needs to be reworked a little bit anyway.

Fixing these issues is also a good excuse for me to show you how to refactor code in SwiftUI. Refactoring is a helpful feature that allows us to rename code or remove and replace different parts of code throughout multiple files in your project without having to search through all your files looking for each instance that needs refactoring and manually changing it.

One thing we want to change is the name of the pathPath constant, which is the first line of code inside the path function that was pasted in. This constant seems to have been named twice because it was exported from Inkscape. However, it should simply be named path.

So, to refactor this, just *Command + click* on the pathPath variable and select **Rename**. You will see Xcode highlight every instance of pathPath in the file, and all you have to do is just type in the new name, path, and hit *Enter*.

That's our first revision of the code that we copied over. The next revision is to change the class that's being assigned to the path constant. Currently, the path constant is assigned as a CGMutablePath() instance, which is a core graphics class used for drawing shapes and lines. Working in SwiftUI though, nearly everything is built with structs, so we need to use the Path() struct instead. Also, change the `let` keyword to the `var` keyword, because we need the `path` variable to be mutable, meaning its value can be changed.

With those modifications done, the first line of the code in your path function should look like the following:

```
var path = Path()
```

Now, let's add one more line of code to this `path` function. At the very end of the function, we need to return the `path` variable, and to do so, we use the `return` keyword, followed by the variable the function must return; so, add this line at the bottom of the `path` function:

```
return path
```

The following are the changes we made to the start and end of the `path` function:

```
func path(in rect: CGRect) -> Path {
    var path = Path()
    path.move(to: CGPoint(x: 33.544579, y: 105.919167))
    path.addCurve(to: CGPoint(x: 3.45976, y: 7.26897),
        control1: CGPoint(x: 8.184458, y: 12.4843), control2:
        CGPoint(x: 7.749718, y: 11.17275))
        •••SHAPE CODE HERE•••
    return path
}
```

When you press *Command + B*, the code should be error-free.

Now let's see what all of that Kite code is actually doing.

The `path()` function will return a shape according to the points, lines, and curves that are drawn inside it. The first line of code inside the `path()` function is creating a path instance; this will draw the shape, and you can think of this variable as the pencil moving along the canvas.

The second line of code is the `move()` function. This is what sets the starting location for the `path` variable to move to. The locations are based on the Cartesian coordinate system and an X and Y location are used to position the `path` variable.

In the third line of code, the `path` variable calls the `addCurve()` function, and this does what it says – it adds a Bezier curve to the path using the specified points. Continuing down our code, we see that the `path` variable also calls the `addLine()` function, and this will add a line to the path using the specified points. The code continues to call these two functions, `addCurve()` and `addLine()`, quite a bit until the `path` variable needs to finish off a particular path in the drawing and close off the ends of that finished line before moving on to the next line in the drawing.

The finished line is closed off using the `closeSubpath()` function and directly proceeded by the `moveTo()` function to start a new line in the drawing. So, as you can see, there are several lines drawn in this code to make up the finished shape.

And finally, at the end of all this code, the `path()` function returns the `path` variable, which now contains a finished shape inside of it, ready to be displayed on the iPhone screen.

Next, continuing to work in the same file, we need to come into the `WEView` struct and add the code to display this shape.

Starting at the top of the struct, add the following variables:

```
//MARK: - VARIABLES
    @State var strokeReset: Bool = true
    @State var startStroke: CGFloat = 0.0
    @State var endStroke: CGFloat = 0.0
```

Next, inside the body property, add a `ZStack`:

```
var body: some View {
    ZStack {
    }
}
```

Inside the `ZStack`, let's add a `Group`, and then the following code to display the shape in the preview:

```
ZStack {
        Group {
            //SHAPE OUTLINE
            WeTextShape()
                .stroke(style: StrokeStyle(lineWidth: 0.5,
                    lineCap: .round, lineJoin: .round))
                .foregroundColor(.gray)
        }
    }
```

Inside `Group`, we call the `WeTextShape` struct and add the `stroke` modifier directly to it. This modifier will create a new shape that has a stroke on it, which is styled according to the `StrokeStyle` function. The `StrokeStyle` function adds a `lineWidth` property of `0.5`, and sets both `lineCap` (the ends of the stroke) and `lineJoin` to `round`; this joins the ends of the stroke with a semi-circular arc. Finally, the color of the stroke shape is set to `gray`.

This completes the shape – we won't add any animation to it, as we just want it to be a stationary shape. Instead, we will add this shape again, directly over the first one, and that's the one we will animate in color. Let's add that now.

Continuing inside the Group view, and directly under the last line of code, add the following:

```
Group {
    //SHAPE OUTLINE
    WeTextShape()
        .stroke(style: StrokeStyle(lineWidth: 0.5,
          lineCap: .round, lineJoin: .round))
        .foregroundColor(.gray)
    //ANIMATING STROKE
    WeTextShape()
        .trim(from: startStroke, to: endStroke)
        .stroke(style: StrokeStyle(lineWidth: 5,
          lineCap: .round, lineJoin: .round))
        .foregroundColor(Color.red)
}.offset(x: 75, y: 50)
)
}
```

And that's the code that will add a second shape, identical to the first one, directly over it.

As we did for the non-moving shape, we called the WeTextView struct to create the shape. Then, we used the trim modifier to trim the shape by a fractional amount based on the values that get passed into its parameters. By passing in the startStroke variable as the location of the start of the stroke animation and the endStroke variable to tell the trim modifier where to stop, a stroked line will be drawn along the shape's path from start to end. The length of that stroke line will depend on the values inside the startStroke and endStroke variables.

As we did with the first shape, we also used the strokeStyle modifier to style the stroke with a width property of 5, and lineCap and lineJoin set to round. This time, we set the color to red so that the moving stroke will stand out as it travels along the gray shape underneath it.

Then, finally, we're using the offset modifier to center the shape inside the preview in the middle from left to right, and toward the top of the iPhone.

Now, the code for the outline and animating the stroke are complete. What's needed next is to use the onAppear modifier to start the animation and set up some timers so that the stroke can proceed at a certain speed. Add the final bit of code right after the closing brace of the ZStack:

```
.onAppear() {
    Timer.scheduledTimer(withTimeInterval: 0.23, repeats:
       true) { timer in
        if (endStroke >= 1) {
            if (strokeReset) {
                Timer.scheduledTimer(withTimeInterval: 0.6,
                   repeats: false) { _ in
                    endStroke = 0
                    startStroke = 0
                    strokeReset.toggle()
                }
                strokeReset = false
            }
        }
        withAnimation(Animation.easeOut) {
            endStroke += 0.12
            startStroke = endStroke - 0.4
        }
    }
}
```

This code might look a little busy to grasp at first, but let's break it down for clarity.

The onAppear() method is called on the ZStack container; this method is triggered when the view appears on the screen. Inside the method, a timer is scheduled using the Timer.scheduledTimer method, which is set to repeat every 0.23 seconds. This is the amount of time it takes for the animation to draw each stroke segment. A stroke segment is how we draw out the shape, in segments, one at a time. You can experiment with this timer's interval value – a larger number will draw the stroke segments slower, and a smaller number will draw the segments faster, creating a smooth animating line around the shape.

Next, we want the animation to repeat, so we set the repeats parameter to true. Within the timer's event handler, the code first checks whether the endStroke variable is greater than or equal to 1. If this is true, the code then checks whether the strokeReset variable is true. If both of these conditions are met, another timer is scheduled using the Timer.scheduledTimer method. This timer is set to run only once, after 0.6 seconds, and within this timer's event handler, the values of endStroke and startStroke are reset to 0, so the stroke animation can once again start at the beginning, and the strokeReset variable is toggled. After the inner timer is scheduled, the strokeReset variable is set to false.

The withAnimation function is different from the animation modifier we have used in past projects. Remember in *Chapter 2*, when we talked about the two types of animations, *implicit* and *explicit*? The withAnimation function is an explicit type of animation and is used to animate changes to the view's state. It is considered an explicit animation because it requires you to specify the animation that you want to use, as opposed to an implicit animation, which would automatically animate changes without the need for additional code.

So, in the body of the withAnimation function, we set the endStroke variable to increase its value by 0.12 after every iteration of the animation. We also set startStroke to a value that is calculated by subtracting 0.4 from endStroke – this computation creates the length and speed of an animating stroke that I think looks pretty good for the "We" shape.

And with that, this animation is complete. So, to summarize the code in the WeView struct, it creates a view that animates a shape, this shape is outlined twice, once with a gray color and a small stroke, and then again, with a red color and a bigger stroke. The animation is controlled by the startStroke and endStroke variables, which are incremented over time. The animation will be repeated once the endStroke variable reaches 1, and there is a 0.6-second delay before the animation starts again.

Now that we have finished with the code, if you click on the **Update Preview** button, you will see that the outline is now a red, five-point line. Again, these two values are very customizable for different looks for this animation. By increasing the value of endStroke in the withAnimation function, you can leave more of the stroke line on the shape or less of it, depending on the look you want to go for.

Play around with the values and experiment. You can create a flashing stroke by increasing the speed, or you can have a very slow-moving stroke. You can stroke the entire shape with a short line, or you can go with a very long line along the whole shape.

That completes our first animation, the "WE" image stroke. Even though that seems like a long process, the whole thing actually only takes a few minutes once you get familiar with the different programs and techniques used. We are going to move on to the heart image now and repeat the same process. After all, practice makes perfect!

Creating a stroke animation on the heart image

Okay, we have animated our first image, so we are going to follow the same process again for two more images. The next image will be a heart – for this one, we will animate a stroke around it as we did with the letters, but also we will add the heart image back into the scene.

If you are following along with the book's project, you can find the heart image in the GitHub repository, where the background has already been removed. However, if you are using your own images, you will need to do this yourself.

After you have prepared your image, now open it with Inkscape so that you can vectorize it. With the image selected in the editor, go to the **Path** menu at the top and choose **Trace Bitmap**; this will trace the image and prepare it for vectorization, as before.

With the image selected on the canvas, if you look at the **Previews** pane at the right, the image has been converted into black and white. That's because, by default, Inkscape selects the **Single Scan** option, the option for black-and-white images. And even though this is a color image, because it's such a simple shape with not many variations of red in it, we don't need the **Multicolor** option; so, **Single scan** will work fine here.

This is also a good opportunity to use the **Smooth Corners** option as well because this shape has (for the most part) smooth corners, and this selection will preserve them.

This is what it should look like so far:

Figure 9.15: The heart image in Inkscape

Also, do you notice that the heart image shown in **Preview** has two white areas inside it? That's the Inkscape algorithm trying to capture the shiny parts of the red heart image on the canvas. We only want to trace the outside perimeter of the heart, which is the area that will be outlined later in the code – we don't want those white areas. To remove those white areas in the preview, slide the **Threshold** slider to the right, just enough so the heart fills up like this:

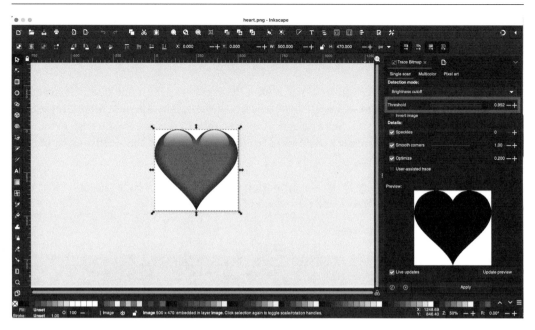

Figure 9.16: Setting the options in Inkscape for the heart image

Now that the heart shape is ready to be vectorized, click the **Apply** button to complete the process, and a new vectorized black heart is placed directly over the red heart image on the canvas. Drag the black heart off to the side, in order to see the red heart under it, then delete the red heart.

Next, position the black heart back over the white canvas and export it like the "WE" image, making sure to choose the **Plain SVG (*.svg)** file type.

Moving away from Inkscape and into the Sketch program, open the new vector image we just exported from Inkscape into Sketch by right-clicking on the image and selecting **Open with Sketch**. We will resize the image again to a width of **250** (again, making sure to click on the lock icon to fix the proportions):

Figure 9.17: Setting the size for the heart image in Sketch

Next minimize the Sketch window, as we only need it running in the background so that Kite can access it, and open the Kite program. In Kite, click on **File**, then **Import**, and then **From Sketch**. You will see the same window as shown in *Figure 9.12*, and you can keep the default settings. Then, click **Import**.

Once the image has been imported, select the image on the canvas, and then click the **Code** button at the top to generate the Swift code we need:

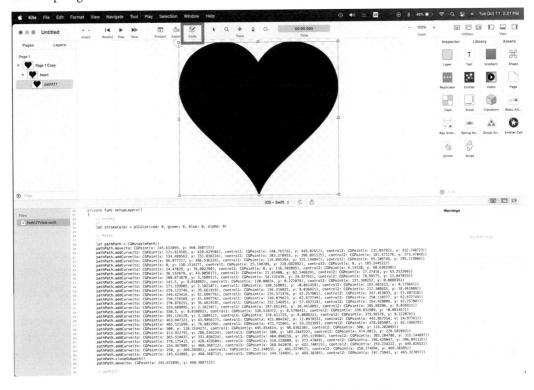

Figure 9.18: Generating the heart's Swift code in Kite

Like we did with the "WE" image code, we just want to copy the code that starts with the `patht Path` name. In the example here, the code we need starts at the `let pathPath = CGMutablePath()` line and ends with `pathPath.move(to)`.

Now back to Xcode – create a new SwiftUI View file, which I will name `HeartView`. Inside the file, we will create a struct to put the code in, call it `HeartShape`, and make it conform to the `shape` protocol, like this:

```
struct HeartShape: Shape {
    func path(in rect: CGRect) -> Path {
    }
}
```

Remember when making the "WE" shape, we used the shape protocol? As before, it requires us to use the `path()` method, which I have added here.

Now, we can paste the Kite-generated Swift code inside this method (again, I will only include the first few lines and the last few lines so as not to take up too much space here; as before, the complete code file and project are available in the GitHub repo):

```
struct HeartShape: Shape {
    func path(in rect: CGRect) -> Path {
        let pathPath = CGMutablePath()
            pathPath.move(to: CGPoint(x: 245.632095, y:
                460.368713))
            pathPath.addCurve(to: CGPoint(x: 221.824585, y:
                420.429504), control1: CGPoint(x: 240.765762, y:
                449.02652), control2: CGPoint(x: 231.057922, y:
                432.740723))
. . . . . . . . . . . . . . . . . . . . . . . . . . . . . . . . . . . . . . . . . . . . . . . .
            pathPath.closeSubpath()
            pathPath.move(to: CGPoint(x: 245.632095, y:
                460.368713))
        }
    }
```

Next, let's refactor the code as we did before. *Command + click* on the `pathPath` instance and choose **Rename**, then simply name it `path`. Also, change the mutability of the `path` constant to a variable by replacing `let` with `var`, and change `CGMutablePath()` to `Path()`. These changes should look like this:

```
var path = Path()
```

The last change to make is at the bottom of the `HeartShape` struct; after the very last line of code, we need to return the path we created, so add the following line of code to the end of the `path` function:

```
return path
```

The code should now build cleanly, and we can move on to animating the outline around the heart. This is similar code to that in the `WEView` file. At the top of the struct, let's add the following variables:

```
//MARK: - VARIABLES
    @State var strokeReset: Bool = true
    @State var startStroke: CGFloat = 0.0
    @State var endStroke: CGFloat = 0.0
```

The `strokeReset` variable will keep track of the animation, `startStroke` will hold a value that sets the `length` property of the stroke at the beginning, and `endStroke` will hold a value that sets the `length` property of the stroke at the end.

Moving into the body property of the struct, let's add the views needed to display and animate our heart outline:

```
var body: some View {
  ZStack {
    Group {
      //SHAPE OUTLINE
      HeartShape()
          .stroke(style: StrokeStyle(lineWidth: 0.5,
            lineCap: .round, lineJoin: .round))
          .foregroundColor(.gray)
      //ANIMATING STROKE
      HeartShape()
          .trim(from: startStroke, to: endStroke)
          .stroke(style: StrokeStyle(lineWidth: 5, lineCap:
            .round, lineJoin: .round))
          .foregroundColor(Color.white)
    }.offset (x: 75, y: -30)
    }.onAppear() {
    Timer.scheduledTimer(withTimeInterval: 0.23, repeats:
      true) { timer in
        if (endStroke >= 1) {
          if (strokeReset) {
              Timer.scheduledTimer(withTimeInterval: 0.6,
                repeats: false) { _ in
                  endStroke = 0
                  startStroke = 0
                  strokeReset.toggle()
              }
              strokeReset = false
          }
        }
        withAnimation(Animation.easeOut) {
            endStroke += 0.12
```

```
            startStroke = endStroke - 0.4
        }
      }
    }
}
```

The code here is almost identical to the code in the WEView file – what's different is the color of the stroke. Here, it is white and we are offsetting the heart to be lower on the screen.

Run the code and you'll see that there is a smoothly animating stroke going around the heart shape.

Again, all the values are for you to explore and experiment with to create the look you want.

But let's do something a bit different for this shape – let's add the actual heart bitmap image right inside the animating heart shape. To do this, add the following code at the bottom of the Group view:

```
Group {
    //SHAPE OUTLINE
    HeartShape()
        .stroke(style: StrokeStyle(lineWidth: 0.5,
          lineCap: .round, lineJoin: .round))
        .foregroundColor(.gray)
    //ANIMATING STROKE
    HeartShape()
        .trim(from: startStroke, to: endStroke)
        .stroke(style: StrokeStyle(lineWidth: 5, lineCap:
          .round, lineJoin: .round))
        .foregroundColor(Color.blue)
    ///HEART BITMAP IMAGE
    Image("heart").resizable().aspectRatio(contentMode:
      .fit)
        .frame(width: 246, alignment: .center)
        .position(x: 125, y:117.5)
}
```

Run the code again and you'll see that it performs as before, only now we've positioned the heart bitmap image inside the stationary stroke, so the animated stroke is tracing the heart image for an interesting look:

Figure 9.19: The stroke around the heart image

We have completed two shapes now, the "WE" letters and the heart. Let's continue and add the final image to the project, the SwiftUI logo.

Creating a stroke animation on the SwiftUI logo image

Now that we have reached the final image, I would like to challenge you by letting you take this one on by yourself. Use the steps we have outlined in the previous two shapes – including removing backgrounds, vectorizing your image, and converting the image into Swift Code – and copy the code into a new SwiftUI View file called `SwiftUILogoView`.

Okay, give it a try, and come back here when you're ready…

How did you do?

After you vectorize a few shapes and gather the code, the process will become very familiar and much quicker. If you have used images other than the ones I supplied for this project, that's perfectly fine; just know that the SwiftUI code for those images will be different from the code I will show here for the SwiftUI logo, but the animating code will be the same.

Here is the SwiftUI code that I got back from Kite for the SwiftUI logo image (and as before, the full code file is available in the GitHub repo):

```
struct SwiftUILogoShape: Shape {
  func path(in rect: CGRect) -> Path {
    var path = Path()
    path.move(to: CGPoint(x: 201.374207, y: 235.109955))
    path.addCurve(to: CGPoint(x: 231.023102, y:
      220.544876), control1: CGPoint(x: 212.656006, y:
      233.244553), control2: CGPoint(x: 222.89035, y:
      228.216904))
    . . . . . . . . . . . . . . . . . . . . . . . . . . . . . . . . . . . . . . . . . . .
    path.addCurve(to: CGPoint(x: 207.854324, y:
      191.140839), control1: CGPoint(x: 209.692215, y:
      193.796051), control2: CGPoint(x: 208.764877, y:
      192.663177))
    path.addLine(to: CGPoint(x: 207.854324, y:
      191.140839))
    path.closeSubpath()
    path.move(to: CGPoint(x: 207.854324, y: 191.140839))
      return path
  }
}
```

I have previously explained how this code creates a shape object in the *Creating a stroke animation on the "WE" image* section; if you would like a refresher on understanding how this works, go back to that section for the details on this code.

We can now move to the top of the file, inside the `SwiftUILogo` struct, and start adding the animation code. I will add the complete code for this final shape:

```swift
struct SwiftUILogoView: View {
    //MARK: - VARIABLES
    @State var strokeReset: Bool = true
    @State var startStroke: CGFloat = 0.0
    @State var endStroke: CGFloat = 0.0
    var body: some View {
        ZStack {
          Group {
            //SHAPE OUTLINE
                SwiftUILogoShape()
            .stroke(style: StrokeStyle(lineWidth: 0.5,
              lineCap: .round, lineJoin: .round))
            .foregroundColor(.gray)
          //ANIMATING STROKE
          SwiftUILogoShape()
            .trim(from: startStroke, to: endStroke)
            .stroke(style: StrokeStyle(lineWidth: 5, lineCap:
              .round, lineJoin: .round))
            .foregroundColor(Color.blue)
        }.offset(x: UIScreen.main.bounds.size.width / 5.5)
          }.onAppear() {
        Timer.scheduledTimer(withTimeInterval: 0.23, repeats:
          true) { timer in
            if (endStroke >= 1) {
                if (strokeReset) {
                    Timer.scheduledTimer(withTimeInterval: 0.6,
                      repeats: false) { _ in
                        endStroke = 0
                        startStroke = 0
                        strokeReset.toggle()
                    }
                    strokeReset = false
                }
            }
```

```
        withAnimation(Animation.easeOut) {
            endStroke += 0.12
            startStroke = endStroke - 0.4
        }
    }
}
}
}
```

This animating code is the same code that we have been adding all along, and if you would like an explanation of how it works, go back to the "WE" shape code for all the details. The minor differences here are that the line is blue, and we are offsetting it lower on the screen.

Give this a run and check out the stroke around the logo.

The final part of the project is to combine all three of the shape structs onto the screen together. Let's do that next.

Combining the animated strokes

There is very little code needed for this, as we are just calling the three shape structs in one place. All you need to do is add the following code to the ContentView struct:

```
struct ContentView: View {
    var body: some View {
        VStack  {
            WeView()
            HeartView()
            SwiftUILogoView()
        }.background(Color.black)
    }
}
```

What we have done here is called all three structs inside ContentView, used a VStack to line up the views vertically, and then added a black background at the end. When you run the code, you will see the following result:

Figure 9.20: The finished project

Now, all three views are animated as being outlined with different colors.

Summary

Nice job finishing this project! To create the finished animation, we learned how to turn bitmap images into vector files, and then how to turn those vector files into code that we can work with using SwiftUI. Also, we learned how to create and animate a moving outline around almost any shape using the `stroke` modifier and timers, and used animation in this project.

Using this project, you can play around with the values. You can make the stroke thicker or thinner, make it move faster or slower, and make it any color of the rainbow.

There are many applications for animating strokes in your apps, too. It can be used for logos, text, and brands, so that they stand out and get noticed; it can be used in game apps to bring the users' attention to different areas of the screen or can be used anywhere you want to make an app come alive. The uses are only limited by your imagination.

In the next chapter, we will learn how to animate lines in a different way to create waves, and then put them together to make an ocean with an animating buoy, complete with sound effects.

10

Creating an Ocean Scene

In this chapter, we will be creating an ocean scene. To do that, we will be revisiting the Shape protocol and path function that we used in the previous project to create the waves, as well as a new SwiftUI property called animatableData, which will help to make our curvy lines animate in a fluid wave-like motion.

We will also add an image of a buoy to our scene and animate it in multiple different ways, including moving it along an anchor point, rotating it around the center of this point, and making it rise up and down along the y-axis – so the buoy looks like it's bobbing in the water.

Finally, we will add some sound effects to the project to help it really come alive.

In this chapter, we will cover the following topics:

- Adding the wave's offset property
- Creating a wave shape using the Shape protocol and Path function
- Adding the wave's animatableData property
- Setting up the ContentView for animation
- Duplicating and animating the wave shape in the ContentView
- Adding an animated floating buoy to the ocean scene
- Adding sound effects

Technical requirements

You can download the resources and finished project from the Chapter 10 folder on GitHub: https://github.com/PacktPublishing/Animating-SwiftUI-Applications.

Adding the wave's offset property

Okay, let's start by creating a new SwiftUI project – I'll be calling it `Making Waves`.

Then, let's add a new file that will be in charge of making the waves for the ocean. Press *Command + N* to create a new file, then select the **SwiftUIView** file, and call it `WaveView`.

Inside this new file, we will make some minor modifications to the structure so that it conforms to the Shape protocol, as we did in the previous project. So, at the top of the `WaveView` struct, right after its name, remove the `View` protocol and replace it with the `Shape` protocol. Also, remove the `body` property as we don't need that here. The file should look like this:

```
struct WaveView: Shape {
}
```

The reason why we removed the `body` property was that it was used to return a view; however, we will be returning a `path` variable that will hold the shape of the wave we want to animate.

The animation we want to create will be a wavy line that moves up and down in a wave-like motion, on the *y* axis. We will need a variable to control this animation movement, so let's add a variable inside the `WaveView` struct to handle this:

```
var yOffset: CGFloat = 0.0
```

It's called `yOffset` because that's what the variable will do: it will offset the line only on the *y* axis. It gets an initial value of `0.0`. Its type is set to `CGFloat`.

We will need another special built-in Swift variable that will dynamically change the value of the `yOffset` variable and make things animate, called `animatableData`, but let's first create the wave shape itself before adding that.

Creating a wave shape using the Shape protocol and Path function

For the wave shape, it's easy – we just need to make three straight lines and one curved line and join them together. Think of it as a rectangle, with the top line of the rectangle being the curvy wave part (skip to *Figure 10.4* to see what I mean).

Before we start adding the wave code, let's first modify the `Previews` struct so that we can see the results of each line of code we add. Modify the code so it looks like the following:

```
struct WaveView_Previews: PreviewProvider {
    static var previews: some View {
        Group {
```

```
WaveView(yOffset: 0.7)
    .stroke(Color.blue, lineWidth: 3)
    .frame(height: 250)
.padding()
    .previewDisplayName("Wave")


        }
    }
}
```

We start off by giving the yOffset parameter in the Previews struct a value of 0.7. This is a simple hardcoded value that allows us to display our wave shape in the previews on the right in Xcode. yOffset works by offsetting two control points in the Bezier curve – one control point will be offset in the up direction for the curvy line and the other control point will be offset in the down direction on the curvy line. The next line of code adds a stroke to the wave shape, so we can see it in the preview, and gives the wave a height of 250 points.

Now, with these changes in the previews, any code we add to the WaveView struct will immediately be visible in the previews. Let's add the wave shape code now, small pieces of code at a time, so we can better understand how the wave shape is formed:

```
func path(in rect: CGRect) -> Path {
    var path = Path()
    path.move(to: .zero)
    path.addLine(to: CGPoint(x: rect.minX,
       y: rect.maxY))
    return path
}
```

The first thing we do is create the path instance; this is the variable that we're going to load up with all the lines that make the wave shape.

The next line calls the move_to method. This is the method that starts the drawing of the shape you're making; in this project, that's the wave shape. The to parameter is asking where on the screen you want to add the first point. For that parameter, we pass in the value of .zero, which is another way of setting the x- and y-axis values to 0. (We could simply write out the values as X: 0 and Y: 0, but using .zero is easier.)

The next line of code calls the addLine function, which simply draws a straight line. Its parameters need an X and Y value to know where to put the next point to draw the line. For those X and Y values, we pass in two helper functions called minX and maxY, which automatically get different points of the screen for us.

The iPhone uses the X and Y coordinate system – X runs from left to right, and Y runs from top to bottom. The top-left corner of the iPhone screen would have the X and Y values of 0, 0. As you move to the right of the screen, the X value increases, and as you move down the screen, the Y value increases. So, by using the `minX` function in the `addLine` parameter, it will place a point at the far left of the screen (the minimum location on the X-coordinate plane). We could hardcode a value instead, such as 50 or 100, but by using the `minX` function, it tells Xcode to place the point over to the far left of the screen. Though this may seem vague, it is helpful when considering that Apple devices have different screen sizes.

> **Note**
>
> The following are the Swift helper functions available for use to place points on the screen without hardcoding them: `minX`, `midX`, `maxX`, `minY`, `midY`, and `maxY`. The `midX` and `midY` functions, as you might imagine, add a point to the middle area of the screen, and `maxX` and `maxY`, when used together, add a point to the bottom-right area of the screen.

Now, the result of that code is visible in the **Previews** window, showing a vertical straight line:

Figure 10.1: The first line

The `move_to` and `addLine` functions have drawn a line down from the middle-left area of the screen to the bottom-left area of the screen. The length of the line is set by the `frame` modifier we used in the `Previews` struct. By adding a bigger value in the `frame` modifier's parameter, you make the line bigger.

Now, with the first line of the wave shape done, let's draw the second line – this will be a horizontal line that starts from the bottom of the first line and stretches to the right, across the screen. We can do this by adding the highlighted line to our existing code:

```
func path(in rect: CGRect) -> Path {
        var path = Path()
        path.move(to: .zero)
        path.addLine(to: CGPoint(x: rect.minX,
          y: rect.maxY))
        path.addLine(to: CGPoint(x: rect.maxX,
          y: rect.maxY))
        return path
    }
```

This line of code calls the `addLine` function again, adding a point to the `maxX` and `maxY` locations. The result should now look like this:

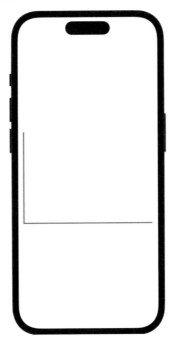

Figure 10.2: The second line

With two lines and half of the wave shape done, let's now add the third line, which is the last straight one. Add the following highlighted line to your existing code:

```
func path(in rect: CGRect) -> Path {
        var path = Path()
        path.move(to: .zero)
        path.addLine(to: CGPoint(x: rect.minX,
          y: rect.maxY))
        path.addLine(to: CGPoint(x: rect.maxX,
          y: rect.maxY))
        path.addLine(to: CGPoint(x: rect.maxX,
          y: rect.minY))
        return path
    }
```

This line of code adds a point to the maxX (far-right) and minY (top-left) parts of the screen, so the result will look like this:

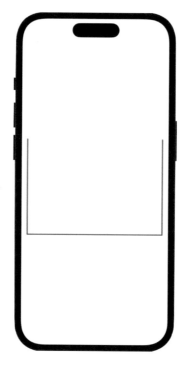

Figure 10.3: The third line

Now that we have three straight lines, we just need to add the wavy line to the top to complete the wave shape. Let's add that now:

```
func path(in rect: CGRect) -> Path {
        var path = Path()
        path.move(to: .zero)
        path.addLine(to: CGPoint(x: rect.minX,
          y: rect.maxY))
        path.addLine(to: CGPoint(x: rect.maxX,
          y: rect.maxY))
        path.addLine(to: CGPoint(x: rect.maxX,
          y: rect.minY))
        path.addCurve(to: CGPoint(x: rect.minX,
          y: rect.minY),
        control1: CGPoint(x: rect.maxX * 0.45,
          y: rect.minY - (rect.maxY * yOffset)),
        control2: CGPoint(x: rect.maxX * 0.45,
          y: (rect.maxY * yOffset)))
        return path
    }
```

Here, we have used the `addCurve` function to create the Bezier curve. This has three parameters.

The first parameter, `to`, is for adding a point to the screen for drawing the curvy line. The previous line of code drew a line that ended at the top-right side of the rectangle, so from there, the `addCurve` function will draw to the `minX` and `minY` location, which is the top left of the rectangle, effectively closing off the shape.

The next two parameters are what are called **control points**, or `control1` and `control2` points, specifically. These parameters are here to accept values that will adjust the amount of curve in a line that pertains to the *y* axis – `control1` will adjust the right portion of the line and `control2` will adjust the left portion of the line.

To understand how these control points work, if we pass in a value of 0 to both parameters, then the line created will be straight, not a curvy one; that's because a value of 0 does not alter those points up or down, thus the line remains straight. But by passing in floating-point values, the control points start to bend the line on the right and left sides by the given amount. The control points do not act on the right and left ends of the line; those are the connection points that close the wave shape. Instead, the control points are equally spaced and offset from the ends.

Looking at the values being used for the control points now, they have been computed to create a line that has a bend going upward on the right side and a bend going downward on the left side. The x values for `control1` and `control2` get their results by multiplying the `maxX` value by 0.45 (this is a hardcoded value and helps shape the bend in the line on the *x* axis).

On the other hand, the y values for `control1` and `control2` are computed a little differently. `control1` gets its value by subtracting the `minY` value by the result of multiplying `maxX` by the `yOffset` variable. `control2` gets its value by multiplying the `maxY` value by the `yOffset` value.

These computations may be a bit unclear at first, but when you complete the project and experiment with different parameter values, you will see how the math works to make the bend in the line move; the amount of movement is related directly to how big or small a value the `yOffset` variable has.

Let's now have a look at the result of adding the control points:

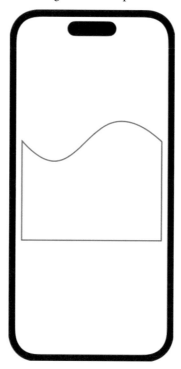

Figure 10.4: The completed wave shape

Now, with all four lines completed, we have created the wave shape. Up next, we will make the shape come alive using a special Swift property called `animatableData`.

> **Note**
>
> When working with the path_in function, as we are doing here, there is also another function that is used to close off the shape we are drawing out: closeSubpath(). This is helpful when closing the ends of a shape without needing to use the addLine() function and passing in X and Y points. We didn't need to use it here because we drew the wave shape out and ended with the curvy line on top. If I drew the curvy line first and wanted to end with a straight line, then I could have used this function to save some code.

Adding the wave's animatableData property

We now have a wave shape that we can duplicate as many times as needed to create a layered ocean scene. However, those waves are still static, meaning they won't do anything unless we have a way of changing the value in the yOffset variable. To accomplish that, we need to add one more important variable to the file here: animatableData.

So, let's add it right under the declaration of the yOffset variable:

```
var animatableData: CGFloat {
    get {
        return yOffset
    }
    set {
        yOffset = newValue
    }
}
```

The animatableData property is an instance of a Swift class called Animatable, and is a built-in Swift property that has a getter and a setter attached to it. Properties with getters and setters do just that: they get a value and set a value.

Using the animatableData property provides a few benefits over animating with a simple @ State property alone:

- It allows you to declaratively specify that a view can be animated, making it clear to other developers (and to the framework) that the view is intended to be animated

- It allows the framework to automatically interpolate between the old and new values, rather than requiring you to manually calculate the intermediate values

- It allows you to use the animation() method to specify how the animation should be performed, such as the duration, curve, and delay

- It allows you to use more advanced animation techniques, such as `animation(_:)` and `transition(_:)`, to specify the animation between different states of the view

In our project, we're using the `animatableData` property to get and set the values of the wave's control points. This getting and setting is happening constantly and thus making the value of the `yOffset` variable change constantly too. Since the `yOffset` variable is being used to create the curvy line inside the `path_in()` function, the result will be that the curvy line dynamically changes too.

With the `animatableData` property in place, and the wave shape completed, we can proceed to the `ContentView`, where we will add the animation to the shape.

Setting up the ContentView for animation

Here, in the `ContentView`, we are ready to use the wave shape and add the animation to it. Let's start by creating a new struct at the bottom of the file, just above the `Previews` struct, and call it `WaveCreation`:

```
struct WaveCreation: View {
    var body: some View {
    }
}
```

This struct is very similar to the `ContentView` struct – it conforms to the `View` protocol, which means it must implement the `body` property. The `body` property itself will return a view, and that will be the animated wave. By the end of the next section, we will have created six waves in total, spaced out neatly inside of a stack.

We will need several variables to get this working, some for the animation and some that allow us to alter the size of the wave curve. Add the following code above the `body` property, inside the `WaveCreation` struct:

```
@Binding var animateOffset: Bool
    var curveOne: CGFloat
    var curveTwo: CGFloat
    var radius: CGFloat
    var shadowX: CGFloat
    var shadowY: CGFloat
    var duration: Double
```

There are seven variables here:

- The first one is a `Binding` variable, which we will use in `ContentView` to start the animation when it is set to `true`.

- The next two variables are called `curveOne` and `curveTwo`, which will be used to set the size of the wave's two curves. Remember the wavy line shape has two curves on it, and they were created using those two control points, one for the left curve of the wavy line and the other for the right curve of the wavy line. The `curveOne` and `curveTwo` variables will allow us to alter the size of those curves on that wavy line; a bigger value will give us a bigger curve, and so a bigger wave.

- Next is the `radius` variable, which allows us to set the radius on a shadow. I want to give each wave a shadow later and so this variable makes that customization easier.

- The placement of these shadows is also important; we can control this placement with two variables, `shadowX` and `shadowY`.

- Finally, the `duration` variable allows us to set the duration of the animation for each wave.

With those variables in place, we only need a few lines of code to complete the `WaveCreation` struct. Those lines are as follows:

```
var body: some View {
    WaveView(yOffset: animateOffset ? curveOne : curveTwo)
        .fill(Color(UIColor.blue))
        .shadow(color: .gray, radius: radius, x: shadowX,
          y: shadowY)
        .animation(Animation.easeInOut(duration:
          duration).repeatForever(autoreverses: true),
          value:animateOffset)
}
```

The first line of code calls the `WaveView` struct, and that requires a value for its `yOffset` parameter. We're passing in one of two values: when the `animateOffset` variable is `true`, we're going to use the `curveOne` variable, which means that one of the curves on the wavy line will be animated on the *y* axis. But when the `animateOffset` variable is `false`, we will then use the `curveTwo` variable, which will control the opposite side of the wavy line on the *y* axis.

The next line of code uses the `shadow` modifier to add a shadow to the wave. Looking at the parameters, the `color` parameter gets a gray color (which will look good against the blue waves), the `radius` parameter sets the size of the shadow, and the X and Y parameters allow us to adjust the shadow up, down, left, and right.

Then, the final line adds the animation – this is an easeInOut timing curve, which means the animation will start slowly, then build up, and when it finishes, it will ease itself out slowly. The duration of the animation will be set using the duration variable, with repeatForever and autoreverses set to true. Then, for the value parameter, that gets the animateOffset variable to start the animation.

Now, rather than just having one wave in our scene, we will call this structure inside the ContentView six times to make the ocean.

Duplicating and animating the wave shape in the ContentView

When creating our ocean, we'll stack six waves in our scene and stagger the animation values so that they animate at different times. Working in the ContentView file now, we'll start by adding a variable inside the ContentView struct that will toggle the animation on:

```
@State private var animateOffset = false
```

Next, let's add a ZStack that will hold all the waves, and inside that, let's set the background to a blue sky color:

```
ZStack {
        //MARK: - BACKGROUND
        Color.blue
            .opacity(0.5)
            .edgesIgnoringSafeArea(.all)
}
```

This code adds a blue color with an opacity of 0.5 (50%) for the background, and then we stretch that background out all the way around the edges of the screen using the edgesIgnoreSafeArea modifier.

We are now ready to add the first wave. So, add the following code directly underneath the edgesIgnoring modifier, inside the ZStack:

```
//MARK: - WAVE 1
    WaveCreation(animateOffset: $animateOffset, curveOne:
        0.05, curveTwo: -0.05, radius: 50, shadowX: 0,
        shadowY: 50, duration: 5.0)
            .opacity(0.8)
            .offset(y: 575)
```

Adding the wave is simple because we have done all of the work already – here, we just call the `WaveCreation` struct and fill some values into its parameters.

The first value is for the `animateOffset` parameter, a Boolean that will start the animation.

Then, the `curveOne` and `curveTwo` parameters require a value for both parts of the wavy line we made in `WaveView`. When you increase the value for one of the curve variables, you increase the height of the wave on one side. If you increase the size of both curve variables, you increase the height for both sides of the wave. Conversely, if you decrease the value for the curve variables by using negative numbers, then the wave gets smaller.

I'm using a small value here of `.05` and `-.05`. That's because this is the first wave in the scene, and it will be further out to sea, so I want this wave to be a little calmer than the waves that are closer to the shore (and the user).

The next parameter is for the radius of the shadow. It's set to `50`, which means it creates a shadow with a size of 50 points. The direction of the shadow will be controlled by the `shadowX` and `shadowY` properties – `shadowX` gets a value of `0` because I don't want to move the shadow on the x axis left or right, but I do want to adjust it on the y axis, and a value of `50` points for the `shadowY` variable will bring the shadow upward by 50 points.

Then, we have the `duration` for the animation. We're setting it to `5` seconds to create the slower, calmer animation that we are aiming for with this first wave.

Finally, We're setting the opacity of this wave to `.8`, so it's slightly less opaque than some of the other waves that we will be adding. Then, we offset this wave using a value of `575` on the y axis, putting it toward the bottom of the screen.

That completes our first wave. To see this animation, all we have to do is toggle the `animateOffset` variable inside the `onAppear` modifier. Add this code right at the end of the `ZStack`:

```
.onAppear() {
        animateOffset.toggle()
    }
```

With that code in place, we can now run the app and see the result:

Figure 10.5: Our first wave

The first wave has a smooth animation flowing back and forth, and we're ready to build our next wave on top of it.

The code for the rest of the waves is nearly identical except for the specific values that we have set in each parameter. Here is the code for the next five waves:

```
//MARK: - WAVE 2
    WaveCreation(animateOffset: $animateOffset,
      curveOne: -0.07, curveTwo: 0.07, radius: 100,
```

```
        shadowX: 0, shadowY: 10, duration: 4.0)
.offset(y: 610)
//MARK: - WAVE 3
    WaveCreation(animateOffset: $animateOffset, curveOne: 0.1,
        curveTwo: -0.1, radius: 30, shadowX: 0, shadowY: 0,
        duration: 3.7)
.offset(y: 645)
//MARK: - WAVE 4
    WaveCreation(animateOffset: $animateOffset,
        curveOne: 0.14, curveTwo: -0.1, radius: 70,
        shadowX: 0, shadowY: 10, duration: 3.5)
.offset(y: 705)
//MARK: - WAVE 5
    WaveCreation(animateOffset: $animateOffset,
        curveOne: -0.05, curveTwo: 0.08, radius: 60,
        shadowX: 0, shadowY: 20, duration: 3.2)
            .opacity(0.8)
.offset(y: 740)
//MARK: - WAVE 6
    WaveCreation(animateOffset: $animateOffset,
        curveOne: -0.05, curveTwo: 0.08, radius: 60,
        shadowX: 0, shadowY: 20, duration: 3.4)
.offset(y: 800)
```

As you can see, the values here are different from those of the first wave – for example, wave 2 has larger values for the curve variables, and the radius is bigger as well; however, the duration of this wave is slightly shorter, with a value of 4 seconds, making the animation a little faster. Waves 3, 4, 5, and 6 also have shorter durations, so we are increasing the speed of the animation for each wave as we move closer to the user's point of view.

The shadows vary too, adding a nice white cresting look to the wave and helping to delineate the waves from each other. I'm using a gray color for the shadows as it's not too pronounced; however, you can try white if you prefer a brighter-looking wave.

Now, go ahead and run the project in the simulator again and check out all the waves animating back and forth in our ocean scene:

Figure 10.6: All six waves together

As with the first wave, the animation is smooth and rhythmic, and by piling up wave upon wave and offsetting each of them a little bit downward, we have created an ocean scene.

Next, we're going to continue adding animations to the scene by adding a buoy that will bob up and down in the water, complete with a blinking light.

Adding an animated floating buoy to the ocean scene

When adding the buoy to our ocean scene, we will be giving it four different animations. It will do the following:

- Have a blinking light at the top of it

- Tilt forward and backward

- Move up and down

- Rotate along its leading anchor

All of these animations will combine to create a realistic-looking bobbing effect that simulates a floating object in an ocean reacting to the waves and current.

First, download the buoy image, which you can find in the Chapter 10 folder in the GitHub repository, and add the image to the Assets catalog. Then, create a new SwiftUI View file, which we will call BuoyView. Inside the file, we will need six variables to get this buoy off the ground and into the water, so add the following code to the BuoyView struct:

```
@Binding var tiltForwardBackward: Bool
    @Binding var upAndDown: Bool
    @Binding var leadingAnchorAnimate: Bool
    @State private var red = 1.0
    @State private var green = 1.0
    @State private var blue = 1.0
```

Here, we are using three Boolean binding variables, which will oversee their respective animations: tiltForwardBackward, upAndDown, and leadingAnchorAnimate. Then, three State variables are used to make a blinking light animation.

We just added some binding variables to the BuoyView struct, which will introduce some errors in the project. The reason why these errors occur is that anytime we add binding variables to the struct we are working in, we will need to add them in the Preview struct as well; otherwise, the previews will complain. The Preview struct's job is to display all the code that's written within the file, so it works hand in hand with the BuoyView struct.

So, modify the Preview struct code to look like the following:

```
struct BuoyView_Previews: PreviewProvider {
    static var previews: some View {
        BuoyView(tiltForwardBackward: .constant(true),
        upAndDown: .constant(true), leadingAnchorAnimate:
        .constant(true))
    }
}
```

We are now, once again, error-free.

Let's now come into the `body` property and add a `ZStack`, then add the buoy image inside of the `ZStack`:

```
ZStack {
        Image("buoy")
    }
```

We should see the buoy in the previews now:

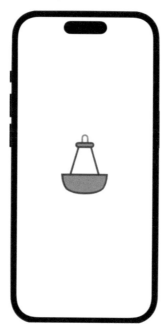

Figure 10.7: The buoy

We're going to work on the blinking light first. In order to achieve this effect, we have to add a rectangle shape, place it on top of the buoy (inside the curved top), then give it some color, and finally toggle that color on and off to make it look like the light is blinking.

Making the buoy light blink

To start the process of creating the light, let's overlay a rectangle on the buoy image. Add the following code to do that, right under the `Image` initializer:

```
ZStack {
        Image("buoy").overlay(Rectangle())
    }
```

This is the `overlay` modifier, which allows us to add a new view over an existing view, to create layers of views.

If you look in your previews, you will see that the rectangle we just added is much too big for what we need. So, there needs to be a little more stylizing and resizing of it. But before we go any further, let's set the color variables to some initial values in the `onAppear` modifier so we can see our work progressing in the previews. Add this code to the end of the `ZStack`:

```
.onAppear() {
            red = 0.5
            green = 0.5
            blue = 0.5
      }
```

I'm setting the `red`, `green`, and `blue` variables to a value of `0.5` (50%). This equal combination of 50% for these RGB colors produces a gray or neutral color, which will look good blinking against the blue sky background later.

Next, coming back to the `Image` initializer, let's add that neutral gray color to the rectangle using another `overlay` modifier and passing in the color variables. Be careful to place the new code directly in front of the overlay's closing brace, like this:

```
ZStack {
            Image("buoy").overlay(Rectangle()
                  .overlay(Color(red: red,green: green,blue:
                  blue)))
      }
```

Now, we have a big gray rectangle, but we don't see the buoy anymore because the rectangle is too big and needs to be resized. We are going to fix that. Add the following rectangle modifiers, which will size and position the rectangle, and place them directly inside the closing brace of the first `overlay` modifier:

```
Image("buoy").overlay(Rectangle()
      .overlay(Color(red: red,green: green,blue: blue))
      //adds a corner radius only to the bottom corners of
         the rectangle
                  .frame(width: 12, height: 17)
                  .position(x: 112.5, y: 19.5))
                  }
```

The `frame` modifier sets the width and height of the rectangle to a small size of `12` by `17`. Then, the `position` modifier places the rectangle at the X and Y coordinates of `112.5` and `19.5`, which is at the top part of the buoy, the area that represents the light.

You can see the rectangle in the following image:

Figure 10.8: The buoy with the rectangle overlay

The rectangle looks good; however, a rectangle is, well, a rectangle. It has sharp corners on all four sides, whereas the top of the buoy has curved corners, as you can see in *Figure 10.9*:

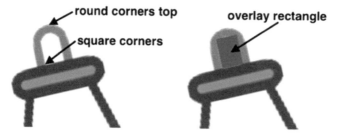

Figure 10.9: A closer look at the rectangle overlay

Using our current rectangle is a bit like fitting a square peg into a round hole. Luckily, SwiftUI does give us a modifier that rounds the corner radius of rectangles, but unluckily, there is still a problem with it: it rounds all four corners when all we want is for the top two corners to be rounded.

We could fix this by adding an extension to the corner radius modifier and altering its behavior so it will only act on two corners by writing numerous lines of code. However, a simpler way of achieving a two-corner radius modifier is by using the `padding` modifier in a unique way.

To do this, after the last variable in the `BuoyView` struct, add a constant to store the radius we want for rounding the two corners of our rectangle:

```
let cRadius = 8.0
```

I'm calling this constant `cRadius`, for the corner radius, and setting it to a value of 8.0 points. The larger you make the corner radius value, the more rounded the rectangle becomes; for our purposes, an eight-point value adds just enough rounding to our rectangle's two top corners to make it fit perfectly within the buoy light.

Add the following code, directly after the second `overlay` modifier, like this:

```
Image("buoy").overlay(Rectangle()
    .overlay(Color(red: red,green: green,blue: blue))
    ///add a corner radius only to the bottom corners
        .padding(.bottom, cRadius)
        .cornerRadius(cRadius)
        .padding(.bottom, -cRadius)
    .frame(width: 12, height: 17)
    .position(x: 112.5, y: 19.5))
```

Here's what the code does. The `.padding(.bottom, cRadius)` line adds eight-point padding to the bottom of the rectangle. Then, we call the `cornerRadius` modifier, which will put a corner radius on all four corners of the rectangle. But since we have an eight-point padding on the bottom of the rectangle, we don't see that corner radius placed on the bottom; we will only see the curved corners at the top of the rectangle, which is exactly what we want.

Finally, we call the `padding` modifier again, and again choose the `.bottom` option to place padding only on the bottom of the rectangle. This time, however, we set a value of -8 points. When we make this option negative, it effectively extends the rectangle downward on the *y* axis – by 8 points – but preserves those two sharp corners that we want at the bottom. This is a pretty neat trick and saves us some time writing code in an extension for the `cornerRadius` modifier. This is the result we see in the previews now:

Figure 10.10: The rectangle overlay now fitting the curved tip of the buoy

The previews show that our gray rectangle now matches the curvature of the top portion of the light and has two sharp corners to match the bottom portion of the light.

To finish off the light and make it blink, we only have to add one line of code after the last line of code in the ZStack:

```
///the animation for the blinking light
.animation(Animation.easeOut(duration:
    1).repeatForever(autoreverses: true),value: red)
```

With that code in place, if you run the previews here in the BuoyView file, you'll see that now we have a blinking light that will blink on and off for a duration of 1 second, repeating forever, or until the app stops:

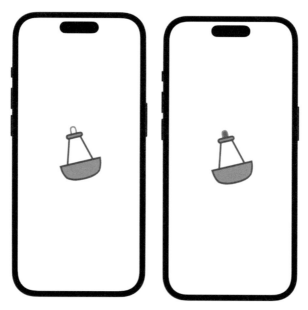

Figure 10.11: The completed buoy with a blinking light

Let's add the animations that make the buoy move now.

Making the buoy move

The first animation that we will add to make the buoy move will be to rotate the buoy along its leading anchor point. To do this, add the following code right after the previous line of code in the `ZStack`:

```
///the animation for the anchor point motion
  .rotationEffect(.degrees(leadingAnchorAnimate ? 7 :
    -3), anchor: .leading)
  .animation(Animation.easeOut(duration:
    0.9).repeatForever(autoreverses: true),
    value: leadingAnchorAnimate)
```

This code uses the `rotationEffect` modifier and will rotate the buoy by either 7 degrees when the `leadingAnchorAnimate` property becomes `true`, or `-3` when it's `false`. For the anchor parameter, we used the `leading` anchor option, which pivots the image around the leading edge, but you can use the `bottom` option as well for a slightly different rotation.

Then, we added the `animation` modifier, setting its `duration` to `0.9` seconds, with `repeatForever`, and `autoreverses` set to `true`.

We will also toggle the `leadingAnchorAnimate` property to `true` in the `onAppear` modifier shortly, but first, let's add the other two animations to the buoy.

The next animation to add will make the buoy tilt forward and backward. Add the code for this right under the previous code:

```
///the animation for the tilt forward and backward
  motion
  .rotationEffect(.degrees(tiltForwardBackward ? -20 :
    15))
  .animation(Animation.easeInOut(duration:
    1.0).delay(0.2).repeatForever(autoreverses:
    true),value: tiltForwardBackward)
```

The is almost identical to the previous code, but the value of `.rotationEffect` is now set to `tiltForwardBackward`. The amount of rotation or tilt forward and back is going to be either `-20` degrees or `15` degrees, depending on the value inside of the `tiltForwardBackward` variable. Also, in the `animation` modifier, we're adding a slight delay of `0.2`, as this will help to add to a real-looking bobbing motion.

Now, to add the final animation to the buoy, which will make the image move up and down, add this line of code directly after the previous code:

```
.offset(y: upAndDown ? -10 : 10)
```

A negative value will move an image up the *y* axis and a positive value will move the image down the *y* axis. So, this code will move the entire buoy image 10 points up or down depending on the upAndDown variable.

The last bit of code we need in the BuoyView file is code that toggles on these three animations in the onAppear modifier. So, add the following code:

```
.onAppear() {
        leadingAnchorAnimate.toggle()
          tiltForwardBackward.toggle()
          upAndDown.toggle()
        red = 0.5
        green = 0.5
        blue = 0.5
    }
```

That completes the BuoyView file, and now we can proceed to ContentView and add the buoy to the scene.

Adding the buoy to the scene

We want to place the buoy slightly in the distance of our ocean scene, so let's add it right after wave 1. Add the following code after the closing brace of the first wave:

```
//MARK: - BUOY
    BuoyView(tiltForwardBackward: $tiltForwardBackward,
      upAndDown: $upAndDown, leadingAnchorAnimate:
      $leadingAnchorAnimnate)
    .offset(y: 205)
```

Inside the BuoyView initializer, we pass in the three binding properties that initiate three separate animations. We add a dollar sign before those binding properties, which tells the compiler that there's a two-way binding between the BuoyView struct and the ContentView struct. Next, using the offset modifier, we can place the buoy at the proper height in the ocean scene.

Now, go ahead and run the project in the simulator to see the animations:

Figure 10.12: The completed animation

Though the code for the waves and buoy work independently, the two elements visually work together to create our ocean scene.

The final element that we can add next is some sound effects. How about the sound of some ocean waves and a buoy bell ringing in the background? That would really complete the project.

Adding sound effects

We already added sound in *Chapter 4*, when building the record player project, and there's nothing complicated about it.

First, start by creating a Swift file (just a Swift file, not a SwiftUI View one), and call it `PlaySound`. Next, drag the M4A sound effects file called `buoyBells` (which you can find on GitHub) and place it into the file navigator.

Inside the `PlaySound` file, the first thing we need to do is import the AVFoundation framework:

```
import AVFoundation
```

The AVFoundation framework gives us access to all the classes and methods needed to add audio to a project.

Next, create an `audioPlayer` object to play our sound file:

```
var audioPlayer: AVAudioPlayer?
```

This `audioPlayer` object is optional, which you can tell by the question mark at the end. It needs to be optional because the sound file may not exist for whatever reason – maybe the file gets corrupted, or the sound file has been downloaded from a server and the internet has timed out – and so this protects the project from crashing.

Finally, under the previous line of code, all we need to do is add a function to handle the audio needs of this project:

```
func playSound(name: String, type: String) {
    if let path = Bundle.main.path(forResource: sound,
      ofType: type) {
        do {
            audioPlayer = try AVAudioPlayer(contentsOf:
              URL(fileURLWithPath: path))
            audioPlayer?.play()
        } catch {
            print("Could not find and play the sound file")
        }
    }
}
```

The function is called `playSound`. It accepts two strings, one to hold the name of the file and another to hold the file's extension type.

The first thing we do is try to access the sound file that's in the app bundle by using the `path_forResource()` function. The app bundle is an internal hidden folder that is created for each app to hold all the necessary files to get the app up and running.

If the file exists with the specified name and type, then the code proceeds into the do block and tries to create the audio player with the path of the file's location stored in the path constant. If, for whatever reason, the file cannot be found or it's corrupt, then the code will fall into the catch block and print out an error.

And that's really it for the PlaySound file. Let's go back into ContentView and add the sound effects to the project. In the onAppear modifier, set the sound to start playing with the following code:

```
.onAppear() {
        animateOffset.toggle()
        playSound(name: "buoyBells", type: "m4a")
    }
```

We also need a way of stopping the sound too, when the app stops running on the device or the user closes the app. The way to make the sound stop is to call the onDisappear modifier, which we can use directly on the closing brace of the onAppear modifier, like this:

```
    .onDisappear()
    {
        audioPlayer?.stop()
    }
```

And with that, the project is complete!

Summary

In this chapter, we created an ocean scene, with moving waves and a bobbing buoy with a flashing light, and added some sounds too.

More specially, you used the Shape protocol, the path function, the animatableData property, and curve variables to make the wave shape come alive. When working on the buoy, we looked at how to combine multiple types of animation to create unique effects, and how to turn different colors on and off to create a blinking effect.

The parameters in this project are highly customizable, so feel free to experiment further – maybe you want to create bigger waves or more of them, create the waves in landscape orientation, alter the shadow to create a horizon, or even replace the buoy with a boat!

Let's keep going. In the next project, we will create a working elevator animation using timers and sound effects.

11

Animating an Elevator

Welcome to the elevator project! In this one, we're going to create a working elevator, complete with sounds, floor lights, a button, and even some images of people inside. We will control the elevator using timers that are available from the Swift timer class, as we have done in previous projects.

To bring these elements together, we'll create a data model using the `@ObservableObject` protocol. Apple recommends making a data model as the place to store and process the data that the application uses. The data model is also separate from the app's user interface, where the views are created. The reason to keep data and the UI separate is that this paradigm fosters modularity and testability. It's easier to find bugs in your logic when the data is not mixed in with UI code. Once we have the data model set up, we can then publish that data anywhere in the app using publishing wrappers, as we will see later.

In this chapter, we will cover the following topics:

- Setting up a project and adding a `Binding` variable
- Assembling the elevator using images and the `GeometryReader` view
- Putting people inside the elevator
- Creating a data model and using the `@ObservableObject` protocol
- Adding the data model functions
- Adding the background, a button, and animating the doors
- Adding floor indicator lights

Technical requirements

You can download the resources and finished project on GitHub: `https://github.com/PacktPublishing/Animating-SwiftUI-Applications`.

Setting up the project and adding a Binding variable

Okay, let's get started! As always, we'll create a new Xcode project (I'm going to call mine `Elevator`).

Next, in the GitHub repo, take all the images from the Chapter 11 folder and drop them into the Asset Catalog. These images include doorDrame, leftDoor, rightDoor, inside, man, man2, man3, and man4.

Then, drop the audio files – doorsOpenClose and elevatorChime – into the Project Navigator.

Next, we're going to need a new file where we can assemble the elevator and add the people, so create a new SwiftUI View file and call it ElevatorAndPeopleView. We only need one variable in this file, which will be the Binding variable. Let's add it at the top, inside the ElevatorAndPeopleView struct:

```
@Binding var doorsOpened: Bool
```

This variable will control the elevator doors opening and closing.

Let's update the Previews so that the code will build without errors. At the bottom of the file, alter the Previews struct so that it looks like the following:

```
struct ElevatorAndPeopleView_Previews: PreviewProvider {
    static var previews: some View {
        ElevatorAndPeopleView(doorsOpened:
            .constant(false), moveMouth: .constant(false))
    }
}
```

The code adds a value of false to both binding properties, and the project once again builds cleanly.

We can now move on to building out the elevator.

Assembling the elevator using images and the GeometryReader view

The next step is to use some of the images from the Assets catalog and make an elevator.

We'll start by adding the inside part of the elevator, which we'll do by adding the following code inside the body property:

```
ZStack {
GeometryReader { geo in
                }
        }
```

First, we have ZStack to hold all the views that will follow, and a GeometryReader view.

The GeometryReader view is a container view that defines its content as a function of its own size and coordinate space. It's a little bit like the other containers that we have used, such as VStack or HStack, but the difference is that GeometryReader has more flexibility because of its proxy parameter, the geo constant (which you can name whatever you want).

This proxy will contain information about the container's size and coordinate space, and we can pass that information to the child views inside GeometryReader, which helps us precisely size and position its children relative to the container. The GeometryReader view also makes the views within it line up perfectly on all iPhone and iPad devices, whatever their size.

We're going to use GeometryReader to size and position all the parts of the elevator, as well as the people inside.

Next, let's add the code that creates the elevator's interior within GeometryReader's body:

```
//MARK: - INSIDE ELEVATOR SCENE
    Image("inside").resizable()
      .frame(maxWidth: geo.size.width,
      maxHeight: geo.size.height)
```

The Image initializer adds the image called inside to the scene, and then uses the frame modifier to set the size of this image to the maximum width and maximum height of the screen. It sets this size using the geo proxy constant we created with the GeometryReader view.

The previews now display the inside of the elevator:

Figure 11.1: The inside of the elevator

Let's continue assembling the elevator by adding doors next. The doors will have animations attached to them so that they slide open and close, and then later, we will add timers to them so that they can operate automatically after an initial button press. So, continuing inside the `GeometryReader` view, add this code for the doors:

```
//MARK: - ADD THE DOORS
HStack {
    Image("leftDoor").resizable()
        .frame(maxWidth: geo.size.width)
        .offset(x: doorsOpened ? -geo.size.width / 2 : 4)
    Image("rightDoor").resizable()
        .frame(maxWidth: geo.size.width)
        .offset(x: doorsOpened ? geo.size.width / 2 : -4)
        }
```

We put the doors in `HStack` because they need to be positioned side by side. The doors are sized using the `frame` modifier and `geo` proxy constant, just as we did with the `inside` elevator image. Both doors also get the `offset` modifier tacked on to them, which will position them on opposite sides of the screen, opening them up fully.

The process to open and close the doors is handled by the `geo` proxy constant. When the `doorsOpened` property becomes `true` for the left door, the `geo` proxy constant will move the door on the *x*-axis, to the left and off the screen. The amount that the door moves is the width of the door divided by 2. The reason why the left door moves to the left and not the right is that we prefix the `geo` constant with a negative sign. When a negative value is used and an object is being offset on the *x*-axis, that object will move to the left, whereas a positive value will move the object to the right.

When the `doorsOpened` property becomes `false`, the `offset` modifier reverses the animation and the left door closes.

For the right door, we do the same thing, except a positive value is used for the `geo` constant, which moves the door to the right along the *X* axis to open it. The values of 4 and -4 that are used for both doors are included to help keep the two doors snug with each other when they are in the closed position.

So far, this is what the scene looks like in the `ElevatorAndPeopleView` file:

Figure 11.2: The elevator doors

We have the elevator's interior and doors placed together, and we have the animation mechanism to operate the doors, but we won't see any motion happening until we call this file inside `ContentView`, and we still have some more assembly to do.

Let's put a frame around the outside of the elevator so that it will look like the actual elevator, and provide a place to add the elevator's button. Add the following code just after the closing bracket of `HStack`, still within the `GeometryReader` view:

```
Image("doorFrame").resizable()
    .frame(maxWidth: geo.size.width, maxHeight:
      geo.size.height)
```

Here, we are adding the `doorFrame` image to the scene, and as we want the frame to go around the entire elevator, we used the same code that we used for the `inside` image – we used the `geo` proxy constant again, and by setting the image at the maximum width and height, the door frame creates a nice border around the elevator doors. This is the result so far:

Figure 11.3: The elevator frame

Now, let's add the animation code that will open and close the doors, and control the speed and delay of the doors when activated later in the `ContentView`. Its only one line of code, and it can be placed right after the closing bracket of the `GeometryReader` view:

```
.animation(Animation.easeInOut.speed(0.09).delay(0.3),
    value: doorsOpened)
```

Here, we use the `animation` modifier. Then, we pass in a value of `0.09` for the `speed` function, which will control how fast the doors open and close. There's also a slight `delay` added of `0.3` seconds, which will delay the door opening and closing just enough to keep things in sync with the floor lights, which we will add soon.

We're getting close to finishing using this file – the only parts left to add are the people images. Of course, you can put the people code into a separate file if you prefer, but since there isn't a lot of code in this file, it will be fine to continue to work here.

Putting people inside the elevator

We'll be adding four characters into our elevator, Let's start with the manOne image – add the following code right after the `frame` modifier near the top of the file, inside the `GeometryReader` view:

```
//MARK: - ADD THE PEOPLE
    Image("manOne")
```

```
.resizable().aspectRatio(contentMode: .fit)
.frame(maxWidth: geo.size.width - 200, maxHeight:
  geo.size.height - 300)
.shadow(color: .black, radius: 30, x: 5, y: 5)
.offset(x: 0, y: 250)
```

What we are doing here is bringing the manOne image into the scene and then adding the correct aspect ratio to the image. Next, we use the frame modifier to set the size for the image, but what's different this time is that we use the proxy constant of GeometryReader to set the size dynamically; when the width and height of an image are set this way, the scene will proportionally scale up or down on all Apple devices to fit the various screen sizes.

I'm trimming off 200 and 300 points for the width and height values so that the image will fit nicely inside the elevator. Once we have the images sized and positioned the way we want, they will scale dynamically when they appear on different devices, so we do need to size and position them initially.

We will then add some shadow with 30 points around the image on the X and Y axes, which gives a nice depth of field for the man when placed inside the shiny metal elevator. And finally, we offset the image on the Y axis so that the feet are on the floor of the elevator.

This is how manOne looks in our elevator:

Figure 11.4: The first man

Since we don't have the animation hooked up yet, to open the door and see inside the elevator while we continue to work, you can simply comment out the door code, and the door images will disappear.

The code for the three remaining people is similar to what we've just added, so I'm going to add the other three images directly under the previous code:

```
Image("manTwo")
    .resizable().aspectRatio(contentMode: .fit)
    .frame(maxWidth: geo.size.width, maxHeight:
      geo.size.height - 290)
    .shadow(color: .black, radius: 30, x: 5, y: 5)
    .offset(x: 40, y: 230)
    .rotation3DEffect(Angle(degrees: 20), axis: (x: 0,
      y: -1, z: 0))

Image("manThree")
    .resizable().aspectRatio(contentMode: .fit)
    .frame(maxWidth: geo.size.width - 100, maxHeight:
      geo.size.height - 250)
    .shadow(color: .black, radius: 30, x: 5, y: 5)
    .offset(x: 130, y: 255)

Image("manFour")
    .resizable().aspectRatio(contentMode: .fit)
    .frame(maxWidth: geo.size.width - 0, maxHeight:
      geo.size.height - 280)
    .shadow(color: .black, radius: 30, x: 5, y: 5)
    .offset(x: -80, y: 265)
```

The code for the manTwo, manThree, and manFour images are largely the same as the code for the manOne image, just with slightly different values for the frame modifier, the offset modifier, and their positions in the elevator.

Regarding the manTwo code, I'm adding a rotation effect to this image because I want to turn this image a little bit toward the left, as he appears to be talking, and it looks a little bit better if we position him in the direction of the person on his right. This is accomplished with the rotation3DEffect modifier; simply turning him 20 degrees on the Y axis is enough to point him in the right direction of the other image.

Here is our elevator full of people:

Figure 11.5: The rest of the people

And that finishes off this file. We can now move on to creating the data model file and adding the necessary functions for the timers and sound effects.

Creating a data model and using the ObservableObject protocol

Let's create a new file – although this time, choose the **Swift** template file rather than the **SwiftUI View** template – and call it DataModel. In this file, we will put the data that we can access from ContentView later, using the @ObservableObject protocol.

To use this protocol, we first need to import the SwiftUI framework:

```
import SwiftUI
```

Next, we need a class to hold all the data, and we also need to make the class conform to the @ObservableObject protocol, so let's add that now. You can name the class anything you want, but many developers like to name the class the same name as the file it is in, so we will do the same, naming the class DataModel:

```
class DataModel: ObservableObject {

}
```

Let's understand what @ObservableObject does.

In previous projects, we used the @State property to pass data to the views and display them to the user, but this is limited because the @State property wrapper can only store values that control the states of a single view; we can't make @State properties and pass them around to other structs, as they work in only one struct.

We also used the @Binding property wrapper, which helped to re-establish the connection to other views or structs with a bidirectional link that the @State property could not provide. However, this would not work globally to hold and pass data to all files in the app.

So, what we need now is an object that can globally control all the app's data and its states and update the views accordingly when there are any changes to the properties, either by user input or changes made by other means, such as downloads from a server or the web.

This is where the @ObservableObject protocol comes in.

The @ObservableObject protocol defines three distinct property wrappers:

- An @StateObject property wrapper that listens for changes in @ObservableObject and receives the new values
- An @ObservedObject property wrapper that listens for changes in the @StateObject property and receives those new values
- An @Published property wrapper that reports all the changes to the system and publishes those changes to the view app-wide

The advantage of using @ObservableObject over the @State property wrapper is, again, that we can update more than one view with any changes, and the state can be checked from views anywhere in the app.

Now, that's a lot to take in, but it will become clearer as we build out the data model. We already have the DataModel class created, and it conforms to the @ObservableObject protocol – that's the first step. Next, we want to declare the properties we need, prefixing them with the @Published property wrapper so that they will hold the various data and states and be published to the views when needed. Let's do that now by adding the following properties inside the DataModel class:

```
@Published var doorsOpened = false
@Published var floor1 = false
@Published var floor2 = false
@Published var goingUp = false
@Published var doorOpenTimer: Timer? = nil
@Published var chimesTimer: Timer? = nil
@Published var doorSoundTimer: Timer? = nil
```

There are several properties here that hopefully are self-explanatory. The four Booleans will be used to let us know when the doors of the elevator are opened, whether floor 1 or floor 2 is the active floor, and whether the elevator is going up or going down. The timers will control the timing of the doors opening and closing, as well as when to play the floor chimes and when to play the door opening and closing sounds.

With the properties listed, we next need a way to access them from other parts of the app. This is done by going up the hierarchy to the `Root` view and injecting an instance of the data model there – the `Root` view is the entry point of the app, the point from which the app starts up.

Let's go into the `App.swift` file in the Project navigator and create an instance of the `DataModel` class there inside the struct, sending a reference to `ContentView`, like this:

```
@main
struct Elevator: App {
    @StateObject private var appData = DataModel()
        var body: some Scene {
        WindowGroup {
            ContentView(appData: appData)
        }
    }
}
```

As I mentioned, this file is the entry point for our app, as denoted by the `@main` wrapper at the top, and it creates the `Root` view window and takes care of creating all the objects we need for the app to start up. Since this file is at the top of the hierarchy, it's the perfect place to create the `DataModel` instance and pass it into the `Root` view, `ContentView`, so it can be available app-wide.

The `DataModel` instance is called `appData`, and it gets prefixed with the `@StateObject` property wrapper – this wrapper will listen for changes in `@ObservableObject` and receive any new values.

Next, the `@StateObject` property wrapper that we called `appData` is injected into `ContentView` by passing it into the `ContentView` initializer to, again, make the data in the data model available throughout the app.

Now, to complete the connection from our data here, and from any view in the project, all we have to do is include an `@ObservedObject` property inside every view that we want to have a connection to this model. The job of `@ObservedObject` is to listen for changes in the `@StateObject` property and receive those new values so that it can update the views.

Let's now go into `ContentView` and add an `@ObservedObject` property to complete the bidirectional binding between the `AppData` class, which holds all the data, and `ContentView`, which is in charge of displaying all of that data on a screen to a user. Add the following property to the `ContentView` struct:

```
struct ContentView: View {
    @ObservedObject var appData: DataModel
            •••••••
}
```

Now, we have an instance of `DataModel`, which will monitor all the data for us; if there are any changes to the data, `ObservedObject` will know about it and update the views accordingly.

Also, if we create more files and need to access the data model from those new files, all we have to do is create another instance of the data model and use it in those files too, like we did with the `appData` instance here, and they will have the same access and be updated with any changes that occur.

We have the instance of the data model ready to be used in `ContentView`, but now we need to add some functions that will take care of setting different timers, which will trigger the doors to open and close, trigger the floor number lights, and also trigger the sound effects at the right moments.

Adding the data model functions

In this section, we will create five functions, and each one oversees a specific task:

- A function to open and close the doors
- A function to play the chimes bell sound that signifies the elevator has reached its destination
- A function to play the door opening and closing sounds
- A function to light up the floor indicator lights
- A function to stop all the timers

Let's start by creating the function that will open and close the doors.

Adding the doorOpenTimer function

Come back into the `DataModel` class, and directly underneath the last variable, add the following function:

```
func openDoors() {
    doorOpenTimer = Timer.scheduledTimer(withTimeInterval:
      8, repeats: false) { _ in
        self.doorsOpened.toggle()
```

```
    }
  }
```

This function is called `openDoors`, and what this does is set the `doorsOpenTimer` object to a value specified by the `scheduledTimer` method. The `scheduledTimer` method will execute the code in its block after a certain amount of time has elapsed – in this case, 8 seconds.

The `scheduledTimerWithInterval` function also has a `repeats` parameter, which lets you repeat the triggering of the code in its body. In the code, we set the `repeats` parameter to `false`, as we only want the code in its body to be triggered when the elevator button is pressed.

The code that it will trigger will involve toggling the `doorsOpened` property to its opposite value. We're going to add a button to the elevator, and we will call this function when that button is pressed. When it's pressed, if the `doorsOpened` property is `true`, it will be toggled to `false`, and vice versa, thus opening and closing the doors as needed.

Adding the playChimeSound function

Let's create another function that will trigger the chimes sound effect; this sound signifies the elevator has reached its destination and will play just before the doors open. Add the following function, directly underneath the previous one:

```
func playChimeSound() {
    chimesTimer = Timer.scheduledTimer(withTimeInterval:
      5.5, repeats: false) { _ in
      playSound(sound: "elevatorChime", type: "m4a")
      }
    }
```

This function is called `playChimeSound`, and it is like the previous function we just added.

When the function is called, it sets the `chimesTimer` property to a value specified by the `scheduledTimer` method, which is `5.5` seconds. After 5.5 seconds have elapsed, the `scheduledTimer` method will call the `playSound` function within its body.

The `playSound` function has two parameters – one for the name of the sound file that we imported into the project, and the other for the file's extension type. However, we haven't created this function yet, so we will get an error!

To fix this, we need to create a separate Swift file, which we will call `PlaySound`. Then, add the following code to this file:

```
import Foundation
import AVFoundation
```

```
var audioPlayer: AVAudioPlayer?
func playSound(sound: String, type: String) {
    if let path = Bundle.main.path(forResource: sound,
      ofType: type) {
        do {
            audioPlayer = try AVAudioPlayer(contentsOf:
            URL(fileURLWithPath: path))
            audioPlayer?.play()
        } catch {
            print("ERROR: Could not find and play the sound
              file!")
        }
    }
}
```

As we've done in previous projects, we imported the AVFoundation framework to have access to the audio classes and methods we need. Next, we created an audio player instance and then added the playSound function.

You should be familiar with how this function works; all we need to do is call this function in any file in which we need to have sound playing, passing the name of the sound file into its sound parameter and its extension type into its type parameter. Now, the playChimeSound function should play error-free.

Now, let's head back to the DataModel class and continue to add the rest of the functions that we need.

Adding the playDoorOpenCloseSound function

When an elevator door opens and closes, it makes a distinctive sound, similar to a mechanical whooshing sound. We want to add that sound to the project, and we'll need a function that can trigger it at the right moment. Let's do that right after the previous function:

```
func playDoorOpenCloseSound(interval: TimeInterval) {
    doorSoundTimer = Timer.scheduledTimer(withTimeInterval:
      interval, repeats: false) { _ in
        playSound(sound: "doorsOpenClose", type: "m4a")
    }
}
```

playDoorOpenCloseSound is a function in which we set the doorSoundTimer property to a value specified by the scheduledTimer method, and the value it will use for the interval parameter will be passed into this function when it gets called in ContentView. When this function is called, it triggers the code in its body after the interval time has passed, and in its body is the playSound function, as we have seen before, which will play the doors' opening and closing sounds.

Adding the floorNumbers function

Up until this point, the functions that we've created have been simple and straightforward, with only one or two lines of code each. But to have the floor indicator lights working correctly, we need to add some more complexity and a little bit of logic.

The objective of this next function is to have the appropriate floor light activate when the elevator reaches its intended floor, and deactivate when the elevator leaves that floor, as a real working elevator would do. So, let's add the following function underneath the previous one:

```
func floorNumbers() {
        ///light up floor 1 as soon as the button is
           pressed, making sure floor 2 is not lit first
        if !floor2 {
            floor1.toggle()
        }
        ///check if the doors are opened, if not, open the
           doors and play the chime sound
        if !doorsOpened {
            openDoors()
            playChimeSound()

        ///going up - wait 4 seconds and turn on the floor
           2 light, and turn off the floor 1 light
            if goingUp {
              withAnimation(Animation.default.delay(4.0)) {
                    floor2 = true
                    floor1 = false
              }
        ///once at the top, and the button is pressed again to
           go down, wait five seconds then turn off the floor 2
           light and turn on the floor 1 light
                withAnimation(Animation.default.delay(5.0)) {
                    floor1 = true
                    floor2 = false
```

```
                              playDoorOpenCloseSound(interval: 8.5)
                    }
            } else if !goingUp {
                withAnimation(Animation.default.delay(5.0)) {
                        floor1 = true
                        floor2 = false
                        playDoorOpenCloseSound(interval: 8.5)
                }
                withAnimation(Animation.default.delay(5.0)) {
                        floor2 = true
                        floor1 = false
                }
            }
        }
    }
```

The function is called floorNumbers, and it starts off by checking various properties to see whether they are true or false.

The first if statement in the function checks to see whether the floor2 property is false – if it is false, then we want to toggle the floor1 property to its opposite value. We always want to make sure that the floor1 and floor2 variables have values that are opposite each other, as they represent the different floors that the elevator goes to.

After that first if statement, there is another if statement. This one checks to see whether the doors are open; if they are not open, then the code will open the doors and play the chimes sound.

Then, inside that if statement is another if statement, which makes this a nested if statement. An if statement will not run the code in its body if the variable it is checking is false; it will just move to the next line of code in the file. This one is checking to see whether the goingUp property is true; if it is true, let's make floor2 true and floor1 false because we want to light up floor2.

This code is all being triggered in the withAnimation function, after a delay of 4 seconds. That's the amount of time to wait before turning on the floor2 light and turning off the floor1 light. The withAnimation function is going to add a default animation, which is just a fade-in/fade-out animation that looks good when turning on and off lights – in our case, the elevator floor lights.

When the elevator reaches the top floor and the button is pressed again to go down, the elevator waits 5 seconds, and then the floor1 light turns on and the floor2 light turns off because the elevator is on its way down. Also, we're going to trigger the open and close door sounds after 8.5 seconds, which is enough time for the elevator to reach the bottom floor, at which point the sound needs to be playing. Again, we're doing this in the body of the `withAnimation` function, so it adds a default fade animation to the lights being turned on and off.

Next, we need to use similar code for when the `goingUp` variable is not `true`, so both states, `true` and `false`, will operate the lights and sounds correctly. We do that in an `else if` statement. `else if` offers another alternative to the `if` statement that proceeds it, should that `if` statement be `false`. So here, `else if` checks whether `goingUp` is `false`; if so, the code turns the `floor1` light on after 5 seconds because the elevator is heading down, turns the `floor2` light off, and then plays the door opening and closing sounds. Otherwise, after 5 seconds, it will do the opposite, turning `floor2` back on and `floor1` off.

This is the logic now in place that is used to operate the timers and trigger the appropriate sounds at the right moment, by using `if` and `else if` statements. Now, the thing with timers is that when a few of them are created, they can overlap with each other and cause unintended consequences in the app, so we need to stop them before creating new ones.

Adding the stopTimer function

We do have a lot of timers firing at various times in the app, and some of these timers can overlap with each other in the background and cause unintended side effects in the app. We need to stop any timer that has served its purpose so that there are no problems. New ones will be created when needed, but they all should be stopped after the completion of their tasks.

So, let's handle the deactivation of all the timers in a separate function. Add the following final function to the file:

```
func stopTimer() {
        doorOpenTimer?.invalidate()
        doorOpenTimer = nil
        chimesTimer?.invalidate()
        chimesTimer = nil
        doorSoundTimer?.invalidate()
        doorSoundTimer = nil
    }
```

This function is called `stopTimer`, and it invalidates all the timers that were created and sets them to `nil`.

Invalidating a timer effectively stops the timer from ever firing again and requests its removal from its run loop. Setting an object to `nil` is equivalent to a variable being set to zero; it makes sure that it is completely stopped. We will call this method inside the elevator button press and make it the first method to be called, thus removing any timers that might still be going.

Now, `DataModel` is complete with all the functions and properties set up to be used anywhere in the app; we're going to use them in `ContentView`. Let's head over there and start to put things together so that we can start to see some results.

Adding the background, a button, and animating the doors

Let's continue and start to fill out `ContentView` so that we can see the elevator, and then we can animate things.

First, we will add a black background to the whole scene. To do this, add a constant at the top just after the `appData` variable to hold some color:

```
let backgroundColor = Color(UIColor.black)
```

Next, inside the `body` property, let's add `ZStack` and call our `backgroundColor` constant, setting the color for the screen:

```
var body: some View {
        ZStack {
            backgroundColor.edgesIgnoringSafeArea(.all)
                }
```

Now, we will need to call the `ElevatorAndPeople` view so that we can make it visible in this file. Add the following code, still working inside `ZStack`, and in fact, all subsequent code we add into this file will be within this `ZStack`:

```
//MARK: - ADD THE PEOPLEANDELEVATOR VIEW
ElevatorAndPeopleView(doorsOpened:
  $appData.doorsOpened)
```

As we've seen before, to show another view in `ContentView`, we simply call it here inside the `body` property and pass in the binding variable that we created to access the model class. Remember that we use the dollar sign to access binding variables, which tells the system that we are bidirectionally connecting to another view.

Note that we can access our data by using the `appData` observed object, and by typing a dot, we can then choose any of the properties or functions within the model file. Here, I'm choosing the `doorsOpened` property, and we will be toggling that on in a button.

And speaking of buttons, let's add the elevator button right now; we'll put it on the left side of the elevator frame, and when pressed, the doors will open and close. Add the following code under the previous line:

```
//MARK: - ELEVATOR BUTTON
    GeometryReader { geo in
      Button(action: {
          appData.doorsOpened.toggle()
      }) {
          ///if the doors are opened, make the button
            white, otherwise make it black
          Circle().frame(width: 10, height: 10)
            .foregroundColor(appData.doorsOpened ? .white
            : .black)
              .overlay(Circle().stroke(Color.red,
                lineWidth: 1))
              .padding(5)
              .background(Color.black)
              .cornerRadius(30)
      }.position(x: (geo.size.width / 33), y:
        (geo.size.height / 2))
```

This code starts off by using `GeometryReader`. As we have seen, using `GeometryReader` will align the views so that they fit perfectly in the scene, and they will resize correctly on other size devices by accessing the `geo` constant inside the closure.

We then create a button inside `GeometryReader` – the button will run all the code in its body when pressed. We want to check out how the doors work first, so I added the code to toggle the `doorsOpened` property when the button is pressed.

Let's look at what else we're doing here with the button code by looking at the button closure, where the styling is being done. The code uses the `Circle` view to create a circle shape for the button. I gave it a dimension of 10 x 10 and then added several modifiers to help with the styling:

- First, we use the `foregroundColor` modifier for the circle, which is either going to be white when the doors are open, or black when they are closed. This is achieved by accessing our model's `ObservedObject` instance, `appData`, and calling up the `doorsOpened` property from the model.

- The next modifier is `overlay`, where we pass in another `Circle` view. Then, by adding the `stroke` modifier, it turns it into a stroked circle (and not a filled circle). The color of the stroke is set to red and has a line width of 1 point. This stroke will look like a small red ring within the button, as you sometimes see in an actual elevator button.

- Then, we use the `padding` modifier, with a value of 5 points.

- Then, we use a `background` color modifier, positioned underneath the red ring.

- Finally, a `cornerRadius` value of 30 is added to the black background color view, as that is by default a rectangle and we need a rounded shape.

- Now, all we have to do is position the button exactly where it needs to be on the elevator frame, and we can do that with the `position` modifier, passing in the `geo` proxy constant, which has the precise size of an iPhone's screen. Here, the code locates the button on the X axis by using the width of the button, and divides the `GeometryReader` (the width of the iPhone screen) by 33; this value will move the button exactly to the left portion of the elevator frame. Now that we have the X location for the button, we need the Y location. Using the `geo` constant again, and dividing `height` by 2, we can place the button in the middle of the frame for the Y axis.

And with that, the button is complete. Let's try out the animation that we have so far:

Figure 11.6: The opening doors and button

Press the button and you should see the doors open; if you press the button again, the doors will close. And the doors work perfectly, opening and closing at a nice pace, and the button changes color when the doors are open.

Let's continue and add floor indicator lights to the elevator.

Adding floor indicator lights

As we know, elevators have lights, usually at the top of the frame, to let people know what floor the elevator is on at any time. Let's simulate that by adding the lights that represent both floors of the elevator, one and two. Add the following code directly after the previous line of code we have just written:

```
//MARK: - ADD THE FLOOR LIGHTS
  HStack {
      Image(systemName: "1.circle")
          .foregroundColor(appData.floor1 ? .red : .black)
          .opacity(appData.floor1 ? 1 : 0.3)
      Image(systemName: "2.circle")
          .foregroundColor(appData.floor2 ? .red : .black)
          .opacity(appData.floor2 ? 1 : 0.3)
  }.position(x: (geo.size.width / 2), y: (geo.size.height *
    0.02) + 2)
      .font(.system(size: 25))
```

We start off with HStack so that we can put two circle images side by side. These are system images, and they have specific names of 1.circle and 2.circle. The first circle represents the first floor, and the second circle represents the second floor.

The color of the first circle light will depend on the floor1 variable – if it's true, it will make the color red; otherwise, if it's false, it will turn it black. The opacity of this circle will also depend on the floor1 variable – again, if true, the circle will have a fully opaque look; otherwise, we will make the opacity .3. We use the same code for both circles.

Then, by putting the position modifier at the end of HStack, we can position both circles directly at the top of the frame and keep the position in place by, again, using the geo proxy. Finally, we will use a font size of 25 for the floor numbers.

That completes the floor indicator lights.

Finally, all we need to do is to call the rest of our functions inside the button body, so that when the button is pressed, all the lights and sounds will work on timers. So, add the following code to complete the project:

```
//MARK: - ELEVATOR BUTTON
    GeometryReader { geo in
        Button(action: {
            appData.stopTimer()
            appData.playDoorOpenCloseSound(interval: 0.5)
            appData.doorsOpened.toggle()
            appData.goingUp.toggle()
            appData.floorNumbers()
        }) {
```

The code accesses the model functions using the `appData` instance and runs each one when the button is pressed.

Now, run the project and you'll see that when the button is pressed, the doors will open and you'll see the people inside. Also, notice that the button changes color and the indicator for the floor lights up, along with chimes and the sounds of doors opening. When the elevator is moving between floors, the doors, lights, and sounds will work on their own, at the right times.

Figure 11.7: The completed project

It's a nice animation, and it really simulates the timing of an actual elevator very well.

Summary

We have now completed our elevator project. Let's look at what we have done.

We used `GeometryReader` and the proxy constant to add images to the project and position them where needed, which will resize all the images in the project dynamically, based on the device that displays them, whether iPhones or iPads.

We created `DataModel` to store all the app's data and functions, and we accessed all that data using the `@ObservableObject` protocol.

We used timers to trigger door and light animations at different moments in the scene, making the animations happen on their own. We also added and styled a button to change color, when pressed, and we made floor lights turn on and off with timers.

The skills learned here can be useful and applied to other projects. For example, if you were putting together a game app that has several levels, maybe you could incorporate an elevator scene into the game to take the user to another level after they have completed a certain skill, or to search for power-ups.

How about a challenge? To take the project further, see whether you can add more floors to the scene. Or how about animating the people inside the elevator using the same techniques we used with the girl on the swing project? Cut up the images and make different parts move in different ways – for example, you could cut up the second man's mouth so it looks like he's talking when the doors open. You could also animate the legs so that they shuffle a little bit inside the elevator, or animate their bodies so that they sway a little, basically simulating human motion.

In the next chapter, we'll start putting together a language-learning game and animate various aspects of the UI to make the game fluid and interesting. We'll also make the game work across three different languages – English, Spanish, and Italian – so that it can appeal to a broad range of language learners.

12

Creating a Word Game (Part 1)

In this project, we will start creating a "complete the word" game, which we will then finish in the next chapter. The word game will require the user to find words using the letters within a given word. To add a little twist to the game, we'll offer it in three different languages – English, Spanish, and Italian.

Some new things that you will learn are how to add and customize a `PickerView`, implement user feedback in a few different ways (including with pop-up alerts, haptics, and sound), and add various animations to the user interface, including spring animations.

So, in this chapter, we will cover the following topics:

- Setting up the project and creating a data model
- Building out the UI by adding a text field and list
- Displaying a character count next to each word in the list
- Checking the entered words for duplicates
- Adding a random word with a button press
- Checking whether the user's entered word is possible
- Checking whether the user's entered word is a real word
- Checking whether the user's entered work is valid
- Creating `HeaderView` with an `info` button
- Creating `PickerView`

Technical requirements

You can download the resources and finished project from the `Chapter 12 and 13` folder on GitHub: `https://github.com/PacktPublishing/Animating-SwiftUI-Applications`.

Setting up the project and creating a data model

First, create a new Xcode project and call it `Find Words`. Then, in the GitHub repository, go to the `Chapter 12` and `Chapter 13` folders; this folder will include three subfolders called `Language Data`, `Images`, and `Sound`. Add the `Images` folder to the Assets catalog, and the other folders to the Project navigator.

Next, we will create a data model file to hold the data for the `https://github.com/PacktPublishing/Animating-SwiftUI-Applications` app – to do this, press *Command + N*, choose the **SwiftUI** file type, and call it `DataModel`. In this file, import SwiftUI by adding the following code at the top of the file:

```
import SwiftUI
```

As we have done before, we add a class to hold all of the properties and methods. We'll call the class `DataModel`, and it needs to conform to the `ObservableObject` protocol in order for us to access this data later on. Then, we'll add the properties we need:

```
class DataModel: ObservableObject {
    @Published var allWordsInFile = [String]()
    @Published var baseWord = ""
    @Published var userEnteredWord = ""
    @Published var userEnteredWordsArray = [String]()
    @Published var letterCount = ""
    @Published var showSettings: Bool = false

    //error properties
    @Published var errorMessageIsShown = false
    @Published var errorTitle = ""
    @Published var errorDescription = ""

    //properties to stpre in user defaults
    @AppStorage ("selectedSegment") var selectedSegment:
        Int = 0
    @AppStorage ("englishIsOn") var englishIsOn: Bool =
        false
    @AppStorage ("spanishIsOn") var spanishIsOn: Bool =
        false
    @AppStorage ("italianIsOn") var italianIsOn: Bool =
        false
```

```
//splash view property
@Published var change = false
}
```

Let's break down the code:

- First, we have an array called `allWordsInFile`, which will hold all of the words needed to play the game. We will use three separate files, one for English, one for Spanish, and one for Italian. This array will be loaded with whichever language is selected to play the game with.

- Next is a `baseWord` property, which will contain the word the user is working with and trying to find new words from.

- Then, we have another property called `userEnteredWord` that will hold the user's word when they type it into the text field.

- Next is another array called `userEnteredWordsArray`, which will hold all of the user's guessed words so that we can keep track of what they have completed so far.

- Next is a property called `letterCount`, which will be used to keep track of the number of letters per word being used so that we can tally an average number of letters per word. For example, if the user is only choosing three-letter words, we will display that word letter average on the screen.

- Next is the Boolean that will open `SettingsView`, allowing the user to change the game's language.

- Next are three error properties we will use to show an alert when the user misspells words or enters duplicate words, which are words that are already in the list.

- Next are what are called `AppStorage` properties. These are used to save the user's language settings in memory, so when they close the app and then come back later, their settings are preserved. When we prefix a property with the `AppStorage` wrapper, a place in memory on the phone will preserve the user settings.

- Next, a property to display a splash screen. A splash screen is an opening scene that the user will see briefly as the app loads in the background.

Let's continue and add all the methods we need for the project now into `DataModel`, right under the properties we just added:

```
//FUNCTIONS
    //starts the game off with a random word by looking in
       the app's bundle for the language file
```

```
func getRandomWord() {
    guard let wordsURL = Bundle.main.url(forResource:
    setWordLengthAndLanguage(), withExtension: "txt"),
    let wordsConverted = try? String(contentsOf:
      wordsURL) else {
    assert(false, "There was a problem loading the data
      file from the bundle.")
        return
    }
    let allWordsInFile =
      wordsConverted.components(separatedBy: "\n")
    baseWord = allWordsInFile.randomElement() ??
      "SwiftUI"
}

//sets the language for the game
func setWordLengthAndLanguage() -> String {
  return ""
}

//adds a new word to the game
func addWordToList() {

}

//check to see if the word is a duplicate
func isWordDuplicate(word: String) -> Bool {
    return false
}

//check to see if the word is possible given the base
  word's letters
func isWordFoundInBaseWord(userGuessWord: String) ->
  Bool {
    return false
```

```
    }

    //check to see if the word is a real word in dictionary
    func isWordReal(word: String) -> Bool {
        return false
    }
    //error message
    func displayErrorMessage(messageTitle: String,
      description: String) {


    }
```

Let's break this code down too:

- We have a method to grab a random word from the language files

- We have a function to set the word length – either 7, 8, or 9 letters – and language – either English, Spanish, or Italian

- There's a function to add the user's word to a list so that they can see all the words that they have found so far

- Then a function to check whether their word is a duplicate; we don't want duplicates in the list

- Then, a function to check to see whether the word is possible given the word they're working with

- We also have a function to check to see whether the word is a real word in the language of choice (we don't want made-up words!)

- And then finally, a function to display an error message to the user if they type in a word that doesn't exist or cannot be made

As you see from the code, I have filled out only one function for now, and the rest of the functions are just known as **function stubs**. A function stub is a declared function but without anything in its body other than a `return` statement. This is helpful because we can still continue writing code in the interface, call these functions stubs, and the code will still build cleanly, even though it won't do anything yet.

We will fill out the body of the other functions soon enough, but let's look at the one function I did add code into – `getRandomWord()`. This function starts by trying to access the app bundle, which is where we placed our language files. When we add files to the project, they are put into the app bundle. The app bundle is a folder where all the app files are stored and used to make the app work. We need to access the bundle and find the path to those language files so we can load the words they contain and use them in the game.

To access them, Swift gives us a method called url (forResource) for locating the path of a file – we simply type the name of the file into the first parameter and the extension into the second parameter. For now, we're just going to load up the seven-letter word file in the English language (but later on, we'll be accessing words of other sizes and other languages' files).

For the extension, I put in txt for a text file. If we find that file, then we proceed to the next step where we attempt to convert that file into a string so that we can manipulate it. If the code is able to complete that task, then it will separate the words in the file using the components (separatedBy) method and pass in the new line character, so each word will be on its own line. This is helpful so we can access these words later, one by one.

Next, we need to get a random word from the file and store it in the baseWord property. Notice that we need to use the ternary operator here. That's because the randomElement function is an optional function. For this reason, it might not have a word to get, so, we offer an alternative word to keep the code from crashing in case there are no words in the file (this would only happen if the file became corrupt, which is rare).

Finally, if we do come across a problem along the way, we'll use the assert function. assert takes two arguments: a condition to check, and a message to display if the condition is false. If the condition is false, the message will be displayed and the app will halt in a debugging environment. In a production environment, the assert statement will be ignored.

We will use the getRandomWord() function later to get a random word that the user can play with and try to find new words from.

Okay, that's all the properties and functions in place, with one function complete.

Now let's go into the App.Swift file and create an instance of the DataModel class, and then inject that instance into ContentView so that the data model is available from anywhere in the app:

```
@main
struct FindWordsApp: App {
    @StateObject private var appData = DataModel()

    var body: some Scene {
        WindowGroup {
            ContentView(appData: DataModel())
        }
    }
}
```

This should be familiar to you – we have created the `DataModel` instance and passed it into the root view, `ContentView`. We will also get an error because we now need to update `ContentView`, and the `Previews`. Let's add the following modifications in `ContentView` and finish off implementing the `Observable` object protocol by adding a `DataModel` instance so that we can pass the data into the views:

```
@ObservedObject var appData: DataModel
Now let's update the Previews at the bottom of the file
  too:
ContentView(appData: DataModel())
```

Then, let's add a property to display a random word at the top of `ContentView`:

```
@State var wordToPlayFrom = "Click for Word"
```

The `wordToPlayFrom` property will be set to a random word, which will be the user's word to start playing with and finding new words to make with. It's being set to a string that will prompt the user to start the game.

Okay, our data model is now set up here in `ContentView`; let's focus on building out the user interface next.

Building out the UI by adding a text field and list

To build out our UI, first, we'll add a text field view so the user can enter their answers, and then we'll add a list view, so all of the user's words can be listed in a table.

To do that, go into the `body` property of `ContentView` and remove the existing boilerplate code for the `Text` and `Image` views, and add the following code:

```
//MARK: - TEXTFIELD - LIST TABLE
    VStack(alignment: .center, spacing: 15) {
        //MARK: - TEXT FIELD AND LIST
            TextField("Enter your word", text:
              $appData.userEnteredWord)
                .textInputAutocapitalization(.never)
              .textFieldStyle(RoundedBorderTextFieldStyle())
                .padding(.horizontal, 55)
                .onSubmit(appData.addWordToList)
          ///List view to display the user input
          List(appData.userEnteredWordsArray, id: \.self) {
```

```
            word in
                Text (word)
              .foregroundColor(.black)
              .font(.system(size: 18))
        }
        .frame(width: 285, height: 190, alignment: .center)
        .cornerRadius(10)
        .foregroundColor(Color.blue)
        .font(.system(size: 50))
    }
```

Here, we added a text field so we can grab the user's input, while changing `.textInputAutocapitalization` to `never` so that auto-capitalize won't capitalize what the user types into the text field. The word files we imported into the project are all written in lowercase, so turning auto-capitalization off helps with accessing those words and checking the letters.

Next, the text field gets a little styling and a little padding, before we call the `onSubmit` modifier and pass the `addWordToList` property into it. What this modifier does is add an action to be performed when the user types in a word and hits *Enter*. That action being performed is a call to the `addWordToList` method that we have in our data model. That method will process the user's input and see whether their word is allowed to be used based on certain criteria, such as whether the word is even possible in the chosen language and whether they make it from the letters present in the base word.

Notice that in order to access our data model, we have to use our `DataModel` instance's `appData` that we created at the top of this file; this gives us access to all the methods and properties we created in `DataModel`.

Continuing with the code, we then move on to the `List` view, which creates a list to display the user's words. This uses the `id` parameter to uniquely identify each word in the `guessedWords` array. When we iterate (loop) through `userEnteredWordsArray`, we need a way of identifying its content – each element in that array has to be unique to be able to use it and fortunately, every word is indeed unique (no two words are the same). So, what the `id` parameter you see here is saying is that it will use the word's own name as its identifier (the `self` part), and we can access the elements in the array.

After that, we did a bit more styling. We set the text color of the words to `black` and their size to `18` points. Then, we set the frame size of the `List` view, as well as changing the color to `blue` and providing a `cornerRadius` property.

Now, if we run the app, we can type words into the text field, but when we press *Enter*, the word isn't being placed into the `List` view:

Figure 12.1: Words typed into the text field

The reason the words are not going into the list is that we just haven't filled out the empty `addWordToList` function in the `DataModel` class yet. Let's fill out that method now with some code that will allow the user's typed-in word to be displayed inside the list:

```
func addWordToList() {
    let usersWord = userEnteredWord.trimmingCharacters(in:
      .whitespacesAndNewlines).lowercased()
    //guard against one or two letter words - they are too
      easy
```

```
guard usersWord.count > 1 else {
    return
}
userEnteredWordsArray.insert(usersWord, at: 0)
userEnteredWord = ""
}
```

Here, we created a `userWord` constant, which is going to store the new word that the user adds to the list. We first check the user's word for white spaces. This way, if the user types some extra spaces in the text field by mistake, the `trimmingCharacters` function will eliminate them. Next, the word is made lowercase using the `lowercased` function.

Then, we use the `guard` statement, which is very similar to the `if` statement, which checks to see whether the word that the user entered has more than one letter. If it does, it will proceed to the next line of code. Otherwise, the method will return right there and not run any more code. When the code "returns" from a method, that means the code is finished running that method, and even if there's more code inside that method, it won't run. The reason why we're checking to see whether there need to be at least two letters in the user's word is because those are too easy. Even though there aren't many one-letter words in any given language, why not simply remove them altogether?

After the user's word has been trimmed and made lowercase, it's then added to `userEnteredWordsArray`, and inserted at index zero using the `insert(at)` method. This index is at the beginning of the array, and the reason why we insert the word at the beginning and don't append it to the end of the array is that we want each new word to appear at the top of the list so that it's readily visible.

Finally, we set the `newWord` property back to an empty string, which effectively clears out the `Text` view when the user presses *Enter*, so they can type in another word when ready.

Now, if we run the project, we can see that when we type words into the text field and press *Enter*, they now appear in the list:

Figure 12.2: Words are now entered into the list

New words will appear at the top of the list. The `List` view, by default, is also scrollable, so the user can easily scroll up and down to see previously entered words.

Let's continue with the UI and display the number of characters each word contains.

Displaying a character count next to each word in the list

I also want to add a number next to each word that indicates how many letters are in the word that the user has entered. Later, we will take this number from each word and add them together to get an average of how the user is doing in terms of the length of words they are entering.

We can put this number inside a circle, and luckily this is very easy, as Swift gives us system images of circles with numbers in them that are already created; all we have to do is call them up. So, back in

ContentView, then inside the List view, let's put the Text view inside of an HStack (so they are side by side), and add an Image view for the number circle:

```
List(guessedWordsArray, id: \.self) { word in
        HStack {
            Image(systemName:
                "\(word.count).circle")
            Text(word)
        } .foregroundColor(.black)
            .font(.system(size: 18))
    }
```

The Image view gets a system image of a circle. The word.count code statement gets the number of letters in the user's word and displays that number inside of a circle. Now if we run the code, all the words that are typed in will have their letter counts displayed in a circle to the left of the given words:

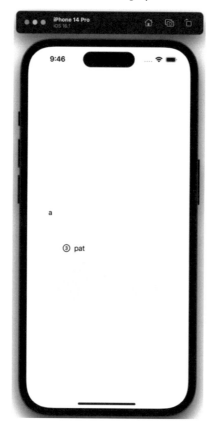

Figure 12.3: The letter count displayed in a circle

Let's move on to now checking the user's words for duplicates.

Checking the entered words for duplicates

Now that we're displaying the words that the user enters, how about we check them to make sure they are real words in a dictionary and that there are no duplicate words in the list? We have all the function stubs in place for these checks, so let's start filling them out.

The first function we'll fill out is `isWordDuplicate`, which we'll modify to look like this:

```
func isWordDuplicate(word: String) -> Bool {
    return userEnteredWordsArray.filter { $0 == word
      }.isEmpty
}
```

What this does is to check `userEnteredWordsArray` to see whether it contains the word the user has typed into the `Text` field. Here's how it works. The `return` statement in this function uses the `filter` method on the `userEnteredWordsArray` array. The `filter` method takes a closure as its argument, which is evaluated for each element of the array. In this case, the closure checks whether the current element of the array (`$0`) is equal to the word passed as an argument to the function.

The result of this `filter` operation is a new array that contains all the elements of `userEnteredWordsArray` that match the given condition. If this new array is not empty, that means that the word already exists in the `userEnteredWordsArray`, so the function returns `false`. If the new array is empty, that means that the word is not duplicated, so the function returns `true`. The `isEmpty` property of the array is used to check whether the array is empty.

Now, just filling out the function is not enough to have it check for duplicates; we have to call this function inside of the `addWordToList` function so that we can use it to check the new words before they are added to the list. Let's do that now – inside the `addWordToList` function, add the following, right after the `userWord` instance is created:

```
func addWordToList() {
    let usersWord =
      userEnteredWord.lowercased().trimmingCharacters(in:
      .whitespacesAndNewlines)
    //is the word a duplicate
    if !isWordDuplicate(word: usersWord) {
    displayErrorMessage(messageTitle: "You already used
      this word", description: "Keep looking!")
    return
```

```
        }

        • • • • • • • • •
    }
```

This code checks the `isWordDuplicate` function to see whether it's returning `true` by using the `!` operator in front of it. Remember, the `isWordDuplicate` function returns a Boolean value, either `true` or `false`, so if this function returns `false`, then the `if` statement runs the code in its body, which is another function called `displayErrorMessage`. This will display an error message to the user telling them that their word is a duplicate (we haven't set up our error messaging system yet, but we will soon!).

Now I'd like you to come back into `ContentView` and run the app, enter a word, and see it appear in the list. Then, try entering that same word again, and you'll notice you're not able to. The `guard` statement stops it from happening because it checks and sees that the word has already been entered into the list.

Next, we want to add a button that will grab a random word from the word files we imported into the project, which gives the user a word to play with and try to find words from.

Adding a random word with a button press

Before we continue with the methods and fill them out, we need a button to provide a random word that the user can play off and try to find words from. After all, it's not a challenge to just type random words and for them to appear in the list currently.

We'll start by supplying a file of thousands of seven-letter words, from which one will be shown on the screen randomly when a button is pressed. We will also give the user the choice to choose a seven-, eight-, or nine-letter word, and the option to select another language later, but right now, let's just stick with seven-letter English words.

If you haven't done so already, go to the GitHub folder, select the `Language` files folder, and drop the contents of that folder into the Project navigator. Once done, select them all, right-click, and choose **New Group From Selection**. Then, name the group `Languages` – this helps keep everything organized in the Project navigator.

Now those files are added to the project and we have already built out the `getRandomWord` function, which will get us a random word from a specified file, so now we need to call this function so that we can show the word to the user – we can do that with a button. Add the following code directly in `VStack`, above the `Text` field code:

```
//MARK: - BUTTON
        Button(action: {
            appData.getRandomWord()
```

```
        wordToPlayFrom = appData.baseWord
    }){
        ZStack {
            Image("background").resizable()
                .renderingMode(.original)
                .frame(width: 125, height: 50)
                .cornerRadius(15)
            Text("New Word")
                .foregroundColor(.white)
        }
    }.padding(7)
        .shadow(color: .black, radius: 2, x: 1, y: 1)
        .shadow(color: .black, radius: 2, x: -1, y: -1)


    Text(wordToPlayFrom)
```

This code creates a button. Inside the `action` parameter for the button, we use our `appData` instance and call the `getRandomWord` function. We also set the `wordToPlayFrom` property to the `baseWord` value because `baseWord` contains the random word that will appear on the screen.

Now every time the button is pressed, a randomized word from our text file is placed into `baseWord`, which then gets placed into the `wordToPlayFrom` property to be displayed.

At the end of the button code, we create a `Text` view that displays `wordToPlayFrom` on the screen. The button is then styled with a wood background image, a slight corner radius, a little bit of shadow, and the words **New Word**.

After adding that code, the button should look like this:

Figure 12.4: A button to create a random word

Now, press the button, and you will get a random word that a user can work with. Also, notice that when you press the button, it actually looks like it's being pressed down; we get this behavior by default, which really adds to the user experience.

The game is coming along, but we want to continue checking the word the user enters to see whether it can be made from the randomized word. Let's do that up next.

Checking if the user's entered word is possible

Looking for duplicate words is not enough. Now that we have generated a random seven-letter word, we want to make sure that the user's entered word can be made from the letters that are in the random word. For example, if the random word is **bookend** and the user types in `books`, that would be invalid because `s` is not in the random word.

Let's go back to the `DataModel` class and add code to the `isWordFoundInBaseWord` function so that we can check that the word can be made from `baseWord`:

```
//check to see if the word is possible given the baseWord
  letters
  func isWordFoundInBaseWord(userGuessWord: String) ->
    Bool {
        var comparisonWord = baseWord
        return userGuessWord.allSatisfy { letter in
            guard let position =
              comparisonWord.firstIndex(of: letter) else {
                return false
            }
            comparisonWord.remove(at: position)
            return true
        }
    }
```

Here's how this function works. The `isWordFoundInBaseWord` function takes a `String` parameter, `userGuessWord`, and returns a `Bool` value indicating whether or not `userGuessWord` can be made by removing letters from the `baseWord` string.

The function starts by creating a `comparisonWord` variable equal to `baseWord`. The `comparisonWord` variable is used to keep track of the remaining letters in `baseWord` that haven't been matched by `userGuessWord`.

Next, the function uses the `allSatisfy` method of `String` to check that all the letters in `userGuessWord` can be found in `comparisonWord`. The `allSatisfy` method iterates over each character in the string and returns `true` if the closure passed to it returns `true` for all characters.

The closure takes a single parameter letter, representing the current letter in `userGuessWord` being processed. It first uses the `firstIndex(of:)` method to find the index of a letter in `comparisonWord`. If a letter is not found in `comparisonWord`, the closure immediately returns `false`, which will make the overall `allSatisfy` call return `false`.

If a letter is found in `comparisonWord`, the closure removes that letter from `comparisonWord` using the `remove(at:)` method. Finally, the closure returns `true`.

If the `allSatisfy` call returns true, the function returns `true`, indicating that `userGuessWord` can be made by removing letters from `baseWord`. If `allSatisfy` returns `false`, the function returns `false`.

The logic for this can be a little tricky to understand at first, but it basically looks at each letter in the user's word and compares it to `baseWord`. Any letter that's not in `baseWord` will cause the method to return `false`, meaning the user's word is incorrect.

Now that we have this method written out, let's put it to work. We need to call this method in the `addWordToList` function, so place this code after the `if` statement's closing brace:

```
func addWordToList() {
        let usersWord =
            userEnteredWord.trimmingCharacters(in:
            .whitespacesAndNewlines).lowercased()
        //is the word a duplicate
        if !isWordDuplicate(word: usersWord) {
        displayErrorMessage(messageTitle: "You already used
            this word", description: "Keep looking!")
        return
        }
        //is the word possible given your base word letters
            to work with?
        guard isWordFoundInBaseWord(userGuessWord:
            usersWord) else {
            displayErrorMessage(messageTitle: "This word is
            not possible", description: "Create only words
            from the letters in the given word")
            return
        }
            userEnteredWordsArray.insert(usersWord, at: 0)
            userEnteredWord = ""
    }
```

What we're doing here is calling the `isWordFoundInBaseWord` function, and it will have `userGuessedWord` passed into it. The function checks whether the word is possible to create – if not, we're going to display an alert message to the user using the `displayErrorMessage` method (again, the alert messages will be created later).

Let's try this out. Come back into `ContentView` and run the program. You will see that you cannot enter a word unless those letters are also present in `baseWord`:

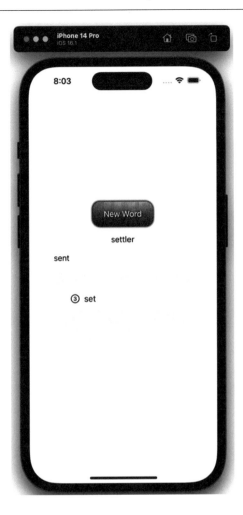

Figure 12.5: Checking whether the word is possible using the base word's letters

Here, I entered `set` into the list because that can be made from **settler**, but I could not enter `sent` because there is no `n` in **settler**. So, we can see that the `isWordFoundInBaseWord` function is working perfectly.

Checking whether the user's entered word is a real word

There is one final check we need to do, and that is to see whether the word is an actual word in the dictionary. This check is important because the user could rearrange letters in `baseWord`, make up their own word, and enter it into the list. We want to prevent that and check each of the words against an actual dictionary. To do that, we can use the `UITextChecker` class. This class has methods and properties we can use to check whether a word is an actual word in the dictionary, and what's especially nice is it will work with misspellings and authenticity in Spanish and Italian as well.

So, let's go into the `DataModel` class and add the following code to the `isWordInDictionary` function:

```
func isWordInDictionary(word: String) -> Bool {
    return UITextChecker().rangeOfMisspelledWord(in: word,
      range: NSRange(location: 0, length:
      word.utf16.count), startingAt: 0, wrap: false,
      language: "en").isNotFound
}
```

We're going to get an error here because I am adding this `isNotFound` property. So, let's fix that error first, and then we can go over what the code is doing. Outside the class's closing brace, add the following extension:

```
extension NSRange {
    var isNotFound: Bool {
        return location == NSNotFound
    }
}
```

Going back now, the `isWordInDictionary` function checks whether a given word exists in the English dictionary. It does so by creating an instance of `UITextChecker` and calling the `rangeOfMisspelledWord` method on it. This method takes several arguments:

- `word`: The word to check for spelling
- `range`: The range of the word to check, specified as `NSRange`
- `startingAt`: The starting position of the word to check within the specified range
- `wrap`: A Boolean value indicating whether to wrap around the end of the range to the beginning when checking for misspelled words
- `language`: The language to use for spell checking – in this case, `"en"` for English

The method then returns an `NSRange` that indicates the range of the first misspelled word found. If no misspelled word is found, the `location` property of the returned range is set to `NSNotFound`.

The `isNotFound` computed property is an extension on `NSRange` that returns `true` if the `location` property is equal to `NSNotFound`, and `false` otherwise. This makes it more readable and allows us to write `isNotFound` instead of comparing the location of `NSNotFound` in the function.

Summing it up, the function creates an instance of the `UITextChecker` class. `UITextChecker` looks through its dictionary for any misspelling to make sure the word is real – if it is in the dictionary, `true` is returned and the word will be entered into the user's list; otherwise, `false` will be returned, and we show a message to the user saying that this is not an actual word in the dictionary.

Now that the function is complete, let's use it. Add the following code directly after the closing brace of the previous guard statement in the addWordToList function:

```
//is the word spelled correctly and a real word in the
   chosen language? - only real words allowed
   guard isWordInDictionary(word: usersWord) else {
       displayErrorMessage(messageTitle: "This is not a
          valid word", description: "Use only real words")
       return
}
```

With that code in place, give the app another go and make up your own word using the given letters in baseWord:

Figure 12.6: Checking whether the word is in the dictionary

Here, I made up a word using the letters from baseWord – tesh – however, I wasn't allowed to add the word to the list because there is no such word in the English language, so we know the function is working.

And that really completes all of the word-checking functionality for the app; we will add pop-up alerts for when a user's word doesn't pass any of those checks.

Let's focus on building out the UI some more. We're going to add a text string at the top that will be the name of the app, and we can style this in a separate file.

Creating HeaderView with an info button

Let's continue building out the UI and add a header title, which will be the name of our app. We can create this header in a separate file so we can keep our ContentView clutter free.

The purpose of HeaderView is twofold – to set the title of the app, and to add an info button that opens a user settings page.

Press *Command + N*, choose a **SwiftUI View** file, and call it HeaderView. Then, add a Binding property in the HeaderView struct:

```
@Binding var showSettings: Bool
Now let's update the Previews struct to satisfy Xcode and so we
can build cleanly again:
HeaderView(showSettings: .constant(false))
        .previewLayout(.fixed(width: 375, height: 80))
```

Next, add the following code inside the body property:

```
ZStack {
        Image("title").resizable()
            .frame(width: 250, height: 50)
            .shadow(color: .black, radius: 1, x: 1, y: 1)

        //info button
        Button(action: {
        }){
            Image(systemName: "info.circle")
                .font(.system(size: 30, weight: .medium))
                .padding(.top, 10)
                .accentColor(Color.black)
        }.offset(x: 160)

    }
```

First, we added a `ZStack` to hold two views, an image displaying the title of the app, and a button that we will set up to take the user to a settings page, where they can choose another language to play the game in. Also added was the `shadow` modifier on the image to help make it stand out a little more.

Inside the button closure, we use the system image of an info circle, then some top padding on it to align the button vertically with the image, and then we colored the button black using the `accent` modifier. After that, we offset the button to the right `150` points so that it's next to the image on the right side of the screen.

When the `info` button is pressed, a settings page will open, giving the user three language options for the game. The `showSettings` property will be used to open up `SettingsView`, but we don't have `SettingsView` yet, so let's make one. Press *Command + N*, choose **SwiftUI View**, and name it `SettingsView`. And just like that, we now have our `SettingsView`. Let's come back into the **HeaderView** and add the code that we need to open up the `SettingsView`.

Inside the button, we need to toggle the `showSettings` state variable, so add the following line of code to the button body:

```
showSettings.toggle()
```

And finally, in order to open up a sheet over another view, we need to call the `sheet` modifier on the button, so add the code to the end of the button's closing brace:

```
Button(action: {
        self.showSettings.toggle()
    }) {
        Image(systemName: "info.circle")
            .font(.system(size: 30, weight: .medium))
            .padding(.top, 10)
            .padding(.horizontal, 10)
            .accentColor(Color.black)
    }.offset(x: 160)
      .sheet(isPresented: $showSettings) {
        //show the settings view
        SettingsView()
    }
```

The `sheet` modifier is used in SwiftUI to open a sheet, which is simply another view that opens by sliding up from the bottom of the screen. The sheet is triggered by the `isPresented` parameter – when the value of `isPresented` becomes `true`, the code in the `sheet` modifier's body will run. In the `sheet` modifier's closure, there is a call to `SettingsView`; this is the view (sheet) that gets presented over `ContentView`. To dismiss the sheet, the user slides it back down with their finger.

To see this in action, we need to add two more lines of code inside `ContentView`. First, go into that file, and add a `State` property that can connect to the `Binding` variable of `HeaderView`. Add this `State` variable right after the previous property at the top in `ContentView`:

```
@State var showSettings: Bool = false
```

I'm calling it `showSettings`, the same as the variable it's binding to from `HeaderView`.

Now, we just need to add a call to `HeaderView` to get the `info` button working. Add this line of code inside `VStack` at the top:

```
HeaderView(showSettings: $showSettings)
```

And that's all we need to get `SettingsView` working. Try it out – press the information button in `ContentView` and `SettingsView` opens:

Figure 12.7: SettingsView

To dismiss the view, simply slide down on the opened view. This "sliding to close" behavior is automatically baked into the sheet modifier, so we don't have to implement it.

So, we have SettingView working, although it doesn't do much right now other than open up and show **Hello, World!** (we will build that out soon enough). Let's continue with the styling of the interface and add a PickerView that the user can press on to set the size of the words they want to play with.

Creating PickerView

A PickerView is a view that displays various options to the user. The picker can either be a single button with a drop-down list, a segmented list with multiple buttons, or a wheel that the user can spin to select an option.

There are two main differences between these three pickers in terms of style. The first is how they appear in your app. The second is the number of options available to the user – the wheel can hold many, many options for the user, whereas a button picker or a segmented control picker is limited by the amount of space on the screen.

Since we will be offering just three options to the user, a seven-, eight-, or nine-letter word option, we'll go with the segmented control.

Adding PickerView

Let's start by adding a new **SwiftUI View** file and calling it PickerView. Next, let's add an instance of the DataModel class at the top of the struct so we have access to the data properties:

```
@ObservedObject var appData = DataModel()
```

Then add a VStack, and inside that, add a topBar image that we have in the Assets catalog, which will help to frame the picker:

```
VStack(alignment: .center, spacing: 10) {
        //bar
        Image("topBar").resizable()
            .frame(width: 280, height: 8)
            .padding(.bottom, 10)
            .shadow(color: .black, radius: 1, x: 1, y: 1)

}
```

In the code, we add the topBar image and put a little padding and shadow around it to help it stand out against the background (which will be added soon). Then, we use 10 points of center spacing on the VStack to keep some space between the views.

Now, add the `Picker` control underneath the last line of code we just added:

```
Picker("", selection: $appData.selectedSegment) {
            Text("7 Letter").tag(1)
            Text("8 Letter").tag(2)
            Text("9 Letter").tag(3)


        }
```

This code adds the picker and uses the `selectedSegment` property in `DataModel`, which is used to keep track of which segment of the picker has been selected by the user. The picker is set to three different titles, and we use the `tag` modifier to distinguish which title goes where on the picker control. Now, the user can choose between 7, 8, or 9 letters for the word they will work with.

This is the default button look, which offers options to the user when pressed:

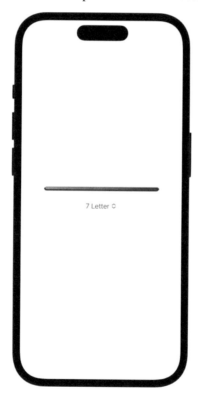

Figure 12.8: The button picker

Let's now look at how we can style the picker to something more suitable for our game.

Styling PickerView

As I mentioned, I feel that segmented control looks better, so let's change the styling to that picker option instead. Add the following code after the closing brace of `PickerView`:

```
.pickerStyle(SegmentedPickerStyle())
.background(RoundedRectangle(cornerRadius: 8)
.stroke(Color.black, lineWidth: 4).shadow(color:
  Color.black, radius: 8, x: 0, y: 0))
.cornerRadius(8)
.padding(.horizontal, 50.0)
.padding(.bottom, 10)
```

We set the picker to the segmented style, and added a rounded rectangle with a corner radius of 8 points, with a black stroke around the picker control to give it a nice border. Then, we finished it off with some shadow and padding, and this is what it looks like:

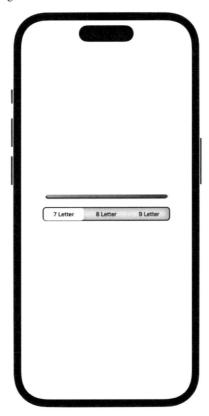

Figure 12.9: The completed PickerView

`PickerView` is done, but to complete the work in the `PickerView` file, let's add a `bottomBar` image to the scene. After the `shadow` modifier, add the following:

```
Image("bottomBar").resizable()
        .frame(width: 280, height: 8)
        .padding(.bottom, 10)
        .shadow(color: .black, radius: 1, x: 1, y: 1)
```

This just sets `bottomBar` like `topBar`, and helps frame out `PickerView` in the UI:

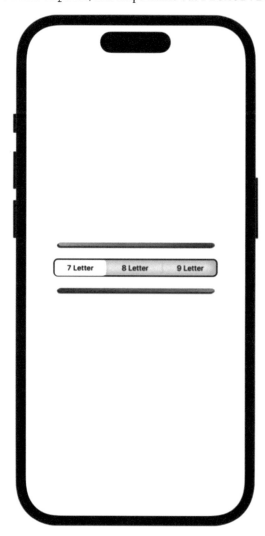

Figure 12.10: The bottom bar image added

Let's go back into `ContentView`, where we need to call `PickerView` to bring it into the scene. Add the following just below the `HeaderView` code:

```
//MARK: - PICKER
PickerView()
```

And now we have our `PickerView` that can offer the user some choices. It doesn't do anything yet because we need to fill out the `setWordLengthAndLanguage` method, so let's do that. Back in `DataModel`, add the following code inside the `setWordLengthAndLanguage` method:

```
//sets the word length and language for the game
func setWordLengthAndLanguage() -> String {
    let language = ["English": "En", "Spanish": "ES",
      "Italian": "It"]
    let wordLength = [1: "7", 2: "8", 3: "9"]
    var dataFile = ""
    var selectedLanguage = ""

    if englishIsOn == true {
        selectedLanguage = "English"
    } else if spanishIsOn == true {
        selectedLanguage = "Spanish"
    } else if italianIsOn == true {
        selectedLanguage = "Italian"
    }

    if let languageCode = language[selectedLanguage],
      let lengthCode = wordLength[selectedSegment] {
    dataFile =
      "\(lengthCode)LetterWords\(languageCode)"
      letterCount = "LR \(lengthCode) letter word -
        \(selectedLanguage) LR"
    }
    return dataFile
}
```

This is how the setWordLengthAndLanguage function works. It starts by defining two dictionaries, language and wordLength:

- The language dictionary maps the names of different languages to their abbreviations. In this case, "English" is mapped to "En", "Spanish" is mapped to "ES", and "Italian" is mapped to "It".

- The wordLength dictionary maps integer values to their corresponding word lengths. For example, 1 is mapped to "7", 2 is mapped to "8", and 3 is mapped to "9".

Next, the function checks the value of the selectedSegment variable. This variable holds an integer that represents the user's selected word length (seven letters, eight letters, or nine letters).

Based on the value of selectedSegment, the function retrieves the corresponding word length from the wordLength dictionary using the square bracket notation, wordLength[selectedSegment]. This gives us the word length as a string, such as 7, 8, or 9.

The function then checks the values of the englishIsOn, spanishIsOn, and italianIsOn variables. These variables hold Booleans that indicate whether the user has selected the corresponding language.

If one of these language variables is true, then the function uses the corresponding language abbreviation (retrieved from the language dictionary) and the word length (retrieved from the wordLength dictionary) to construct the filename of the data file that contains the words for that language and word length. For example, if the user has selected English with seven letters, the filename will be 7LetterWordsEn.

The function sets the value of the letterCount variable to a string that provides a description of the selected language and word length, such as 7 letter word - American English.

Finally, the function returns the constructed filename as a string.

There's one other bit of code we need to add to ContentView in order to get the language word count string working for the picker control. Add the following code directly after the shadow modifier of the button:

```
//MARK: - WORD TO PLAY FROM
    VStack {
        //word letter count string
        Text("\(appData.letterCount)")
            .font(.system(size: 18, weight: .regular,
              design: .serif))
            .foregroundColor(Color.white)
            .bold()
            .shadow(color: .black, radius: 1, x: 1, y: 1)

    }
```

In this code, we added a VStack and then displayed the letterCount property in a Text view by using the appData instance. Then, we applied a font size and weight and a white foreground, made it bold, and added a shadow to the Text view. What I want you to do now is to cut out the Text view that displays the wordToPlayFrom property, and paste it inside the VStack just added, at the very end. This keeps both text views horizontally organized.

Now, to test the picker out and see it display the letter word string, as well as a word in a different language, we need to come to our data file and set one of the language variables to true; just for testing purposes, we will later toggle these variables in the settings page. So, in DataModel, change the spanishIsOn variable to true, like this:

```
@AppStorage ("spanishIsOn") var spanishIsOn: Bool = true
```

Now, come into ContentView and select the length of the word that you want to use from the picker control. Press the button and you will see a Spanish word of the length you chose and the letterCount string displaying the chosen language's flag and picker selection for the word size:

Figure 12.11: Choosing the word size and language for the game

You can check it for the other two languages as well by just setting one of those languages to `true` and keeping the others set to `false`. Also, if you don't set one of the `AppStorage` variables to `true`, then the picker will not pick the length of the word; it will default to an eight-letter word (this behavior will work itself out when we finish adding the rest of the code in the next chapter).

After you're done testing things out, make sure to set the `data` variable back to `false`.

Summary

So, we've come to the end of this chapter, and have done quite a bit of work.

We started building out our game, allowing the user to enter words to play the game, and adding checks to validate their choices. We also added a button that the user can press to bring up a random word from a file of thousands of words, a button that brings up a settings page, a picker control, and a letter count string.

Next, we will continue building out the app, specifically building out the user interface, the settings page so it contains those three buttons that the user can select for the languages, and adding error messages when the user's entered word is not valid. So, let's continue with the second part of this project in the next chapter.

13

Creating a Word Game (Part 2)

In the first part of our project, we put together a good portion of the interface and implemented much of the game's functionality, so we currently have a working game that can list all the user's entered words.

Let's continue here in the second part of the project, finishing off the settings screen so that the user can select the language of their choice, and adding more elements to the UI to help make it more polished – for example, adding user feedback.

In this chapter, we will cover the following topics:

- Creating a settings screen
- Styling the UI
- Implementing user feedback with alerts
- Adding a Footer View to display more information
- Adding haptics and button sounds

Technical requirements

You can download the resources and finished project from the `Chapter 13` folder on GitHub: `https://github.com/PacktPublishing/Animating-SwiftUI-Applications`.

Creating a settings screen

Now that we can set the word length, let's put together the settings view so that the user can click on the info button and actually change the language from there. We want to create three buttons – one for each language – and a fourth button, the **Done** button, which users can use to complete their selection and dismiss the page.

So, inside `SettingsView`, we'll first need a variable to access `DataModel`. Add this observed object variable at the top of the `SettingsView` struct:

```
@ObservedObject var appData = DataModel()
```

Next, let's add a title for this page called `Language Settings` in the body property:

```
VStack {
        Text("Language Settings")
            .font(.title).bold()
            .padding(.top, 20)
    }
```

Here, we simply add the `Text` view with a little padding and bold font, all inside of `VStack`.

Next, let's add a `Form` view and a `Section` header view inside `VStack` to group the buttons that we will be adding. Place this code just under the `padding` modifier:

```
        Form {
            Section(header: Text("Select a language")) {
            }
        }
```

The `Form` view is a container that's commonly used to group controls together, and the `Section` header will add some header text to each grouping. This is what `SettingsView` looks like so far:

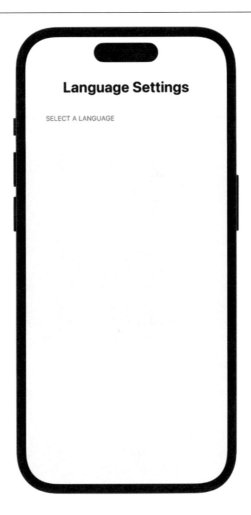

Figure 13.1: Styling the SettingsView using the Form and Section header views

Next, we will add buttons to let the user select a language.

Adding the language buttons

The buttons we will create will be styled with a wood image background and some text applied to them. Let's do the button styling in a separate struct.

Add the following struct anywhere in the file, as long as it's not inside the `SettingsView` struct (I usually create other structs just above the `Previews` struct):

```
//style the button with a background and text
struct configureButton: View {
```

```
    var buttonText = ""
    var body: some View {
        ZStack {
            Image("background").resizable()
                .frame(width: 70, height: 35)
                .cornerRadius(10)
            Text(buttonText)
                .foregroundColor(.white)
                .shadow(color: .black, radius: 1, x: 1, y: 1)
        }
    }
}
```

We're calling the configureButton struct, and inside it, we create a string variable that will hold the text for the button. Then, we're using the background image in the Assets Catalog and setting its size and cornerRadius value. After that, we add a Text view with white color and shadow, all done inside of ZStack so that they overlay each other.

Let's proceed to add the first button, which will let the user play the game in the English language. Add the following code inside the Section header braces:

```
var body: some View {
    VStack {
        Text("Language Settings")
            .font(.title).bold()
            .padding(.top, 20)
        Form {
            Section(header: Text("Select a language")) {
                VStack(alignment: .center, spacing: 10) {
                    HStack {
                        //english button
                        Button(action: {

                        }){
                            configureButton(buttonText: "English")
                        }
                        Spacer()
```

```
        //english flag
        Image("engFlag").resizable()
            .border(Color.black, width: 1.5)
            .frame(width: 50, height: 30)
      }
    }
  }
}
}
}
```

In this code block, we added `VStack` with a center alignment and a spacing of 10 points. This will keep each button vertically spaced from each other by 10 points.

Along with creating a button to select the English language, I want to add a flag for the chosen country's language as well. We do this in `HStack` – the button will be on the left, and the flag will be on the right of the screen. Next, I call the `configureButton` struct in the button closure, which will set the button to the word **English** and give it the wood background image. For the flag, I added a small border around it with a 1.5-point width, so it has a nice defined edge, and since this is associated with the English button, we will use the American flag image.

Now you can try it out; press the **English** button and see what happens. Note that the whole row will flash with each button press, which is not exactly the behavior we're going for. This happens because we made a custom button that does not have the same behavior as a default button. Instead, it would be nice just to have the button flash on its own, and not the row. We can achieve this by using the `ButtonStyle` protocol to control what flashes when the button is pressed.

Let's do that. Add the following code underneath the `configureButton` struct:

```
struct ButtonFlash: ButtonStyle {
    func makeBody(configuration: Configuration) -> some
View {
    configuration.label
        .shadow(color: .black, radius: 2, x: 2, y: 2)
        .opacity(configuration.isPressed ? 0.3 : 1)
  }
}
```

This struct is called `ButtonFlash`, and it uses the `ButtonStyle` protocol. This is a protocol that applies interactive behavior and custom appearance to buttons. The `ButtonStyle` protocol requires that we use the `makeBody` method to configure the behavior and look for the button label.

In the code, we're only calling two modifiers in the makeBody function – shadow and opacity. The opacity modifier will check the isPressed property to see whether it's true. If it is true, that means the button has been pressed, so we can change the opacity to .3, which will make the button fade out slightly. Otherwise, if the button is not pressed, the button will remain at full opacity.

All we need to do next is call the buttonFlash structure on the button, like this:

```
HStack {
        //english button
        Button(action: {

        }){
            configureButton(buttonText: "English")
        }.buttonStyle(ButtonFlash())
        Spacer()

        //english flag
        Image("engFlag").resizable()
            .border(Color.black, width: 1.5)
            .frame(width: 50, height: 30)
    }
```

The buttonStyle protocol automatically creates a new modifier for us, also using buttonStyle, which we can access like any other modifier by using dot syntax and then passing in the name of our new struct, ButtonFlash.

Now, the button has a new look. It has a shadow around its text that gives it a sort of 3D look:

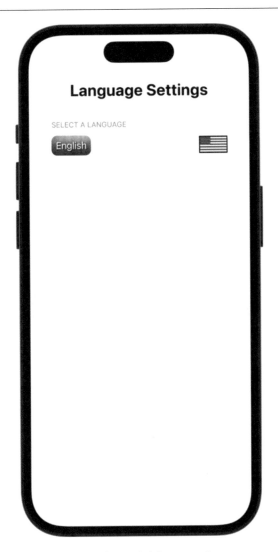

Figure 13.2: The English language button

When you press the button, the modifiers will help make it look like it's actually being pushed down. Also, it will just look like the button is being pushed, rather than the whole row.

Now, with the configuring and styling of the button complete, let's add two more buttons for the other languages. Add this code right after the closing brace of HStack:

```
Divider()
    HStack {
        //English button
```

```
                Button(action: {

                }) {
                    configureButton(buttonText: "Spanish")
                }.buttonStyle(ButtonFlash())
                Spacer()

                //Spanish flag
                Image("esFlag").resizable()
                    .border(Color.black, width: 1.5)
                    .frame(width: 50, height: 30)
            }
        Divider()

        HStack {
            //Italian button
            Button(action: {

            }) {
                configureButton(buttonText: "Italian")
            }.buttonStyle(ButtonFlash())
            Spacer()

            //italian flag
            Image("itFlag").resizable()
                .border(Color.black, width: 1.5)
                .frame(width: 50, height: 30)
        }
```

The code starts with `Divider`, which is a very thin line that delineates the first button from the second one. Then, we use another `HStack`, similar to what we've just added for the **English** button. The only changes we make here are for the text of the button so that it says **Spanish**, and the flag so that it is the flag of Spain. After that, we use another `Divider` and then create our **Italian** button.

Now, the buttons are complete, but they don't do anything when they're pressed other than look nice. We need to make them functional and actually select the individual languages. This is simple – we just have to access our data model and change the language properties to the correct value, either `true` or `false`.

Let's start with the **English** button. Inside the body of the button, add the following code:

```
appData.englishIsOn = true
appData.spanishIsOn = false
appData.italianIsOn = false
```

What we are doing here is accessing `DataModel` and changing `englishIsOnProperty` to `true` because the **English** button was just pressed. At the same time, we want to make sure that the Spanish and Italian properties are set to `false`. Now, if the **English** button is pressed, only that data file will be used to make a new random word.

Let's add similar logic inside the **Spanish** button:

```
appData.englishIsOn = false
appData.spanishIsOn = true
appData.italianIsOn = false
```

For the **Spanish** button, we want to make sure that the other two languages' properties are set to `false`, and that the Spanish property is set to `true`.

Finally, let's add the following code to the **Italian** button:

```
appData.englishIsOn = false
appData.spanishIsOn = false
appData.italianIsOn = true
```

Now, all the buttons are complete, and they will implement the user's chosen language.

Adding a checkmark

However, we can improve the design a little bit here. Currently, when the user presses the language buttons, there's no indication that the button selected anything. How about we add a checkmark next to the flag for the selected language?

Let's add another struct that will make checkmarks for the buttons. Add the following struct under the `ButtonFlash` struct:

```
//add a checkmark
struct addCheckmark: View {
    var isLanguageOn: Bool = false
    var body: some View {
        VStack{
            Image(systemName: "checkmark.circle")
```

```
                    .imageScale(.small).foregroundColor(.green)
                    .font(Font.largeTitle.weight(.regular))
                    .opacity(isLanguageOn ? 1.0 : 0)
            }
        }
    }
```

I'm calling the struct addCheckmark and then creating a Boolean to check which language has been selected. Inside the body of the struct, we create a small checkmark, color it green, and set the opacity of the checkmark to either fully visible or hidden, depending on whether the isLanguageOn property is true or not.

Now, we can call this struct inside each HStack, so a checkmark will be placed toward the flag side. For the sake of brevity, I will add the checkmark code to the first HStack, but you need to add it to all three HStack instances as well, in the same location that I use here:

```
VStack(alignment: .center, spacing: 10) {
        HStack {
            //english button
            Button(action: {
                appData.englishIsOn = true
                appData.spanishIsOn = false
                appData.italianIsOn = false
            }){
                configureButton(buttonText: "English")
            }.buttonStyle(ButtonFlash())
            Spacer()
            //english - checkmark appears when
              englishIsOn is true
            addCheckmark(isLanguageOn:
              appData.englishIsOn)
            //english flag
            Image("engFlag").resizable()
                .border(Color.black, width: 1.5)
                .frame(width: 50, height: 30)
        }
        Divider()
```

The code calls the addCheckmark struct, and a checkmark is added to each button when pressed.

If you now run the app from `ContentView`, you will see that you can press the information button to bring up the settings screen, select a language, and then dismiss the screen by sliding it down.

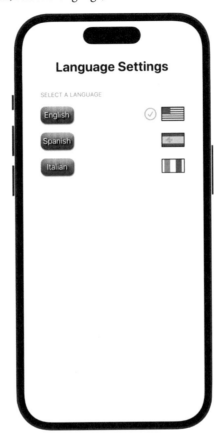

Figure 13.3: The language buttons complete

Also, if you stop the app and run it again, note that your selection choice will remain, as we store these settings internally in user defaults by using the `@AppStorage` property wrapper in the data model.

We're just about done with the settings view, but I'd like to add one more modification here – how about giving the user another way of dismissing the settings screen by adding a dismiss button, instead of just sliding down from the top?

Adding a dismiss button

For the dismiss button, we'll need a property that can access the app's environment. The environment is the part of the app that is generated automatically for us, and it's where we can access system-wide settings such as the color scheme or layout direction.

It's in this environment where we need to dismiss a screen, and to do so, we first need to create a variable using the @Environment wrapper. Add this underneath the ObservedObject property at the top of the SettingsView file:

```
//dismiss the SettingsView
    @Environment(\.presentationMode) var presentationMode
```

Now, we will use this property to dismiss the view. Add this final HStack just after the closing brace of the last HStack in the file:

```
//MARK: - DISMISS BUTTON
    HStack(alignment: .center) {
        Spacer()

        Button(action: {
            presentationMode.wrappedValue.dismiss()
        }){
            HStack {
                Image(systemName: "checkmark")
                Text("Done")
                    .padding(.horizontal, 5)
            }.padding(8)
                .shadow(color: .black, radius: 1,
                    x: 1, y: 1)
        }.foregroundColor(Color.white)
            .background(Color.green)
            .cornerRadius(20).shadow(color:
                .black, radius: 1, x: 1, y: 1)
            .buttonStyle(ButtonFlash())

        Spacer()
    }
```

Firstly, we used two Spacer instances at the top and bottom of the code to align the button in the center of this HStack.

Inside the button, the presentationMode property on the wrappedValue property will gain access to the setting screen data, and then a call to the dismiss function will close the settings screen.

The button is styled with a checkmark, and the text says **Done**. It also has a little bit of padding and shadow, a green color, and finally, it calls the `ButtonFlash` function so that it flashes like the other buttons.

Now, run the app from `ContentView`, and you can see that the dismiss button works perfectly:

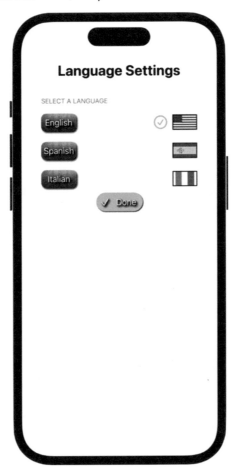

Figure 13.4: The Done button

This completes `SettingsView`. Let's go back to `ContentView` and continue styling the UI.

Styling the UI

In `ContentView`, let's add some more features for the user; we'll a background, some animations to the game, as well as a word count and language display label. Adding some more styling will help the UI come alive.

Adding the background

We'll start by adding a background to the scene. We currently have a title and buttons that are styled with a wooden look, so let's continue the wooden theme and use a wood image as a background. Add the following code after the closing brace of VStack:

```
.background(Image("background").resizable()
        .edgesIgnoringSafeArea([.all])
        .aspectRatio(contentMode: .fill)
        .frame(width: 500, height: 800))
```

This code sets a wooden image as the background and uses the edgesIgnoringSafeAreas modifier to stretch the background out to fill the screen. Also, the aspect ratio is set to fill, and it sets a frame to size this background image:

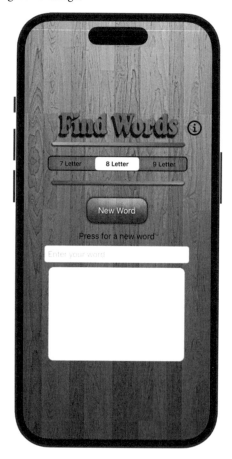

Figure 13.5: A wooden background

The background looks good, but it does introduce a small problem – we need to change the color and size of the `wordToPlayFrom` property, as its black color makes it hard to see against the wood background. Let's do that now. Just after the button code, we can style this `Text` view to make it look better:

```
//MARK: - WORD TO PLAY FROM
  Text("\(wordToPlayFrom)")
        .font(.custom("HelveticaNeue-Medium", size: 38))
        .foregroundColor(.white)
        .shadow(color: .black, radius: 1, x: 1, y: 1)
```

The code adds a custom `Helvetica` font with a size of `38` points, while changing the color of the text to white and adding a shadow so that it stands out a little more. This is what it looks like:

Figure 13.6: The styled base word

That looks much clearer now!

Adding animations to the game word

How about we also add some animation to the new word? We can use the `scaleEffect` modifier to flip the word horizontally as it comes into view.

Let's first add a property to track this animation, right after the other properties in `ContentView`:

```
@State private var horizontalFLip = false
```

Now, in the WORD TO PLAY FROM Pragma Mark, and right after the `shadow` modifier, add the following code:

```
.scaleEffect(x: horizontalFLip ? -1 : 1, y: 1)
.scaleEffect(x: horizontalFLip ? -1 : 1, y: 1)
.animation(.spring(dampingFraction:0.8),value:
   horizontalFLip)
```

By calling the `scaleEffect` modifier twice, each call will flip the text horizontally by 180° so that it completely makes one revolution, horizontally, as it enters the screen. It also gets a `spring` animation applied to it, which will make it grow and shrink just a little bit; you can control the growth and shrinkage by setting the `dampingFraction` parameter to a lower or higher value.

As well as this, we want the animation to start when the button is pressed because that's when a new word appears on the screen, so let's toggle the `horizontalFlip` Boolean inside the button:

```
//MARK: - BUTTON
    Button(action: {
        appData.getRandomWord()
        wordToPlayFrom = appData.baseWord
        horizontalFLip.toggle()
    }){
```

Before we try it out, let's go a bit further with the new incoming word – we'll add pointing hands on each side of the new word and add a `spring` animation as well. Let's put the `Text` view that is displaying `wordToPlayFrom` into `HStack`, like this:

```
HStack {
    Text(wordToPlayFrom)
        .font(.custom("HelveticaNeue-Medium", size: 38))
        .foregroundColor(.white)
        .shadow(color: .black, radius: 1, x: 1, y: 1)
        .scaleEffect(x: horizontalFLip ? -1 : 1, y: 1)
```

```
            .scaleEffect(x: horizontalFLip ? -1 : 1, y: 1)
            .animation(.spring(dampingFraction:0.8),value:
              horizontalFLip)

      }
```

Next, let's add some pointing hand images that will point to the word to play from. The first image is the system image called hand.point.right, and it goes inside HStack just above the Text view code, and the next image is called the hand.point.left image, which gets placed below the Text view code, again, all inside the HStack view we just added:

```
//MARK: - WORD TO PLAY FROM
  HStack () {
        //right hand image
        Image(systemName: "hand.point.right")
            .foregroundColor(.black)
            .font(.system(size: 30))
            .animation(.spring(dampingFraction:0.2),value:
              horizontalFLip)


        Text(wordToPlayFrom)
            .font(.custom("HelveticaNeue-Medium", size: 38))
            .foregroundColor(.white)
            .shadow(color: .black, radius: 1, x: 1, y: 1)
            .scaleEffect(x: horizontalFLip ? -1 : 1, y: 1)
            .scaleEffect(x: horizontalFLip ? -1 : 1, y: 1)
            .animation(.spring(dampingFraction:0.8),value:
              horizontalFLip)


        //left hand image
        Image(systemName:"hand.point.left")
            .foregroundColor(.black)
            .font(.system(size: 30))
            .padding(-4)
            .animation(.spring(dampingFraction:0.2),value:
              horizontalFLip)

      }
```

The code starts off with a system image of a hand that's pointing right, setting the foreground color to black and setting the image size by using the `font` modifier. Then, we add the spring animation to it, which has a damping fraction of `.4` (again, the larger the value, the less spring animation there will be).

Then, we go to the left-hand image and do the same thing, setting its size and color, as well as a little padding to position it a bit more to the left. Also, the `value` parameter in the `spring` animation will be the `horizontalFlip` Boolean property and toggled inside the button's body, which is how the animation gets triggered.

Now, give the app another go – you'll see that every time you hit the button to add a new word, not only does the word flip horizontally, and stretch and shrink, but also the two hands bounce in and out as the word enters the screen:

Figure 13.7: Animating the base word, plus the hand images

Before we continue with more enhancements, let's fix one issue we have, which is that the `letterCount` string only appears on the UI when the button is pressed. It's much better to always have it on the UI and just update it when the button is pressed. We can fix that with one line of code, a call to the `getRandomWord` function in `ContentView`. Let's add that call down at the bottom of `VStack`, just after the `frame` modifier of the background:

```
.onAppear (perform: appData.getRandomWord)
```

The `onAppear` modifier will call the `getRandomWord` function and populate the `letterCount` string so that it always stays on the screen:

Figure 13.8: The word length and flag string displayed

Next, we need to implement the alert system to give the user feedback about any words that don't get accepted into the list.

Implementing user feedback with alerts

The user can get a random word and try and make some words out of that word in the language of their choice, but there are certain checks that we've put in place that will stop those words from entering the list. Now, we need to let the user know why a certain word is not acceptable, using SwiftUI alerts.

Let's go back into DataModel and fill out the displayErrorMessage function stub with the appropriate code to get a message alert. Add the following code right into the method:

```
//error message
    func displayErrorMessage(messageTitle: String,
        description: String) {
        errorTitle = messageTitle
        errorDescription = description
        errorMessageIsShown = true
    }
```

The code takes the messageTitle string and assigns it to the errorTitle property. Then, it takes the description string and assigns it to the errorDescription property. After that, the errorMessagesIsShown Boolean is set to true because at this point the function has been triggered, and we'll need to have this property set to true in order to initiate the alert message.

Next, the displayErrorMessage function needs to be called in the right place. If you remember from when we set up the addWordToListist method earlier and added the method stubs in the data model, we also made a call to the displayErrorMessage method. Here is a look at the complete addWordToList method that has a call to displayErrorMessage, so there is nothing for us to do there:

```
    func addWordToList() {
    let usersWord =
        userEnteredWord.lowercased().trimmingCharacters(in:
        .whitespacesAndNewlines)

    //guard against single letter words - they are too easy
    guard usersWord.count > 1 else {
        return
    }
    //is the word a duplicate
```

```
    guard isWordDuplicate(word: usersWord) else {
        displayErrorMessage(messageTitle: "You already used
            this word", description: "Keep looking!")
        return
    }
    //is the word possible given your base word letters to
      work with?
    guard isWordFoundInBaseWord(userGuessWord: usersWord)
      else {
        displayErrorMessage(messageTitle: "This word is not
            possible", description: "Create only words from
            the letters in the given word")
        return
    }
    //is the word a real word in the dictionary? - only
      real words are allowed
    guard isWordInDictionary(word: usersWord) else {
        displayErrorMessage(messageTitle: "This is not a
            valid word", description: "Use only real words")
        return
    }
    userEnteredWordsArray.insert(usersWord, at: 0)
    userEnteredWord = ""
}
```

Here's a quick refresher on how the addNewWord function works.

First, the word is made lowercase – that's because all the word files are lowercase, and it's how we can compare words. Then, we trim out any whitespaces that they might have typed into the text field.

The next line of code guards against single-letter words – again, there is only a handful of those in any given language, and there's no point in including them in the game here.

Then, we start to check the user's word to see whether it's a duplicate word. If it is, that means they added that word to the list already, so the displayErrorMessage function will display an error message of **You already used this word**, along with an instruction that says **Keep looking**.

The next guard statement checks whether the word is even possible to make, given the letters the user is working with. If it's not possible, the displayErrorMessage function will be called and display the **This word is not possible** error, along with an instruction that says **Create only words from the letters in the given word**.

Next, the `displayErrorMessage` function will be called if the word is not a real word in the chosen language, showing the user an alert that says **This is not a valid word**, along with an instruction that says **Use only real words**.

Finally, after the user's word has been processed and gone through all those checks, it's entered into `userEnteredWordsArray`. Remember, an array's elements are indexed, starting from 0, which is the beginning of the array. The index is how we access different elements in an array, so in the `insert(at)` method, we pass in the "0" value, which means inserting the user's word into the list at the beginning of the list, the top. This way, as the user enters words, they will always be placed at the top of the list so they are visible on the screen, and if there are many words, the user can scroll up through the list to see them.

The final line of code sets the user-entered word back to an empty string, ready to start the process again.

Now that we have the error alerts all set up, we just need to add the `alert` modifier to make it functional. We can add it right after the `onAppear` modifier in `ContentView`, like this:

```
//add the alert popup
.alert(isPresented: $appData.errorMessageIsShown) {
    Alert(title: Text(appData.errorTitle), message:
      Text(appData.errorDescription), dismissButton:
      .default(Text("OK")))
}
```

The `alert` modifier has a parameter called `isPresented`, and this will present an alert message when the `errorMessageIsShown` Boolean variable becomes `true`. When it does become `true`, the code in the alert body – this being the error title and description – gets executed.

Now, try it out. Enter a word that is already in the list, and you should see a popup like this:

Figure 13.9: An alert message for duplicate words

If you enter a word that is not possible given the letters you have, you will see this alert:

Figure 13.10: An alert message for words that are not possible using the given word

And finally, if you enter a word that does not exist in the chosen language's dictionary, you will see this alert:

Figure 13.11: An alert message for words that are not real

Now, we have three different checks on the user's words, just to give them feedback and let them know where they went wrong. The user can then press the **OK** button to dismiss the alert and continue playing.

Let's now continue with the UI and add a footer view to display some more information about the user's progress in the game.

Adding a Footer View to display more information

The Footer view that we will add will contain two pieces of information – first, how many words the user has found so far, and second, what their letter average is for each found word.

To do this, create a new **SwiftUI View** file and call it `FooterView`. This will contain the `Text` views we need to display that information.

Now let's get to work and add some code. Add the following properties inside the `FooterView` struct:

```
struct FooterView: View {
    //MARK: - PROPERTIES
    @ObservedObject var appData = DataModel()
    @Binding var userEnteredWordsArray: [String]

    var foundWords: Double {
        let wordCount = userEnteredWordsArray.count
        //if theres no words in the array, return 0
        if wordCount == 0 {
            return 0
        }
        var letterAverage = 0
        //get a total of all the letters in each word
        for letterCount in userEnteredWordsArray {
            letterAverage += letterCount.count
        }
        return Double(letterAverage / wordCount)
    }
```

●●●●●●●

As you recall, when we add a `Binding` variable to a struct, we need to include it in the `Previews` struct; otherwise, we will get an Xcode error. Modify the `Previews` struct as such to keep Xcode happy:

```
struct FooterView_Previews: PreviewProvider {
    static var previews: some View {
        FooterView( userEnteredWordsArray: .constant(["0"]))
            .previewLayout(.fixed(width: 350, height: 125))
    }
}
```

Okay, we are now error-free, so let's go back to the `FooterView` struct and review the code we just added there.

There's a `userEnteredWordsArray` property that we will use to bind to the `ContentView` struct later.

Next, we have a computed property called `foundWords`. A computed property is a property that has a body and runs code in its body when the property is accessed. The `foundWords` property displays how many words the user has found so far by using the `count` property, which will return the number of elements in `userEnteredWordsArray`. If there are no words in the array, it will return `0`.

Next, inside the `foundWords` computed property, we create a variable called `totalLetters` and use it to hold all the letters of the user's word. To get all those letters, we use a `for in` loop to iterate through the array, storing the amount of letters from each word the user enters on the list back in the `totalLetters` variable.

Finally, the `foundWords` computed property returns all the letters from every word divided by the number of words entered, which returns the average amount of letters per word.

Now, let's go into the body property and start designing two text views that will display this information. Add the following code:

```
VStack {
    HStack(spacing: 80) {
        ZStack {
            Image("background").resizable()
            .frame(width: 80, height: 50)
            .clipShape(Capsule())
            .shadow(color: .black, radius: 1, x: 1, y: 1)
            .shadow(color: .black, radius: 1, x: -1, y: -1)

            Text("\(userEnteredWordsArray.count)")
            .frame(width: 50, height: 20)
            .font(.system(size: 25))
            .padding(20)
            .foregroundColor(.white)
            .font(.system(size: 80))


            Image("foundWords").resizable()
            .aspectRatio(contentMode: .fill).frame(width:
              100, height: 70)
            .shadow(color: .black, radius: 1, x: 1, y: 1)
            .offset(y: 40)
            .padding(.horizontal, -10)
            .padding(.bottom, -10)
        }
    }
}
```

The first thing we do is style the background that the text will be placed over. We use the `background` image from Assets catalog and set its size to a width of `80` points and a height of `50` points. Then, we use the `clipShape` modifier to turn the rectangle into a capsule and add some shadow to the image. Note that we're using the `shadow` modifier twice here – this gives the image a more defined border than just a single call would.

Next, the text gets added, and by calling the `count` property on `textField`, we can show how many words the user has found so far. Then, we set the font size and add some padding and a foreground color of white.

We're putting the images all inside three stacks:

- First, inside `VStack` to hold all of the views vertically on the screen and line them up accordingly

- Then, inside `HStack`, which will put the two `textField` instances we need side by side horizontally

- Finally, `ZStack` so that we can position the text directly over the background image

Finally, we add the `foundWords` image, size it up, and give it a little bit of shadow and some padding so that we can offset it downward from the text.

Now, we can add the other text, which will display the average amount of letters per word. Just after the closing bracket of the `ZStack`, add the following code:

```
ZStack {
        Image("background").resizable()
            .frame(width: 80, height: 50)
            .clipShape(Capsule())
            .shadow(color: .black, radius: 1, x: 1, y: 1)
            .shadow(color: .black, radius: 1, x: -1, y: -1)

        Text("\(foundWords, specifier: "%.0f")")
            .frame(width: 50, height: 20)
            .font(.system(size: 25))
            .padding(20)
            .foregroundColor(Color.white)
            .font(.system(size: 80))

        Image("letterAverage").resizable()
            .aspectRatio(contentMode: .fill)
            .shadow(color: .black, radius: 1, x: 1, y: 1)
```

```
                    .frame(width: 100, height: 70)
                    .offset(y: 40)
                    .padding(.bottom, -10)
    }
```

This code replicates the previous `Text` view we added, only this time we're displaying the `foundWords` computed property, which will show the letter average from the `foundWords` array, and using the format specifier, it will format the text view to two decimal places.

Now, we can call `FooterView` inside `ContentView`. Let's go back there and add a call to `FooterView` at the end of the code in the main `VStack`:

```
//MARK: - FOOTER VIEW
    FooterView(userEnteredWordsArray:
       $appData.userEnteredWordsArray)
```

Now, go ahead and try the app. Every word that you enter into the list will be counted on the bottom-left side of the screen, and the average amount of letters per word that you are getting will be displayed on the bottom-right side:

Figure 13.12: Displaying the found words and letter average

From the figure, we can see that the given random word is **cambering**, and I found 4 related words so far, so the footer view displays those **4** found words. The letter average for those words is also displayed, **4** letters per word.

Before we move on to more feedback, let's just do one more check in the `addWordToList` function. I want to be able to stop the user from entering single-letter words, and that's very easy to do. There are many single-letter words in any given language, so it's not really a big deal, but we might as well prevent them anyway. Code inside the `addWordToList` function just after `userWord` is declared:

```
//guard against one letter words - they are too easy
        guard usersWord.count > 1 else {
            return
        }
```

We're checking the count of `usersWord` to see whether it's greater than 1; if not, we won't allow single-letter words in the list and the function will just return right here. Give it a try and you'll see that you cannot enter single-letter words.

Up next, in the spirit of giving the user feedback, we'll continue and add haptics and audio to the game.

Adding haptics and button sounds

Haptics are a form of sensory feedback that works by accessing the internal vibration hardware on an iPhone, providing a physical response when the phone is being used. You are probably familiar with haptics, as it's felt every time we set our phones to vibrate. We won't use a full vibration but just a brief one that the user can feel every time they click on a button.

The best place to add such code is in the button itself, so let's do that. We're going to use the `UIImpactFeedbackGenerator` class for this, and it is actually quite simple to implement. First, inside `ContentView`, we need an instance of that class underneath all the properties that we already added:

```
//haptic feedback
var hapticImpact = UIImpactFeedbackGenerator(style:
  .medium)
```

We have set the `hapticImpact` variable style to `medium`, but you can set the vibration to `heavy`, `light`, `ridged`, or `soft`.

Now, to use this, we just simply call this variable inside the button like this:

```
//MARK: - BUTTON
Button(action: {
```

```
hapticImpact.impactOccurred()
appData.getRandomWord()
```

• • • • • • •

And that's it – every time the **New Word** button is pressed, the user will feel a slight vibration on their finger. In order to try this out, you actually have to run this on a device, as you cannot use haptics in the simulator.

Since we've implemented haptics here with the ContentView button, how about we also add it to the SettingsView language buttons? Let's go into SettingsView and add the same code as we did here. First, create an instance of the UIImpactFeedbackGenerator class at the top of the file, in SettingsView:

```
//haptic feedback
    var hapticImpact = UIImpactFeedbackGenerator(style:
        .light)
```

Now, in each of the three language buttons, add the following code:

```
hapticImpact.impactOccurred()
```

And that's it – it's very easy to implement tactile feedback for the user.

And how about one other form of feedback that we are already familiar with – audio? We can add a button click sound to the **New Word** button, so not only does the user feel the button being pressed but they also hear it.

We have already done this several times, so for the sake of brevity, I won't go over the code; instead, you can simply refer back to many of the other projects in which we've added audio (such as our record player project).

As we always do, we create a new **SwiftUI** file called PlaySound and add the following code to the file:

```
import Foundation
import AVFoundation
var player: AVAudioPlayer?

func playSound(sound: String, type: String) {
    if let path = Bundle.main.path(forResource: sound,
      ofType: type) {
        do {
        player = try AVAudioPlayer(contentsOf:
```

```
        URL(fileURLWithPath: path))
    player?.play()

    } catch {
        print("Could not load audio file")
    }
  }
}
```

Now that we have our sound file, all we need to do is use it inside the body of the **New Word** button:

```
playSound(sound: "buttonClick", type: "m4a")
```

And that completes the sound.

Now, the user has three forms of feedback when they press the **New Word** button – they see the button being pressed because, during the press, the button changes its form, they feel the impact with their finger because we accessed the internal vibration motor of the phone, and they hear a clicking sound. This feedback all comes together to give the user a more enriched and tactile experience when interacting with the app.

Summary

In this project, we built a complete app from start to finish and included different animations along the way.

We organized properties and functions in a data model, created separate header and footer views, implemented a picker control, and created some specific functions that can process and check a word's authenticity within three different languages. We also implemented user feedback in three different ways – in the form of pop-up alerts to the user, in the form of haptic feedback, and as audio. Plus, we've added three languages to the game to make it educational for users learning languages.

How about taking the gamer further by adding some more animations to it, by revisiting previous projects and using code that you already implemented into different areas of the game? For example, if the user gets a certain number of words in their list, they could be rewarded with points that get displayed in an animated label at the top. Alternatively, we could add another button that will ask the user to find only words that are palindromes.

In the next chapter, we will build another game – this time, a color-matching game.

14
Creating a Color Game

In the last chapter, we built a game where the user had to find words by using the letters of a larger word. In this project, we will continue the "finding" theme and build another game, where the user must find colors within a broader color.

The goal of this project will be to generate a random RGB color and then have the user manipulate separate sliders for each of the individual RGB values in order to completely match that random color. For example, there will be one slider for red, one slider for green, and one slider for blue, with each slider containing a range from 0 to 255 (the range of each RGB value). Then, the user will have to adjust those sliders to see whether they can find the exact RGB random color.

We will also add three difficulty levels to the game, from easy to extreme. And if the user is skilled enough to work out the individual RGB values in the given color, we will display a shower of confetti over the user interface.

In building this game, you will learn about adding pre-built animations to a project using Swift packages, which includes the aforementioned confetti animation for when the user gets a high score. We will also add a spring animation to SwiftUI sliders and make them visible when needed, and invisible when not.

So, in this chapter, we will cover the following topics:

- Understanding colors
- Creating the `Title` View
- Creating the target and guess circles
- Creating the `Picker` View
- Creating the target and guess rectangles
- Making the color sliders
- Keeping track of the user's score with a button
- Showing the user's score in an `Alert` View

- Resetting the game
- Adding a background
- Adding confetti using Swift packages

Technical requirements

As always, you can find the code and download the completed project from the `Chapter 14` folder on GitHub: `https://github.com/PacktPublishing/Animating-SwiftUI-Applications`.

Understanding colors

Before we begin, let's just have a quick look at colors. There are two color models that you may be familiar with, primary colors and RGB colors.

Primary colors are the basic colors from which all other colors can be derived. In traditional color theory, the primary colors are red, blue, and yellow. Primary colors are used in many different fields, such as art, printing, and graphic design.

RGB (which is short for Red, Green, and Blue) colors make up a color model in which the colors are combined to create different intensities of red, green, and blue light that can be displayed on electronic displays and devices, such as computers, TVs, phones, and tablets.

RGB colors are represented by their red, green, and blue components, each of which has a value between 0 and 255. The value 0 represents the absence of that color, while 255 represents the maximum intensity of that color. By varying the values of the RGB components, a wide range of colors can be created. For example, (255, 0, 0) represents pure red, (0, 255, 0) represents pure green, and (0, 0, 255) represents pure blue. Combinations of these colors can create many different colors and hues of colors.

We will be adding three sliders, which will represent each RGB color, and the user has to manipulate those sliders to find a target color by combining different amounts of those RGB colors.

Let's jump right in and get this game off the ground. We'll start by adding a title to the user interface.

Creating the Title view

Let's get started by creating a new Xcode project – I'm calling it **Find the Colors**. We will build this project from the top down, with all of the code placed in a `VStack` to organize the views vertically.

The first objective here will be to give the UI a title; it's not a lot of code, but we'll still put it in its own file anyway. So, create a new SwiftUI View file, and call it `TitleView`, then add the following code to the body property:

```
struct TitleView: View {
    var body: some View {
        HStack {
            Text("Find").foregroundColor(.red)
            Text("The").foregroundColor(.green)
            Text("Color").foregroundColor(.blue)
        } .foregroundColor(.blue)
            .fontWeight(.black)
            .font(Font.system(size: 35, design: .serif))
    }
}
```

Inside the `HStack`, there are three `Text` views, each with different colors – `"Find"` with the red color, `"The"` with green, and `"Color"` with blue – all colored using the `foregroundColor` modifier.

After the `HStack`, three additional modifiers are applied to the view. The first is `.foregroundColor(.blue)`, which sets the text color of all the `Text` views to blue. The next is `.fontWeight(.black)`, which sets the font weight of all the `Text` views to bold. And lastly, `.font(Font.system(size: 35, design: .serif))` sets the font and size of all the `Text` views to 35 points with a Serif design font.

Next, we'll go back into `ContentView` and display the title by adding the following code:

```
struct ContentView: View {
    var body: some View {
        VStack {
            //MARK: - TITLE
            TitleView().padding()
        }
    }
}
```

I also added some `padding` so the `Title` view won't be too close to the notch at the top of the iPhone when we finish adding all the views.

And now, we can see the colorful title that starts off the UI:

Find The Color

Figure 14.1: Game title

With that, we can move on to the next part of the UI, the target and guess circles.

Creating the target and guess circles

The next task is to create two colored circles:

- One circle will be the target circle, which will show a randomly generated color; because it is an RGB color, the user will need to combine three RGB values to find this target color.

- The other circle will be their "guess" circle – kind of like a sketchpad, where the user can see their current progress as they manipulate the sliders.

These two circles will be created in their own SwiftUI file, so let's make them now. Press *Command + N*, select **SwiftUI View**, and call it `TargetAndGuessCircleView`.

We want to use this file inside of `ContentView` – in order to do so, we will need some `Binding` variables inside the struct:

```
struct TargetAndGuessCircleView: View {
    //target variables
    @Binding var redTarget: Double
```

```
@Binding var greenTarget: Double
@Binding var blueTarget: Double

//guess variables
@Binding var redGuess: Double
@Binding var greenGuess: Double
@Binding var blueGuess: Double

//picker variable
@Binding var selectedPickerIndex: Int
```

• • • • • • •

There are seven variables needed for this file – three variables for the target circle, three variables for the guess circle, and one integer (which we will use for a `Picker` view) will allow the user to select a difficulty level.

After adding those `Binding` properties, we notice we have an error in the `previews` struct. Remember that when we add these variables to a file, the `previews` struct always has to be updated with some dummy data in order for it to work again. So, modify the `previews` struct so it looks like this:

```
struct TargetAndGuessCircleView_Previews: PreviewProvider {
    static var previews: some View {
        TargetAndGuessCircleView(redTarget: .constant(0.3),
        greenTarget: .constant(0.2), blueTarget:
        .constant(0.7), redGuess: .constant(0.7),
        greenGuess: .constant(0.4), blueGuess:
        .constant(0.7), selectedPickerIndex: .constant(2))
    }
}
```

After that, let's go back into the body property. We want to add a `ZStack` so that we can overlay the target circle over the guess circle. We can create these two circles with the following code:

```
ZStack {
    //MARK: - GUESS CIRCLE
    if selectedPickerIndex == 0 {
        Circle()
            .fill(Color(red: redGuess, green: greenTarget,
```

```
                blue: blueTarget, opacity: 1.0))
            .frame(height: 200)
    }
    else if selectedPickerIndex == 1 {
        Circle()
            .fill(Color(red: redGuess, green: greenGuess,
                blue: blueTarget, opacity: 1.0))
    .frame(height: 200)
    }
    else if selectedPickerIndex == 2 {
        Circle()
            .fill(Color(red: redGuess, green: greenGuess,
                blue: blueGuess, opacity: 1.0))
            .frame(height: 200)
    }

    //MARK: - TARGET CIRCLE
    Circle()
        .fill(Color(red: redTarget, green: greenTarget,
          blue: blueTarget, opacity: 1.0))
        .frame(height: 80)
}
```

Inside the ZStack, we start off with the guess circle; this will be the bigger circle, with the frame height set to 200. Here, we're using an if else statement and checking the selectedPickerIndex variable to see what difficulty level the user has chosen. If they've chosen **Easy**, the index will be equal to 0; in that case, we will supply the green and blue RGB target colors to the user, so they only have to work out the red RGB target value. If they've selected **Hard**, the index will be 1; in that case, we only supply the user with the blue RGB value, and they have to work out the red and green values themselves. Finally, if the user selected the **Extreme** option, the index will be 2; in that case, we don't supply the user with any RGB target values and they have to work out the individual target color value themselves.

Next, we create the target circle – this will be the randomly generated colored circle that the user has to try and match by manipulating the sliders. Notice that we're creating this circle much smaller, only 80 points, and because we are in a ZStack, this circle will be on top of the guess circle. The reason for this overlaying of circles is that as the user is trying to work out the colors, their guess circle will change in color and they can better visualize how close they are to the target color.

Lastly, at the end of the ZStack, we're using the onAppear modifier. This modifier will run an action every time the ZStack gets redrawn; if the ZStack gets redrawn, it means the user chose to play a new game (using a button that we will create later) and the sliders will go back to **0**.

That finishes up the TargetAndGuessCircleView file. Let's go back into ContentView and add the State variables that we need in order to display TargetAndGuessCircleView:

```
//target variables
    @State var redTarget = Double.random(in: 0..<1)
    @State var greenTarget = Double.random(in: 0..<1)
    @State var blueTarget = Double.random(in: 0..<1)
    //guess variables
    @State var redGuess: Double
    @State var greenGuess: Double
    @State var blueGuess: Double
    //picker variable
    @State var selectedPickerIndex = 1
```

There are seven State properties, one for each of the Binding properties we made in the previous file. The variables are each set to a random double value between 0 and 1 using the Double. random(in: 0..<1) method. The function will generate a new random number every time it's called, meaning that every time the user starts a new game, a new random value will be used to pick an RGB value.

Continuing from here, we notice that there's an error in the Previews struct of ContentView. This is a familiar error – it is Xcode telling us that we declared a property in the ContentView struct, yet we are not including it here in the Previews struct. Let's fix that by inputting some data into the Previews struct, like so:

```
ContentView(redGuess: 0.5, greenGuess: 0.5, blueGuess: 0.5)
```

That will fix the error in ContentView, but we also need to update the Swift file that contains the main startup code for the project. That file will be named the same as what you named your app – I named this project Find the Color, so in the Project Navigator to the left of Xcode, there will be a file with a Swift extension, called Find_The_ColorApp.swift.

Click on that Swift file, and update the code to the following:

```
@main
struct Find_The_ColorApp: App {
  var body: some Scene {
      WindowGroup {
```

```
            ContentView(redGuess: 0.5, greenGuess: 0.5,
                blueGuess: 0.5)
        }
    }
}
```

We can now go back into `ContentView`, call the `TargetAndGuessCircleView` file, and pass in the appropriate `State` variables. Add the following code directly underneath the title code:

```
//MARK: - TARGET AND GUESS CIRCLES
    TargetAndGuessCircleView(redTarget: $redTarget,
        greenTarget: $greenTarget, blueTarget: $blueTarget,
        redGuess: $redGuess, greenGuess: $greenGuess,
        blueGuess: $blueGuess, selectedPickerIndex:
        $selectedPickerIndex)
```

This is how the UI should look now:

Figure 14.2: Target and guess circles

Let's continue by adding the `Picker` view to allow the user to select the difficulty for the game.

Creating the Picker view

To create the `Picker` view, let's make a new SwiftUI View file called `PickerView` for this purpose.

Inside this file, we need to add a `Binding` property so that we can use it inside `ContentView`, as well as add an array of titles for the picker:

```
@Binding var selectedPickerIndex: Int
@State var levels = ["Easy 😊", "Hard 🙁", "Extreme!
    😬"]
```

The code here has a `Binding` variable to hold the value of `selectedPickerIndex`; that way, we can keep track of which button on the picker the user has selected. Then, we have a `State` array of titles that we will use on the individual picker buttons, along with an appropriate emoji signifying the difficulty level.

Next, as we've done before, update the `Previews` struct with some dummy data, to satisfy Xcode:

```
struct PickerView_Previews: PreviewProvider {
    static var previews: some View {
        PickerView(selectedPickerIndex: .constant(1))
    }
}
```

With the previews up and running, we can now create and style the `Picker` control. Move into the body property and add this code:

```
var body: some View {
  VStack {
     Picker("Numbers", selection: $selectedPickerIndex) {
            ForEach(0 ..< levels.count, id: \.self) {
              index in
                Text(levels[index])
            }
        }
        .pickerStyle(SegmentedPickerStyle())
        .background(Color.yellow)
        .cornerRadius(8)
        .padding(.horizontal)
        .shadow(color: Color.black, radius: 2, y: 4)
```

```
                .padding(.top)

        Text("Difficulty Level: " +
          "\(levels[selectedPickerIndex])").bold()
            .padding(5)
            .animation(.easeInOut(duration: 0.2), value:
              selectedPickerIndex)
      }
    }
  }
```

This is what we are doing here.

The code adds a `Picker` component and a `Text` component. The `VStack` is used to arrange the `Picker` and `Text` components vertically. `Picker` is used to display a list of options, with the options being the elements in the `levels` array; it takes two arguments: `Numbers` and `selection: $selectedPickerIndex`, where `Numbers` is the label for the picker and `$selectedPickerIndex` is a state variable that keeps track of the currently selected option.

The `ForEach` loop is used to iterate through the `levels` array, creating a new `Text` component for each element in the array. Each `Text` component is configured to display the corresponding element from the `levels` array.

The `pickerStyle` method is used to change the appearance of the picker to a segmented picker style. We have used the `background`, `cornerRadius`, `padding`, and `shadow` modifiers before, and these apply various visual styles to the picker.

The `Text` component is used to display the difficulty level in the UI under the `Picker` component. It takes the `"Difficulty Level: "` + `"(levels[selectedPickerIndex])"` string and makes it bold, then applies some padding and animation to it. The animation is added so that instead of the difficulty level string appearing and disappearing instantly, it will ease in and out with a `0.2`-second duration, for a smoother transition in the UI.

Now, we have a `Picker` component that can be used to select the difficulty level of the game, and a `Text` string to display that level.

The result is shown here:

Figure 14.3: The segmented picker

With the `Picker` control done, move back into `ContentView` and call `PickerView` directly under the target and guess circle code:

```
//MARK: - PICKER
    PickerView(selectedPickerIndex: $selectedPickerIndex)
```

That code will add the `PickerView` file into the UI under the target and guess circles. The result is shown here:

Figure 14.4: The picker in the UI

Now, if you click on the picker, you will see that the guess circle changes color; it won't change to more than three shades of colors, as the picker displays a random color from each RGB value while the preview is running. If you stop the preview and restart it, another set of three random colors will be displayed.

Shortly, we will implement sliders to change the guess circle colors, and change the target circle color when the user starts a new game. Before that, let's continue with the next part of the UI, making target and guess rectangles. I'll explain what they are for next.

Creating the target and guess rectangles

So far, we have given the user a guess circle so they can see how close they are coming to the target color. Let's do something similar to that and give them another visual cue – let's create a guess rectangle and a target rectangle, and put them directly under the `Picker` control. We can also add an RGB value indicator, so they can see the actual values of each slider as they change, which can be helpful when they're trying to figure out how much of the slider they need to move and in which direction.

Start by creating a new file to make these rectangles, called `TargetAndGuessRectView`. This file will contain very similar code to the `TargetAndGuessCircleView` file, which means adding the needed `Binding` properties:

```
@Binding var redTarget: Double

@Binding var greenTarget: Double

@Binding var blueTarget: Double

@Binding var redGuess: Double

@Binding var greenGuess: Double

@Binding var blueGuess: Double

@Binding var selectedPickerIndex: Int
```

You should be familiar with these `Binding` variables, as we've created them before in the `TargetAndGuessCircleView` file. Actually, you can refactor all the code and combine the two guess and target files into one file if you'd like, or create a data model and make the properties available to all the files... I'll leave that as a challenge for you.

Moving on, we need a combination of VStacks and HStacks to position the `Rectangle` and `Text` views. Add this code to the body of the file (I'll explain it all next):

```
var body: some View {
  VStack {
     HStack {
         //MARK: - TARGET RECTANGLE
         VStack {
             Rectangle()
                 .foregroundColor(Color(red: redTarget,
                     green: greenTarget, blue: blueTarget,
                     opacity: 1.0))
                 .cornerRadius(5)
                 .padding(.init(top: 0, leading: 10,
                     bottom: 0, trailing: 0))
```

```
                    .frame(height: 40)
            Text("Target Color to Match").bold()
    }
    //MARK: - GUESS RECTANGLE
    VStack {
        if selectedPickerIndex == 0 {
            Rectangle()
                .foregroundColor(Color(red: redGuess,
                    green: greenTarget, blue:
                    blueTarget, opacity: 1.0))
                .modifier(rectModifier())
        }
        else if selectedPickerIndex == 1 {
            Rectangle()
            .foregroundColor(Color(red: redGuess,
                green: greenGuess, blue: blueTarget,
                opacity: 1.0))
            .modifier(rectModifier())
    }
        else if selectedPickerIndex == 2 {
            Rectangle()
                .foregroundColor(Color(red: redGuess,
                    green: greenGuess, blue: blueGuess,
                    opacity: 1.0))
                .modifier(rectModifier())
        }
        HStack {
            Image(systemName: "r.circle.fill")
                .foregroundColor(.red)
            Text("\(Int(redGuess * 255.0))")
                .font(.callout)
            Image(systemName: "g.circle.fill")
                .foregroundColor(.green)
            Text("\(Int(greenGuess * 255.0))")
                .font(.callout)
            Image(systemName: "b.circle.fill")
```

```
                                .foregroundColor(.blue)
                    Text("\(Int(blueGuess * 255.0))")
                            .font(.callout)
                    }
                }
            }
        }
    }
}


struct rectModifier : ViewModifier {
    func body(content: Content) -> some View {
        content
            .cornerRadius(5)
            .padding(.init(top: 0, leading: 0, bottom: 0,
                trailing: 10))
            .frame(height: 40)

    }
}
```

Here's a breakdown of what the code is doing.

The first VStack contains a rectangle with the color determined by the values of redTarget, greenTarget, and blueTarget. It also has a corner radius of 5 and padding on the leading edge, with a height of 40. Below the rectangle, there is a Text view displaying the "Target Color to Match" string in bold font.

The second VStack contains a rectangle with the color determined by the values of redGuess, greenGuess, and blueGuess, and is modified by the rectModifier struct (more on the rectModifier struct in a moment). The color of the rectangle is determined by selectedPickerIndex, which is an integer value. If selectedPickerIndex is 0, the color is determined by redGuess, greenTarget, and blueTarget. If selectedPickerIndex is 1, the color is determined by redGuess, greenGuess, and blueTarget. If selectedPickerIndex is 2, the color is determined by redGuess, and greenGuess, blueGuess. Below the rectangle, there is an HStack containing an image and text displaying the values of redGuess, greenGuess, and blueGuess, respectively.

Now the target and guess rectangles are in place, as well as the three Text views that will display the RGB values as the user works the slider, let's continue and look at that last bit of code, the rectModifer struct.

The `rectModifier` struct is a `ViewModifier` that modifies the `Rectangle` view. It is a struct that conforms to the `ViewModifier` protocol and defines a single method, `body(content: Content) -> some View`, which takes a single argument content of the `Content` type and returns a modified version of that content wrapped in a `view`.

In this specific case, the struct is modifying the appearance of a `rectangle` view. The modifications are made by chaining together a series of view modifiers on the `content` parameter in the `body` method, such as setting the corner radius to `5`, adding `padding` to the trailing edge, and setting the height of the rectangle to `40`.

When `rectModifier()` is called, it is passed the `rectangle` view as the `content` parameter, and it applies the modifications defined in the struct to that `rectangle` view, returning the modified version of that view. In other words, `rectModifier()` is a simple way to package a set of modifiers that can be applied to any view, and it provides a way to reuse the same set of modifiers on multiple views, saving on coding time and readability.

Here is the result of what we just coded:

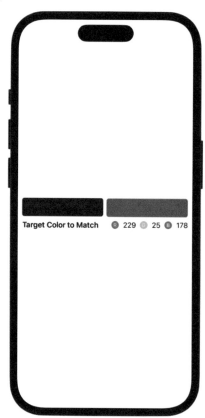

Figure 14.5: Target and guess rectangles

The sliders will now display the RGB values for the user.

Now, it's time to go back into the ContentView and make a call to this file directly underneath the Picker code so that we can display these two rectangles and text in the main UI:

```
//MARK: - TARGET AND GUESS RECTANGLES
    TargetAndGuessRectView(redTarget: $redTarget,
        greenTarget: $greenTarget, blueTarget: $blueTarget,
        redGuess: $redGuess, greenGuess: $greenGuess,
        blueGuess: $blueGuess, selectedPickerIndex:
        $selectedPickerIndex)
```

Again, this is familiar code – we are simply calling TargetAndGuessRectView and passing in the appropriate State variables. Here is the result:

Figure 14.6: Target and Guess Rectangles in the UI

We just need the sliders, and a button to check the score, so let's do that now.

Making the color sliders

To start creating the sliders, make a new SwiftUI View file and call it `SliderView`.

As the sliders are only used to manipulate the guess circle, we won't need any `Target` variables in this file. Instead, we just need three `Guess` variables, as well as a variable to track the value of the picker control, which you can add like this:

```
@Binding var redGuess: Double
@Binding var greenGuess: Double
@Binding var blueGuess: Double
@Binding var selectedPickerIndex: Int
```

Again, we need to update the `Previews` struct, because it's giving us this error: **Missing arguments for parameters redGuess, greenGuess, blueGuess, selectedPickerIndex in call**. This error is telling us, as it has before, to include the `Binding` variables in its `SliderView` struct initializer. Let's give it what it wants, by updating `Previews` with the following code:

```
struct StyleTheSliders_Previews: PreviewProvider {
    static var previews: some View {
        SliderView(redGuess: .constant(0.5), greenGuess:
            .constant(0.5), blueGuess: .constant(0.5),
            selectedPickerIndex: .constant(1))
    }
}
```

With the previews operational again, let's continue by making a separate struct for the creation of the slider itself. Add `CreateSlider` outside and underneath the `SliderView` struct:

```
struct CreateSlider: View {
    @Binding var value: Double
    var color: Color
    var body: some View {
        HStack {
            Text("0")
                .bold()
                .foregroundColor(color)
```

```
            Slider(value: $value, in: 0.0...1.0)
            Text("255")
                .bold()
                .foregroundColor(color)
        }.padding(.init(top: 10, leading: 10, bottom: 10,
          trailing: 10))
    }
}
```

This code defines a new SwiftUI struct called `CreateSlider` that takes in two parameters: a `Binding` variable called `value` of the `Double` type, and a variable called `color` of the `Color` type.

Here is what each line of code does.

As we've seen before, `@Binding var value: Double` is a property wrapper that creates a two-way binding between the struct's `value` variable and another variable. This allows the struct to read and write the value of the variable that it is bound to.

`var color: Color` creates a variable called `color` that is of the `Color` type.

`Text("0")` creates a `Text` view with a value of 0, and gets the following modifiers placed on it: `.bold()` makes the text bold, and `foregroundColor(color)` sets the color of the text to the `color` variable passed to the struct.

Then we add the slider, `Slider(value: $value, in: 0.0...1.0)`. This creates a `Slider` view that reads and writes its value to the `value` property. The `in` parameter sets the range of the slider to go from `0.0` to `1.0`.

Then, we add another `Text` view, add the text `255`, and put some padding on it using `.padding(. init(top: 10, leading: 10, bottom: 10, trailing: 10))`. This is a `View` modifier that adds a padding of `10` points to the top, leading, bottom, and trailing edge of the view.

With the slider created, we will need to call this `CreateSlider` struct several times inside the `SliderView` struct and add some styling to it as well. So, back up into the `SliderView` struct, add the following code:

```
var body: some View {
    //MARK: - SLIDERS FOR THE GUESS CIRCLE
    VStack {
        //red slider - this slider will always be visible
          and represents the "Easy" option on the picker
        CreateSlider(value: $redGuess, color: .red)
            .background(Capsule().stroke(Color.red,
```

```
            lineWidth: 3))
        .padding(.horizontal)
        .accentColor(.red)
        .padding(5)


switch selectedPickerIndex {
case 1:
    //green slider - shown when the "Hard" option
      is selected
    CreateSlider(value: $greenGuess, color: .green)
        .background(Capsule().stroke(Color.green,
          lineWidth: 4))
        .padding(.horizontal)
        .accentColor(.green)
        .padding(5)
case 2:
  //blue slider - this is shown when the
    "Extreme" option is selected
      CreateSlider(value: $greenGuess, color:
        .green)
          .background(Capsule().stroke(Color.green,
            lineWidth: 4))
          .padding(.horizontal)
          .accentColor(.green)
          .padding(5)


      CreateSlider(value: $blueGuess, color: .blue)
          .background(Capsule().stroke(Color.blue,
            lineWidth: 4))
          .padding(.horizontal)
          .accentColor(.blue)
          .padding(5)
    default:
        EmptyView()
    }
```

```
        }
    }
```

Let's break this code down. It starts off by defining a SwiftUI view called `SliderView` that uses a `VStack` to lay out three sliders for adjusting the values of the `redGuess`, `greenGuess`, and `blueGuess` properties. The struct has a `VStack` used to organize three sliders vertically.

Those three sliders are added by calls to the `CreateSlider` view. The `CreateSlider` view uses the `background` modifier and a capsule shape in order to outline the slider with a red color.

Next up is a `switch` statement – since we are using one for the first time, let me explain what it is and the difference between using a `switch` statement and an `if else` statement.

So, an `if else` statement is used to evaluate a Boolean expression and execute a block of code if the expression is `true`, and another block of code if the expression is `false`. It can be used for any type of condition or comparison. A `switch` statement, on the other hand, is used to match a value or expression against multiple possible cases and execute a block of code for the matching case.

A `switch` statement is typically used for matching against multiple possible values for a single variable or expression and is often used for situations where multiple conditions need to be checked in a more concise and readable way. For example, when you have multiple conditions with multiple `if else` statements, you can use a `switch` statement over `if else`. It makes the code more readable and easier to maintain.

> **Note**
>
> In general, `if else` statements are good for complex conditions, while `switch` statements are good for simple conditions. In Swift, you can use either, depending on what you are trying to accomplish.

So, going back to our code, the `switch` statement checks the `selectedPickerIndex` value to see whether it is equal to 1; if so, it means the user selected the **Hard** level, so we need to add a green slider to the UI. If the `selectedPickerIndex` value is equal to 2, it will create both the green and blue sliders, because the user has selected the **Extreme** option, so all sliders will be visible. Lastly, if `selectedPickerIndex` is not 1 or 2, it will return an empty view.

Next, the `CreateSlider` struct is used to create the sliders, and it takes two arguments, `value` and `color`. It displays the minimum and maximum values of the slider and it uses the `color` argument to change the color of the `"0"` text view and the `"255"` text view.

`SliderView` uses the `CreateSlider` struct to create the sliders for RGB colors. The `selectedPickerIndex` binding is used to decide which sliders to show, based on the user's selection.

SliderView is now complete, so let's use it inside ContentView. Add the following code just after the Picker code:

```
//MARK: - SLIDER
  Spacer()
  SliderView(redGuess: $redGuess, greenGuess:
    $greenGuess, blueGuess: $blueGuess,
    selectedPickerIndex: $selectedPickerIndex)
      .scaleEffect(1)
      .animation(.interactiveSpring(response: 0.4,
        dampingFraction: 0.5, blendDuration: 0.5), value:
        selectedPickerIndex)
  Spacer()
```

This code calls the SliderView struct and fills in the Binding variables, then adds a spring animation to the sliders as they appear and disappear in the UI. The interactiveSpring animation is a type of animation that simulates the behavior of a spring, and takes three parameters:

- response: This value controls the stiffness of the spring. A lower value will result in a softer spring, and a higher value will result in a stiffer spring. A value of 0.4 will provide a moderate stiffness.

- dampingFraction: This value controls the damping of the spring, which is a measure of how quickly the spring's oscillations will die out. A lower value will result in a spring with less damping, and a higher value will result in a spring with more damping. A value of 0.5 means that the spring's oscillations will die out relatively quickly.

- blendDuration: This value controls the duration of the animation's blending. A lower value will result in a shorter blend duration, and a higher value will result in a longer blend duration. A value of 0.5 seconds is a moderate blend duration.

As well as the interactiveSpring animation, we're using the scaleEffect modifier and passing in a value of 1. What this does is help smooth out the animation as each slider appears and disappears. Go ahead and try it out. If you click on the picker control to choose a difficulty level, each slider will appear and disappear on the screen with a springy animation to it:

Figure 14.7: The sliders

As you move the sliders, the guess circle color will update smoothly, and the RGB values will change in the RGB text string.

The last UI component to add is a button that will let the user check their score as they play.

Keeping track of the user's score with a button

To make this a game, the user needs a way to check their progress and see a number that reflects how close they are to a perfect score/color match.

Let's add a button right after the `SliderView` struct's `Spacer()` in `ContentView`:

```
//MARK: - BUTTON
    Button(action: {



    }) {
        Text("Check Score")
            .foregroundColor(.black)
            .padding(EdgeInsets(top: 12, leading: 20,
              bottom: 12, trailing: 20))
            .background(Color.yellow)
            .cornerRadius(20)
            .shadow(color: Color.black, radius: 2, y: 4)
    }
```

This code creates a `Button` view, which we have named `Check Score`. The button gets styled with a black foreground, yellow background, padding, a corner radius, and finally, a black shadow to make the button stand out a bit.

The body of the button is currently empty right now, but what we want to do is to put some code in there that will trigger an alert and show the user their current score, so that they know how close they are to the target value.

To do this, we need to create a function that calculates a score. So, at the bottom of the `ContentView` struct, add this code:

```
func calculateScore() -> Int {
        let redDiff = redGuess - redTarget
        let greenDiff = greenGuess - greenTarget
        let blueDiff = blueGuess - blueTarget
        let easyDifference = redDiff * redDiff
        let hardDifference = easyDifference + greenDiff *
          greenDiff
        let extremeDifference = hardDifference + blueDiff *
          blueDiff
        let calculatedDifference: Double
        switch selectedPickerIndex {
            case 0:
                calculatedDifference = sqrt(easyDifference)
```

```
            case 1:
                calculatedDifference = sqrt(hardDifference)
            case 2:
                calculatedDifference =
                    sqrt(extremeDifference)
            default:
                calculatedDifference = 0.0
        }
        return Int((1.0 - calculatedDifference) * 100 +
            0.5)
    }
```

This code defines a function named `calculateScore` that returns an `Int` value. This function is used to calculate a score based on the difference between the `guess` values of `red`, `green`, and `blue`, and the `target` values of `red`, `green`, and `blue`.

Here's how it works. The function first calculates the difference between the `guess` values and the `target` values for `red`, `green`, and `blue`. Next, it calculates `easyDifference` by getting the square root of the `redDiff` variable. Next, it calculates `hardDifference` by adding the square of the `greenDiff` variable to `easyDifference`. Then, it calculates `extremeDifference` by adding the square root of `blueDiff` to `hardDifference`.

After that, it uses a `switch` statement to determine which level of difficulty is currently selected, and assigns the `calculatedDifference` variable a value based on that:

- If `selectedPickerIndex` is 0, then `calculatedDifference` is the square root of `easyDifference`
- If `selectedPickerIndex` is 1, then `calculatedDifference` is the square root of `hardDifference`
- If `selectedPickerIndex` is 2, then `calculatedDifference` is the square root of `extremeDifference`
- If `selectedPickerIndex` is any other value, then `calculatedDifference` is set to 0.0

Finally, it returns an `integer` value that is calculated by taking (1.0 - `calculatedDifference`) * 100 + 0.5, which is the final score.

This function is used to calculate a score based on how close the `guess` values are to the `target` values. The smaller the difference between the values, the higher the score will be. If the `guess` value is equal to the `target` value, the user gets a perfect score of 100.

Now, the `calculateScore` function is complete; let's use it to show the user their score in an `Alert` view.

Showing the user's score in an Alert view

To create an `Alert` view, we first need a state variable to keep track of the alert and trigger it when the `state` value changes. At the top of the file, underneath the other variables we created, add the following `State` variable:

```
//user feedback variable
    @State var showAlert = false
```

Then, we need to add the `Alert` modifier after the `Button` code's closing brace:

```
.alert(isPresented: $showAlert) { () -> Alert in
        Alert(title: Text("Your Score"), message:
          Text("\(calculateScore())"),
              primaryButton: Alert.Button.default(Text("New
                Game?"), action: {
          // Start a new game?
        }),
            secondaryButton:
              Alert.Button.destructive(Text("Continue
                Playing"), action: {
          // Continue with the present game

        }))
    }
```

The code creates a title, a message, and two buttons – a primary button and a secondary button.

The title will be the message to the user, and the message will be the user's score. We're doing that by calling the `calculatedScore` function inside a `Text` view using string interpolation; remember, the `calculateScore` function returns an integer, and that value will be shown to the user as their current score.

Then, the primary button will prompt the user to start a new game, while the secondary button will prompt the user to continue playing.

To trigger the alert, we need to toggle the `showAlert` variable to `true` inside the `Button` body, like this:

```
Button(action: {
        showAlert = true
    }) {
```

Now, we can try the game out. Slide the sliders and try to get as close to the target circle color as you can, then press the **Check Score** button to see your score:

Figure 14.8: Alert view showing the user's score

From this screen, if the user presses **Continue Playing?**, the game will continue from where it left off. However, if they press **New Game?**, nothing will happen – that's because we haven't added any logic to start a new game yet. Let's do that next.

Resetting the game

We want to give the user the opportunity to start a new game, and we can do that by adding a `reset` function to the file. This function will reset the sliders to **0** and generate another random target color for the middle target circle.

Add the following function underneath the `calculateScore` function:

```
//MARK: - RESET THE GAME
    func reset() {
        redTarget = Double.random(in: 0..<1)
        greenTarget = Double.random(in: 0..<1)
        blueTarget = Double.random(in: 0..<1)
        redGuess = 0.0
        greenGuess = 0.0
        blueGuess = 0.0
    }
```

This function creates new random colors and stores them in the `Target` variables. It also resets the `Guess` variables back to 0, which will move all the sliders back to their starting points on the left.

Let's call the `reset` function inside the `Alert` modifier's secondary button, like this:

```
.alert(isPresented: $showAlert) { () -> Alert in
  Alert(title: Text("Your Score"), message:
    Text("\(calculateScore())"),
        primaryButton: Alert.Button.default(Text("Continue
          Playing?"), action: {
                }),
        secondaryButton: Alert.Button.destructive(Text("New
          Game?"), action: {
      // Start a new game?
      reset()
  }))
```

Now, when we press the secondary button, **New Game?**, a new game starts with a new target color, and the sliders are set back to their starting position:

Figure 14.9: Starting a new game

The sliders are set back to zero, and a new random target color is generated and shown.

Let's finish this project by adding two more things – a background, and a confetti animation that will appear when the user gets a perfect score of 100.

Adding a background

First, the background. You can find the resource for this project in the `Chapter 14` folder on GitHub (it's the only asset in the folder); just drag and drop the `background` image file into the Asset Catalog. After you've done that, add the following code in `ContentView`, after the closing brace of the main `VStack`, like this:

```
.background(Image("background").resizable().edgesIgnoringSa
    feArea(.all))
```

Here, we are using the `background` modifier, passing the name of the image, resizing it, and setting `edgesIgnoringSafeArea` to stretch it out throughout the whole screen. It's a subtle background, but it has a nice pattern to it that I think works as a backdrop for the colorful UI:

Figure 14.10: Background added

Now, let's look at Swift packages, and how to make some confetti.

Adding confetti using Swift packages

A Swift package is pre-built software that we can use in any of our projects, in which all the coding work has been done for us; all we have to do is configure it in our project.

To add a Swift package, in Xcode, go to the **File** menu and select **Add Packages…**:

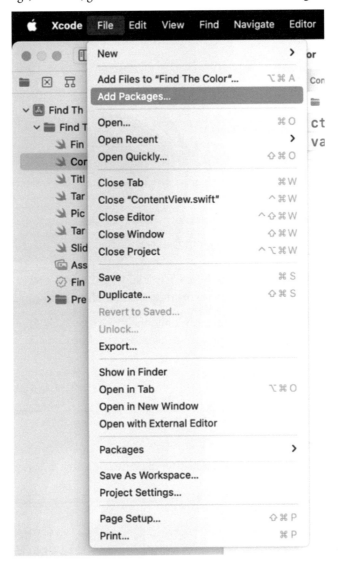

Figure 14.11: Add Packages…

In the **All Sources** window, enter `https://github.com/simibac/ConfettiSwiftUI.git` in the search box:

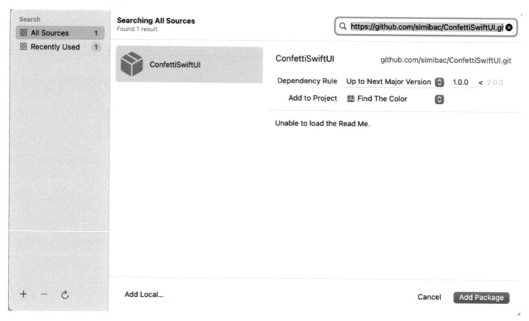

Figure 14.12: Adding the URL

When the **Add Package** button is clicked, Xcode will add the Confetti package to the project. The Confetti package contains all the code needed to create all kinds of confetti, dispersed in different ways.

Now, we need to import the Confetti framework into the `ContentView` file at the top:

```
import ConfettiSwiftUI
```

Next, we need a variable that can trigger the confetti (placed after the other project variables):

```
//confetti variable
    @State var counter = 0
```

Now, we can call the `confettiCannon` initializer in `ContentView` just after the target and guess rectangle code, like this:

```
//MARK: - CONFETTI CANNON
    .confettiCannon(counter: $counter, num: 100, colors:
      [.pink, .red, .blue, .purple, .orange], rainHeight:
      1800.0, radius: 500.0)
```

This code calls the confettiCannon initializer, using the counter variable to trigger the animation. The number of pieces of confetti being created will be 100, and the colors array lets you add the colors that you want the confetti to be. rainHeight will set how high the confetti goes upward, and the radius will set how wide the confetti spreads.

> **Note**
>
> I filled out the variables for our example; however, you can play around with these values and configure them the way you like. There are many parameters that the creator, Simon Bachmann, has built into the confettiCannon initializer, so it's very customizable. For a full list, follow this link: https://github.com/simibac/ConfettiSwiftUI#parameters.

Finally, we want to trigger the confetti in the Button body only when the user scores a perfect 100. So, add the following code into the Button body, right after the showAlert variable is set to true, and then we can test out the animation:

```
Button(action: {
        showAlert = true
        //if a score of 100 is achieved, make the confetti
          fall by adding 1 to the counter variable
        if calculateScore() == 100 {
                counter += 1
                    }
```

This is just a simple if statement that checks whether the calculateScore function returns 100. If so, we add 1 to the counter variable, which will trigger the animation.

And if you're wondering how adding a value of 1 triggers the confetti cannon, well, that's how the Confetti package is configured –when a value of 1 is added to its counter variable, it triggers the confetti.

Okay, now when the user gets a score of 100, the confetti cannon will shoot the confetti from the middle of the screen upward, and the confetti will slowly rain down the entire interface, all the way past the bottom of the screen:

Figure 14.13: Confetti animation

And that's the color-matching game finished.

Summary

In this project, we learned about RGB colors, `switch` statements, implementing a `Picker` view, adding a `Slider` view, and creating a `reset` function, as well as using Swift packages to import pre-built code into our project.

Play around with the code, and think of ways that you can take the game further. For example, maybe you want to play a sound effect when a perfect score is reached, such as a "pop" sound, or maybe you want to display the score on a label in the UI rather than having to click a button to check it. There are many different things that you can do to add more fun to the project.

The next chapter will look at some advanced animations we can create by integrating the SpriteKit framework into our SwiftUI projects. SpriteKit gives us a particle system that creates all kinds of very realistic effects and animations that you can use in your projects.

15

Integrating SpriteKit into Your SwiftUI Projects

In this chapter, we will dive deeper into the world of animation in SwiftUI and create some mini-projects, highlighting different animations that can be made using other techniques and the SpriteKit framework. Some of the animations will be simpler, some will be more complex, and some will be dynamic and interactive animations too.

You will learn how to take advantage of the power of **SpriteKit** and **particle emitters**. SpriteKit is a game development framework that provides a convenient and efficient way to create 2D games for iOS and macOS platforms. Particle emitters, on the other hand, are powerful tools in the SpriteKit framework that allow you to create special effects such as fire, smoke, rain, wind, explosions, and more. These emitters will bring life to your apps, making them visually stunning and engaging for users.

So, here are the topics we will cover in this final chapter:

- Animating pipe smoke
- Animating coffee steam
- Animating rocket fire
- Animating a blizzard
- Animating rain
- Animating a magic wand

Technical requirements

You can find the completed projects and their code in the Chapter 15 folder on GitHub: https://github.com/PacktPublishing/Animating-SwiftUI-Applications.

Animating pipe smoke

In this project, we will create a smoke effect using SpriteKit's **Smoke** template, and make it come out of an image of a pipe. This is a good first project, as it's not too complicated and gets you familiar with creating the needed **SpriteKit Scene (SKS)** particle file and how to configure it.

Let's get started, first create a new SwiftUI project, and call it `Pipe Smoke`. We are going to need a couple of images for this project so you can grab them over at GitHub (`Chapter 15 | Pipe Smoke`) and add them to the project's Assets catalog. Now it's time to create a SpriteKit particle file.

Creating a SpriteKit particle file

Next, let's create a new file; this will be a SpriteKit particle file. The **SpriteKit Scene (SKS) particle file** is a scene file that has information about the particle system it contains, such as the shape, size, and position of the particle emitter, as well as the type of particles that will be emitted, their behavior, and movements.

To create an SKS particle file, in Xcode, you simply need to go to **File | New | File | SpriteKit Particle File**, or press *Command + N* to bring up the template options, and scroll down until you come to a template called **SpriteKit Particle File**.

Now, we need to choose the type of template we want. There are several options and we're going to explore them individually in separate projects, but the one we want now is **Smoke**:

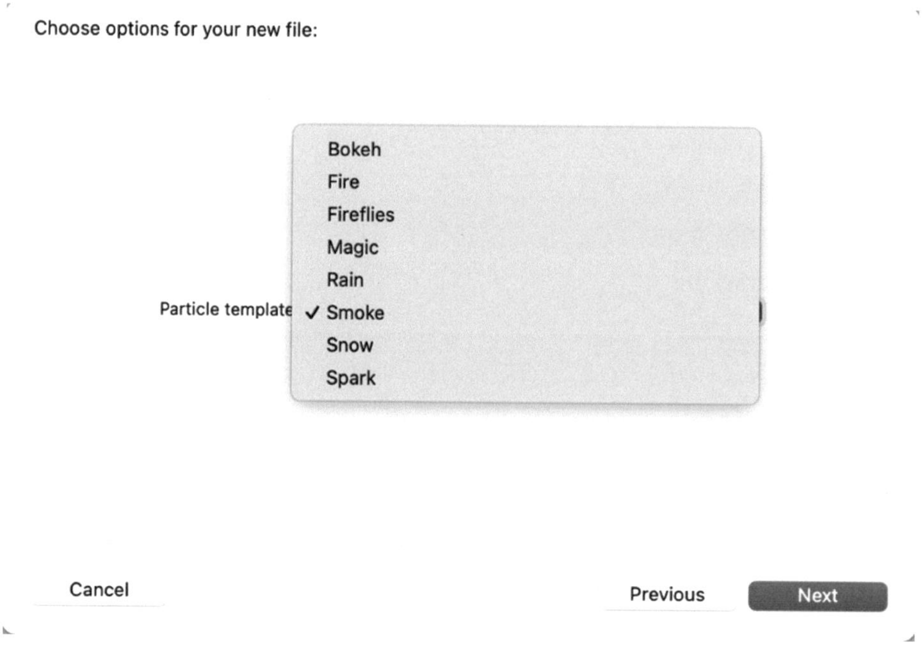

Choose options for your new file:

Bokeh
Fire
Fireflies
Magic
Rain
Particle template ✓ Smoke
Snow
Spark

Cancel   Previous   Next

Figure 15.1: Particle template options

Once you click **Next**, name the file `Smoke`, choose a save location, and then click **Create**:

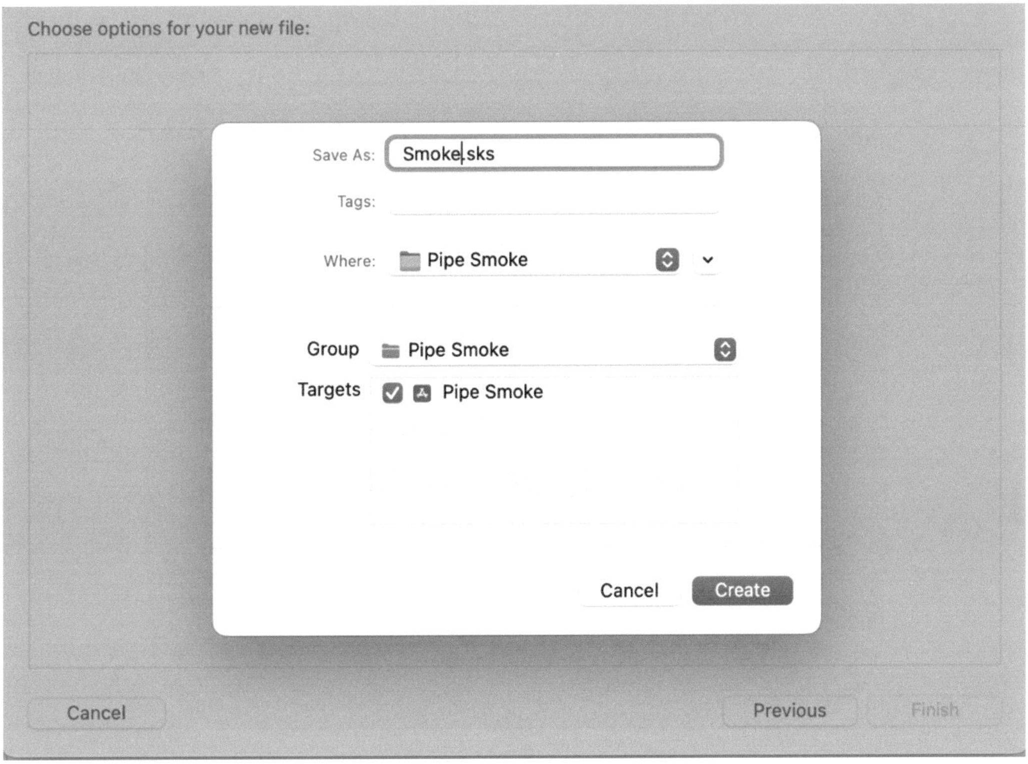

Figure 15.2: Creating the Smoke.sks file

Now, you will see a new particle file in your Xcode editor that has a smoke animation playing. That's because we chose the **Smoke** template, so the particles are pre-configured to produce smoke. This smoke will need to be adjusted so it's not as wide and thick. We want the effect to be thin and small enough that we can make it come out of a pipe.

To configure the smoke, go to the right side of Xcode and you'll see four buttons; if you click on the fourth button, you open up the **Attributes** panel, which is where we can configure our particle file to create an infinite number of effects:

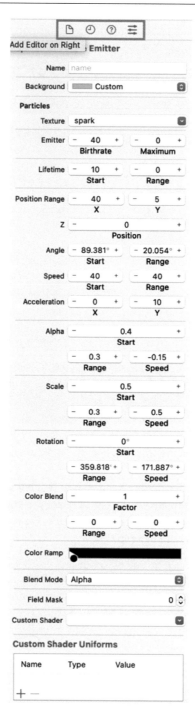

Figure 15.3: Xcode's Attributes panel

There are quite a few settings in this panel, and since we will be creating different particle files in this chapter, it's a good idea to have an understanding of what each field does. So, I will explain each field in order for you to create this first project in the chapter, and you can use these definitions for reference as you continue working through the other projects.

Name

The **Name** field is used to give a unique identifier to the particle emitter so that you can easily reference it within your code or in the editor. The field is a string value that you can set to anything you like, as long as it's unique within the file. By giving your particle emitters descriptive names, they will act as a reminder of what they do and how they're used in your project.

Additionally, you can use the **Name** field to access the particle emitter and modify its properties programmatically in your code.

Background

The **Background** field lets you set the background color of the editor. Sometimes, it's useful to adjust this color to help make the particles stand out more.

Texture

The **Texture** field is used to specify the image file that will be used as the particle texture. The particle texture is essentially the appearance of the particles, and you can use any image file you like to create a wide range of particle effects. For example, you could use a simple dot or circle image for a simple particle effect, or a more complex image with multiple shapes and colors for a more elaborate effect. When you specify a particle texture in the **Attributes** panel, it will be used for all of the particles in the particle emitter.

Emitter

Emitter is the object that defines the characteristics of a particle, such as its initial position, speed, and lifetime.

The **Emitter Birthrate** field specifies the number of particles that are emitted per second. It determines how quickly the particles will be generated by the emitter – a higher birthrate will result in more particles being emitted in a shorter amount of time, while a lower birthrate will result in fewer particles being emitted over a longer period of time.

The **Emitter Maximum** field sets the maximum number of particles that can exist at one time in the particle system. If **Birthrate** is set to a high value and **Maximum** is set to a low value, the emitter will emit particles at the specified rate until the maximum limit is reached. Once the maximum number of particles has been reached, the emitter will stop emitting new particles until some of the existing particles have disappeared. This allows you to control the overall number of particles in your particle system and optimize performance.

Lifetime

The **Lifetime** fields specify the amount of time that each particle in a particle system will be active before it disappears.

The **Lifetime Start** field specifies the length of time for which each particle will exist in the particle system. It determines how long each particle will stay visible in the scene before disappearing. A higher value will result in particles staying visible for a longer period of time, while a lower value will result in particles disappearing more quickly.

The **Lifetime Range** field sets the range of values that the **Lifetime** property can take. Instead of specifying a fixed value for the lifetime, you can specify a range of values, and the particle system will randomly choose a value from that range for each particle that is emitted. This allows you to add variation to your particle system, making it look more organic and natural. For example, if you set **Lifetime Start** to **1.0** and **Lifetime Range** to **0.5**, each particle's lifetime will be a random value between 0.5 and 1.5 seconds.

Position Range

The **Position Range** fields specify the range of values for the initial position of the particles in each dimension – **X**, **Y**, and **Z** – allowing you to create particle systems that emit particles from a random position within a defined area. The particle system will randomly choose a position from within the specified range for each particle that is emitted, which can help add variety and realism to your particle systems.

Angle

The **Angle** fields in an SKS particle file control the initial direction and spread of particles when they are emitted. **Angle Start** sets the starting direction of the particles, while **Angle Range** determines the range of possible directions; the system then randomly chooses an angle within the range for each particle emitted. **Angle Start** is measured in degrees, with 0 degrees pointing to the right, and **Angle Range** specifies the spread of angles in a counterclockwise direction, again measured in degrees.

Speed

The **Speed** fields control the initial speed and variation of particles when emitted in an SKS particle file. **Speed Start** sets the starting speed, while **Speed Range** specifies the possible range of speeds; a random speed is then chosen within the specified range for each emitted particle.

Adjusting these fields allows you to create various particle effects, with a higher value resulting in faster particles and a lower value in slower particles. For example, setting **Speed Start** to **100** and **Speed Range** to **0** will emit particles at a constant speed, while setting **Speed Start** to **50** and **Speed Range** to **25** will create particles with varying speeds between 25 and 75. These values are generally understood to be points per second.

Acceleration

The **Acceleration X** and **Acceleration Y** fields control the acceleration of the particles in the *x* and *y* directions respectively. For example, you could set **Acceleration X** to **0** and **Acceleration Y** to **-100** to create a particle system that is affected by gravity, causing the particles to fall downward. Alternatively, you could set **Acceleration X** to **50** and **Acceleration Y** to **0** to create a particle system that moves to the right at a constant rate.

The **Acceleration X** and **Acceleration Y** fields are specified in points per second squared; positive values will cause the particles to accelerate in the positive direction, while negative values will cause the particles to decelerate or accelerate in the opposite direction.

Alpha

Alpha in an `.sks` file refers to the opacity or transparency of particles in a particle system. The alpha value controls how much of the particle is visible, with a higher value making the particle more visible and a lower value making the particle more transparent.

The **Alpha Start** field specifies the starting alpha value for the particles, which can be used to control their initial transparency. The **Alpha Range** field specifies the range of possible alpha values that the particles can take, and when the particle emitter emits a particle, it will choose a random alpha value within the specified range. The **Alpha Speed** field specifies the rate at which the alpha value of the particles will change over time, and can be used to control the rate of fade-in or fade-out of the particles; a positive value for this field will cause the particles to fade in over time, while a negative value will cause the particles to fade out over time.

By adjusting the **Alpha Start**, **Alpha Range**, and **Alpha Speed** fields, you can control the transparency of the particles over their lifetime and create a wide range of particle effects. For example, you could set **Alpha Start** to **1** and **Alpha Range** to **0** to emit particles with a constant alpha value or set **Alpha Start** to **1**, **Alpha Range** to **0**, and **Alpha Speed** to **-0.5** to emit particles that fade out over time.

Scale

The **Scale** fields control the size of the particles over their lifetime. The **Scale Start** field specifies the starting size of the particles, which can be used to control their initial size. The **Scale Range** field specifies the range of possible sizes that the particles can take, and when the particle emitter emits a particle, it will choose a random size within the specified range. The **Scale Speed** field specifies the rate at which the size of the particles will change over time, and can be used to control the rate of growth or shrinkage of the particles; a positive value for this will cause the particles to grow over time, while a negative value will cause the particles to shrink over time.

As an example of using **Scale**, you could set **Scale Start** to **1** and **Scale Range** to **0** to emit particles with a constant size or set **Scale Start** to **1**, **Scale Range** to **0.5**, and **Scale Speed** to **0.1** to emit particles that grow over time.

Rotation

The **Rotation Start** field specifies the starting rotation of the particles, which can be used to control their initial orientation. The **Rotation Range** field specifies the range of possible rotations that the particles can take, and when the particle emitter emits a particle, it will choose a random rotation within the specified range. The **Rotation Speed** field specifies the rate at which the rotation of the particles will change over time, and can be used to control the rate of rotation of the particles; a positive value will cause the particles to rotate clockwise, while a negative value will cause the particles to rotate counterclockwise.

You could set **Rotation Start** to **0** and **Rotation Range** to **0** to emit particles with a constant orientation or set **Rotation Start** to **0**, **Rotation Range** to **180**, and **Rotation Speed** to **180** to emit particles that rotate rapidly over time.

Color Blend

The **Color Blend** fields control the color of the particles over their lifetime.

The **Color Blend Factor** field specifies the amount of color blending that will be applied to the particles. When the particle emitter emits a particle, it will choose a random color blend factor within the specified range. The particle's color will be blended with the color of the particle's texture according to this blend factor.

The **Color Blend Factor Range** field specifies the range of possible color blend factors that the particles can take. A value of **0** will result in no color blending, while a value of **1** will result in full color blending.

The **Color Blend Factor Speed** field specifies the rate at which the color blend factor of the particles will change over time, and can be used to control the rate at which the particles' color will change. A positive value for the **Color Blend Factor Speed** field will cause the color of the particles to change over time, while a negative value will cause the color of the particles to change in reverse.

Looking an example, you could set **Color Blend Factor** to **0**, **Color Blend Factor Range** to **0**, and **Color Blend Factor Speed** to **0** to emit particles with constant color, or set **Color Blend Factor** to **1**, **Color Blend Factor Range** to **1**, and **Color Blend Factor Speed** to **0.1** to emit particles that change color rapidly over time.

Color Ramp

The **Color Ramp** field is used to specify a range of colors that particles can take on over their lifetime. The colors are defined using a ramp, which is a gradient that blends two or more colors.

Color Ramp allows you to create particle effects with changing colors. By default, particles will be emitted with a single color, but by adjusting **Color Ramp**, you can set the particles to a fixed range of colors, change color over time, or randomize the color within a range. For example, you could set **Color Ramp** to shades of red and yellow to create a fire effect or shades of blue and white for a snow effect.

Additionally, **Color Ramp** can be used to create different blending modes, such as additive or subtractive blending. The blending mode determines how the colors of the particles are combined with the colors of the background or other particles in the scene.

Blend Mode

Blending is a process that combines the colors of the particles with the colors of the objects behind them on the screen. The **Blend Mode** field determines how the colors of the particles and the background will be combined.

There are several blend modes available in SpriteKit, the choice of which depends on the desired visual effect for the particles. For example, the **Alpha** blend mode will blend the colors of the particles and the background by taking the alpha channel of the particle's color into account. The **Add** blend mode will add the colors of the particles and the background together. The **Multiply** blend mode will multiply the colors of the particles and the background together.

By adjusting the blend mode, you can control how the colors of the particles are blended with the colors of the objects behind them and create a wide range of particle effects.

Field Mask

Field Mask takes an integer value that is used to specify a masking bit-field, and the bit-field defines which properties of the particle are affected by the mask. For example, if the bit-field includes the position bit, the mask will affect the position of the particles. If it includes the color bit, the mask will affect the color of the particles. By setting the value of **Field Mask**, you can control which properties of the particles are affected by the mask. This allows you to create complex and sophisticated particle effects.

For example, you could set **Field Mask** to include the position bit, which would cause the mask to affect the position of the particles, and create particles that follow a specific path or shape. Otherwise, you could set **Field Mask** to include the color bit, which would cause the mask to affect the color of the particles, and create particles with a specific color scheme or pattern.

Custom Shader

The **Custom Shader** field allows you to specify a custom shader to be used to render the particles.

A **shader** is a program that runs on the GPU and is used to define the appearance and behavior of the particles. By using a custom shader, you can create complex and sophisticated particle effects that would be difficult or impossible to achieve using the built-in properties of the particle emitter.

For example, you could use a custom shader to create particles that respond to changes in the environment, such as light or shadows, or create particles that change shape or appearance over time. To use one, you need to write the shader code in a language such as **OpenGL Shading Language** (**GLSL**) and then specify the shader code as the value of the **Custom Shader** field. Once you have specified the custom shader, SpriteKit will use it to render the particles, giving you complete control over the appearance and behavior of the particles. By combining custom shaders with other properties of the particle emitter, such as **Birthrate**, **Lifetime**, and **Position Range**, you can create a wide range of sophisticated and visually stunning particle effects.

Now, we have looked at all of the customization fields for the particle system. I know it can be a bit overwhelming, which is why I defined each field in the file so you can refer to it when you're building your particle system.

Let's use the following values to alter the smoke so it is similar to the smoke that you would see coming from a pipe. I have worked out all the values; you just need to fill them in:

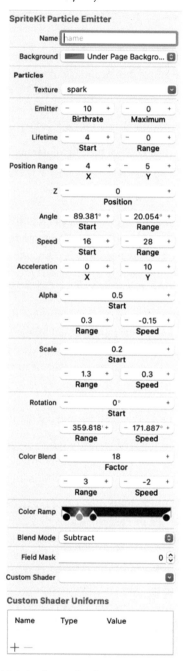

Figure 15.4: Attributes for the pipe smoke animation

Make sure your file has those same values as well before proceeding, which will give you the correct smoke you need to come out of the pipe.

Integrating the Smoke file into a SwiftUI View

Before we get started with this section, a little bit of explanation is needed as to what the SpriteKit framework is all about and how it works. As I mentioned at the beginning of this chapter, SpriteKit is a game development framework that provides a convenient and efficient way to create 2D games for iOS and macOS platforms. Using the SpriteKit framework, you can create different sprites for your animation or game.

A sprite is represented by the SKSpriteNode class, which is a node that can display a textured image. A sprite can be thought of as a single frame of an animation and it can be moved, rotated, and scaled and have physics applied to it. A single sprite can also have multiple textures, allowing it to change appearance. In a game, sprites are used to represent characters, objects, and backgrounds.

You can create a sprite by initializing SKSpriteNode with an image or texture and then adding it to an SKScene. Once added to a scene, a sprite can be manipulated using various properties and methods, such as position, scale, and rotation, and you can also add actions, physics, and gestures to it.

SKView is a UIView subclass that is used to display and interact with SpriteKit scenes. It acts as the container for an SKScene and provides the necessary infrastructure for displaying and animating sprites. An SKScene is a container for all the sprites in a SpriteKit-based project. It is responsible for updating and rendering the sprites, and also provides a way to handle user interactions with the sprites. A scene can also contain other nodes such as labels and shapes in addition to sprites. Each scene can have its own set of sprites, physics, and interactions. You will become more familiar with sprites and nodes as we progress through the projects in this chapter.

Let's do some coding now. Go into ContentView, and we will create a smoke view struct in which we can use our Smoke.sks file. The first thing we need to do is import the SpriteKit framework so that we have access to the classes and methods. Add this line of code at the top of ContentView:

```
import SpriteKit
```

Now, let's create that SmokeView struct I mentioned by adding this under the ContentView struct:

```
struct SmokeView: UIViewRepresentable {
    func makeUIView(context:
      UIViewRepresentableContext<SmokeView>) -> SKView {
        let view = SKView(frame: CGRect(x: 0, y: 0, width:
          400, height: 400))
        view.backgroundColor = .clear
```

```
    let scene = SKScene(size: CGSize(width: 400,
      height: 600))
    ///set the scenes background color to clear because
      we will set the color in the ContentView.
    ///You can also use any other valid color like
      UIColor.lightGray, UIColor.green,
      UIColor.init(red: 1, green: 1, blue: 1, alpha:
      0.5) or any other UIColor initializer.
    scene.backgroundColor = UIColor.clear
    guard let smoke = SKEmitterNode(fileNamed:
      "Smoke.sks") else { return SKView() }
    smoke.position = CGPoint(x: scene.size.width / 2,
      y: scene.size.height / 2)
    // set the blend mode - scale - range
    smoke.particleBlendMode = .screen
    smoke.particleScale = 0.01
    smoke.particleScaleRange = 0.05
    ///add the smoke to the scene
    scene.addChild(smoke)
    view.presentScene(scene)
    return view
  }
  func updateUIView(_ uiView: SKView, context:
    UIViewRepresentableContext<SmokeView>) {
    /// Update the smoke in this function if you need to
  }
}
```

Here's how the SmokeView struct works, line by line. Bear in mind that the SpriteKit framework uses methods and classes we have not used before, so the code may seem unfamiliar at first; as you work through the chapter though, you will understand it very quickly because it is Swift code after all, and is very readable:

- This code starts off by defining a struct named SmokeView, which is used to display the smoke effect that we configured in the Smoke.sks file. The struct conforms to the UIViewRepresentable protocol. This allows the struct to be used as a SwiftUI view.

- Next, we add the `makeUIView` method, which is required by the `UIViewRepresentable` protocol. It creates and returns `SKView`, which is used to display the smoke effect.

- Then, we create an instance of `SKView` with a specified frame (size and position). This frame is used to determine the size of the smoke effect.

- We set the `backgroundColor` property of the `SKView` instance to `clear`. This means that the background of the view will be transparent and will not have a solid color background; this way, any underlying views or graphics can show through.

- We create an instance of `SKScene` with a specified `size` property, which determines the size of the smoke effect, and a background `color` value of `clear` so that the background of the smoke effect will be transparent.

- Next, we create an instance of `SKEmitterNode` using the particle system defined in the `Smoke.sks` file. The guard `let` statement is used to check whether the file was loaded correctly and if not, it returns an empty `SKView`.

- Then, we position the smoke effect in the center of the scene; set the blend mode to `SKBlendMode.screen`, which will make the smoke blend with the background; set the initial scale of the smoke particles, which will make the particles smaller and thinner; and set the range of the scale of the smoke particles.

- The `addChild` method is called on the `scene` instance, passing in the `smoke` node as an argument. This adds the particle emitter node as a child node to the scene, meaning it will be displayed in the scene.

- The `presentScene` method is called on the `view` instance, passing in the `scene` instance as an argument. This sets the scene as the currently displayed scene in the view.

- Then, the `return` keyword returns the `view` instance.

- The `updateUIView` function is called when the view needs to be updated, such as when the view's state changes. In this code, we leave it empty, as it is not needed in our example.

To summarize, the code creates and returns an `SKView` instance that displays a SpriteKit particle emitter as a SwiftUI view. Now, we have a `SmokeView` ready to go and display the smoke.

Let's come into `ContentView` and add a background for the scene, and a smiley image that has a pipe in his mouth. Then, we will call the `SmokeView` we just created to put the smoke into the pipe. To do this, modify `ContentView` like so:

```
struct ContentView: View {
    var body: some View {
        ZStack {
            ///adding the pipe image and setting the size
              and scale to fit on it
            Image("pipe")
                .resizable().frame(width: 350, height: 350)
                .scaledToFit()
            ///calling and positioning the SmokeView
            SmokeView()
                .offset(x: -140, y: 105)
        }.background(Image("background"))
    }
}
```

What we have done here is create a `ZStack` and put our image of the smiley, which is called `pipe`, into the scene. Then, we resized it with `width` and `height` values of `350` points and called our `SmokeView`.

Next, we positioned the smoke so that it is directly above the pipe and appears to come out of the pipe, achieved with the `offset` modifier. Finally, we add the background right onto the `ZStack`, and the project is finished.

If you run the project, you'll see realistic pipe smoke coming out of the pipe:

Figure 15.5: The pipe smoke animation

Now that you know how to create smoke and have a basic foundation of how to get the SpriteKit particle system operational in our SwiftUI project, let's continue and solidify what you know and use the **Smoke** template once again, but vary the values to create a different effect.

Animating coffee steam

In this next project, we'll modify the particle system file to create steam that we can use to create a steaming cup of coffee animation. Well also look at a technique where we can place the steam directly inside the coffee by overlapping images. To get started, create a new project and call it `Coffee`, and then we'll move on to creating the SpriteKit particle file.

Creating the Smoke SpriteKit particle file

To create the file, like before, press *Command + N*, choose the **SpriteKit Particle File** template, and let's pick **Smoke** from the particle template options again (yes, **Smoke** again, but we will make it look like steam this time).

Now, we will modify the various properties to create our animation. Change all the properties in your SKS file to look like the following figure:

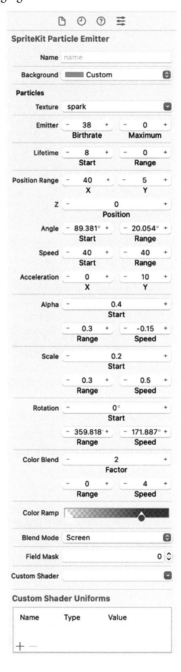

Figure 15.6: The attributes of the coffee steam animation

All of those properties have been explained in the previous project. If you're unclear as to what each one does, revisit that section for a refresher.

Creating the Coffee Steam struct

Next, let's go back into the ContentView file and we'll start assembling the project. In the previous project, we learned how to use the .sks file inside the SwiftUI view, and we're going to do almost the exact same thing here too. The first thing we did was create a separate struct and use the UIViewRepresentable protocol to use the .sks file within a SwiftUI view. So, in this project, underneath ContentView, add the following struct:

```
struct CoffeeSteam: UIViewRepresentable {
    func makeUIView(context:
      UIViewRepresentableContext<CoffeeSteam>) -> SKView {
        let view = SKView(frame: CGRect(x: 0, y: 0, width:
          400, height: 400))
        view.backgroundColor = .clear
        let scene = SKScene(size: CGSize(width: 400,
          height: 600))
        ///set the scenes background color to clear - we
          only want the particles seen
        scene.backgroundColor = UIColor.clear
        guard let steam = SKEmitterNode(fileNamed:
          "CoffeeSteam.sks") else { return SKView() }
        steam.position = CGPoint(x: scene.size.width / 2,
          y: scene.size.height / 2)
        /// set the blend mode - scale - range
        steam.particleBlendMode = .screen
        steam.particleScale = 0.01
        steam.particleScaleRange = 0.05
        ///add the smoke to the scene
        scene.addChild(steam)
        view.presentScene(scene)
        return view
    }
    func updateUIView(_ uiView: SKView, context:
      UIViewRepresentableContext<CoffeeSteam>) {
```

```
    /// Update the steam in this function if you need to
    }
}
```

I explained this code in the previous project, but I will go over it again to help solidify your understanding:

- The code starts off by defining a custom SwiftUI view named `CoffeeSteam`, which is used to display the steam effect that we configured in the `CoffeeSteam.sks` file. The struct conforms to the `UIViewRepresentable` protocol. This allows the struct to be used as a SwiftUI view.

- Next, we add the `makeUIView` method, which is required by the `UIViewRepresentable` protocol. It creates and returns an `SKView`, which is used to display the steam effect.

- We create an instance of `SKView` with a specified frame (size and position). This frame is used to determine the size of the steam effect.

- We set the `backgroundColor` property of the `SKView` instance to `clear`. This means that the background of the view will be transparent and will not have a solid color background; this way, any underlying views or graphics can show through.

- Then, we create an instance of `SKScene` with a specified size, which is used to determine the size of the steam effect, and set the background color to `clear`; this way, the background of the steam effect will be transparent too.

- Next, we create an instance of `SKEmitterNode` using the particle system defined in the `CoffeeSteam.sks` file. The guard `let` statement is used to check whether the file was loaded correctly and if not, it returns an empty `SKView`.

- Then, we position the steam in the center of the scene; set the blend mode of the steam to `SKBlendMode.screen`, which will help to make the steam blend in with the background; set the initial scale of the steam particles to help them resemble a steam effect; then, we set the range of the scale of the smoke particles. (Again, refer to the previous project where I defined each of these property fields in the SKS file).

- The `addChild` method is called on the `scene` instance, passing in the `steam` node as an argument. This adds the particle emitter node as a child node to the scene, meaning it will be displayed in the scene.

- The `presentScene` method is called on the `view` instance, passing in the `scene` instance as an argument. This sets the scene as the currently displayed scene in the view.

- Then, the `return` keyword returns the `view` instance.

- The `updateUIView` function is called when the view needs to be updated, such as when the view's state changes. In this code, we leave it empty, as it is not needed in our example.

So, all that code creates and returns an `SKView` instance that displays a SpriteKit particle emitter as a SwiftUI view. Noticed that I am setting some of the properties in code here? You have the option of setting the properties in the SKS file by adjusting the values there, or you can set them in code here; however, remember that when you set them in code, they override anything you set in the SKS file.

Filling out ContentView

Now, we can just do a little work in `ContentView` and display the steaming cup of coffee. If you haven't already done so, drop the assets into the Asset Catalog that you can find in the `Chapter 15` folder titled `Coffee Steam` on GitHub.

Let's modify `ContentView` to look like the following:

```
struct ContentView: View {
  var body: some View {
    ZStack {
        Image("background")
             .resizable().frame(width: 600, height: 900)
             .aspectRatio(contentMode: .fit)
        ZStack {
            ///adding the whole cup
            Image("cup")
                .resizable().frame(width: 350, height: 300)
                .aspectRatio(contentMode: .fit)
            ///calling and positioning the SmokeView
            CoffeeSteam().offset(x: 15, y: 80)
            ///adding the altered cup
            Image("cup 2")
                .resizable().frame(width: 350, height: 300)
                .aspectRatio(contentMode: .fit)
        }.offset(y: 250)
      }
    }
  }
```

The code declares a `ZStack` that will hold our views. Inside `ZStack`, we add a background image, resize it, and set the aspect ratio on it.

Then, the code declares another `ZStack`, where we placed the first image titled `cup`, resizing it and setting its aspect ratio as well.

Next, we called the `CoffeeSteam` struct and offset it a little bit so it's centered in the middle of the cup.

And after that, we added the cup 2 image. This second image is used to make the steam appear as though it's coming out of the center of the cup. So, what we're essentially doing is sandwiching the animating steam in between two coffee cup images, in which one of the cup images has a little cut out in it; when we place the steam in between these two, we can create a nice steaming effect that appears to be originating from inside the coffee cup.

Finally, I called the offset modifier on the ZStack to position everything on the *y*-axis.

Now, run the project and you will see the steaming effect that's coming right off the surface of the coffee. Also notice how the back of the cup glistens with the steam as it rises, as it would do in a real cup of coffee.

Figure 15.7: A cup of steaming coffee

Now, we have completed two projects using the **Smoke** particle template – creating pipe smoke and coffee steam – and we understand how to manipulate the particles in very different ways. Let's continue and move on to the next project, where we'll use a different particle system: fire.

Animating rocket fire

The SpriteKit Fire particle template generates particles that are typically colored shades of orange, yellow, and red, which give the impression of glowing embers and flames. The particles may also have a slight degree of transparency to mimic the flickering and shifting quality of a real fire. In terms of behavior, the particles are designed to move upward with a certain amount of randomness, representing the movement of hot air and flames.

Rather than creating some simple flames, though, we're going to animate a rocket!

Press *Command + N*, then choose the **SpriteKit Particle File** template. After that, pick the **Fire** particle template and name the file `Rocket`. Xcode will go ahead and create the fire particles that you can see them running in the editor.

Now, let's create the SwiftUI view that will bring this `.sks` file into our SwiftUI project.

Adding FireView

To create the view, press *Command + N* and make a `SwiftUIView` file. Then, call it `FireView`. Then, import SpriteKit, and add the following code at the top of the file:

```
struct FireView: UIViewRepresentable {
    func makeUIView(context:
      UIViewRepresentableContext<FireView>) -> SKView {
        let view = SKView(frame: CGRect(x: 0, y: 0, width:
          400, height: 400))
        view.backgroundColor = .clear
        scene.backgroundColor = UIColor.clear
        guard let fire = SKEmitterNode(fileNamed:
          "Fire.sks") else { return SKView() }
        fire.position = CGPoint(x: scene.size.width / 2, y:
          scene.size.height / 2)
        ///use the particlePositionRange property to
          constrain the fire particles so they are not so
          wide and can fit under the rockets exhaust
        fire.particlePositionRange = CGVector(dx: 5, dy: 0)
        ///add the fire to the scene
        scene.addChild(fire)
        view.presentScene(scene)
        return view
    }
```

```
func updateUIView(_ uiView: SKView, context:
  UIViewRepresentableContext<FireView>) {
    /// Update the fire in this function if you need to
}
}
```

I'm not going to go over this code because we have done this already, but you can refer back to the previous SpriteKit projects for all the explanations, and how we use the `UIViewRepresentable` protocol.

If you run a code in the previews, you'll see that it works great and the fire is the correct dimensions to fit under the rocket. However, notice that the fire is upside down. Let's look at how we can fix this so it looks like a proper thrust to place underneath a rocket.

Adding RocketView

Let's now create one more view that we can use to put together the rocket and the fire, then rotate the fire around so it's properly oriented under the rocket. Press *Command + N*, create a new SwiftUI View file, and call it `RocketView`. Then, add the following code inside the struct:

```
struct RocketView: View {
    @State private var rocketAndFireOffset: CGFloat = 0
    var body: some View {
        ZStack {
            FireView().rotationEffect(Angle(degrees:
              180.0)).offset(y: 60)
                ///move the fire upwards by changing y
                  offset
                .offset(x: 0, y: -rocketAndFireOffset)
                /// position the fire at the bottom
                  center of the screen
                .position(x:
                  UIScreen.main.bounds.width/2, y:
                  UIScreen.main.bounds.height)
            Image("rocket")
                .resizable().aspectRatio(contentMode:
                  .fit).frame(width: 100, height: 200)
                ///move the rocket upwards by changing
                  y offset
                .offset(x: 0, y: -rocketAndFireOffset)
```

```
                ///position the rocket at the bottom
                   center of the screen
                .position(x:
                   UIScreen.main.bounds.width/2, y:
                   UIScreen.main.bounds.height)
            ///rotate the fire and offset it so its
               under the bottom of the rocket
        } .animation(Animation.linear(duration:
          8).repeatForever(autoreverses: false),value:
          rocketAndFireOffset) // increase the duration
        of the animation
            .onAppear {
               rocketAndFireOffset =
                  UIScreen.main.bounds.height * 1.3 //
                  move the rocket off the top of the
                  screen, by increasing the offset
            }
        }
    }
```

First, we create a `rocketAndFire` offset variable that we can use to move both the rocket and the fire upward on the screen.

Then, inside the `ZStack`, we take `FireView` and rotate it 180°, and offset it on the *y*-axis, which makes the fire extend further out from the rocket, which we will add shortly. Then, we animate the fire upward by changing the `y-offset`, and positioning the fire in the center of the screen on the *x*- and *y*-axes using the `UIScreen` property.

Then, we can add the `rocket` image, resize it, and animate it upward by offsetting the *y*-axis using the `rocketAndFire` variable. Next, we just need to position the rocket in the center of the screen using the `UIScreen` property.

Finally, we can add the animation to the closing brace of the `ZStack`, which will act on both `FireView` and the rocket image. Let's give it a duration of 8 seconds, and make it repeat forever with no auto-reverse.

Now, we can launch the rocket in the `onAppear` method by changing the value of the `rocketAndFire` property. When the view appears, the rocket will lift off and continue off the top of the screen and come back up from the bottom and keep flying.

All we have to do now is add the background!

Putting things together inside ContentView

Inside `ContentView`, we need very little code to get our rocket into space:

```
struct ContentView: View {
    var body: some View {
        ZStack {
            ///add the RocketView to the scene
            RocketView()
        }.background(Image("background")
            .resizable()
            .scaledToFill().edgesIgnoringSafeArea(.all))
    }
}
```

And that's it. Inside the `ZStack`, we added `RocketView()` to the scene, and then we added the background image right onto `ZStack`.

Check it out in the previews and you'll see that we now have a rocket flying in space:

Figure 15.8: Our rocket blasting off

By leveraging the power of particle systems, we were able to create a realistic and dynamic visual effect that brings our rocket to life. We explored the various parameters and properties of the emitter to fine-tune the look and feel of the thrust and learned how to integrate it with our SwiftUI view.

Looking at another example, we're going to return to another effect that we've already seen before – snow – but modify it so it creates a blizzard-like effect.

Animating a blizzard

In this next project, we're going to create a blizzard scene, and add a wind effect to make the snow blow from different directions. We will also use that wind to make the branches of a tree blow as well, by combining images and animating them. We created a snow scene in the breathing flower project in *Chapter 6*, but this time, we're going to create this snow scene using a particle file, which gives us more options for making and controlling the snow.

Let's start by creating a new project and calling it Snow. Then, we will get right to work creating the SKS file that we need for the snow – this time, though, we'll create two files.

Creating two Snow SpriteKit particle files

For this project, we will create two SpriteKit files – both will be from the **Snow** template, but we will use different values so the snow blows from different directions and at different velocities.

To create the first file, press *Command + N*, choose the **SpriteKit Particle File** template, choose **Snow** from the particle options, and save it as Snow. Now, let's configure the particle properties so we can create a nice heavy snowfall. Use the same values from the following figure:

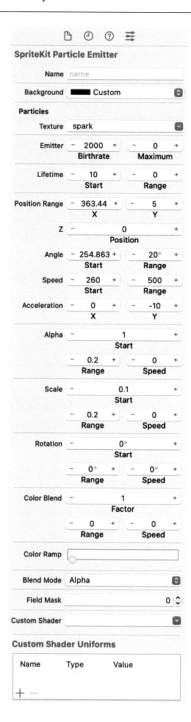

Figure 15.9: The attributes for the Snow file

And that creates the desired snowfall we are going for. To help you in designing your unique snowfall, the following is a guide for making adjustments:

- **Particle Lifetime**: Set the lifetime to a relatively long time so that the particles stay on the screen for a while

- **Particle Birthrate**: Increase the birthrate to generate more particles per second, which will create a denser snowfall effect

- **Particle Size**: Increase the size of the particles to make them appear larger and more prominent on the screen

- **Particle Speed**: Decrease the speed of the particles to make them fall slower and more gently

- **Particle Color**: Change the color of the particles to white or light blue to make them look more like snowflakes

- **Emitter Shape**: Change the emitter shape to a rectangle or a line to make the snowfall appear more natural

- **Emitter Position**: Adjust the emitter's position to start the snowfall from the top of the screen

If you look at that snow in the editor, you can see that it has a pretty heavy effect, just what we need for our scene. Now, let's create the second file with different values for the snow; we'll then combine both of these SKS files into one SwiftUI view that we can use to create a nice blizzard effect.

Follow the same steps to create a second file, but this time, call it `Blustery`. Now, let's alter the attributes to the following values:

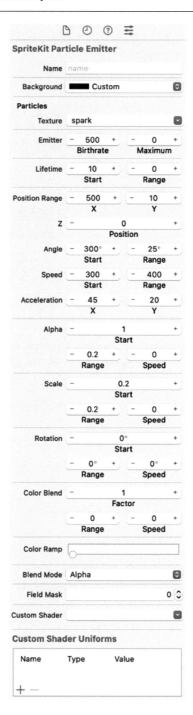

Figure 15.10: The attributes for the Blustery file

This new file has different **Birthrate**, **Angle**, and **Acceleration** values to make the snow blow from different directions, as well as lift the snow up a little bit as if being carried by the wind. When we combine the two SKS files together, which will create a nice blizzard effect.

So, let's do that now; we'll need to create a struct in which you can put these two files together.

Creating a view that combines the two SKS files

Working inside the ContentView file, first, add the SpriteKit import. Then, create a new struct called SnowView after the ContentView struct. (You could create separate files and keep things neat in the project navigator, but I'm just going to put the rest of the code into the ContentView file for this project.)

With SnowView created, add the following code within it:

```
struct SnowView: UIViewRepresentable {
  func makeUIView(context:
    UIViewRepresentableContext<SnowView>) -> SKView {
      let view = SKView(frame: CGRect(x: 0, y: 0, width:
        400, height: 400))
      view.backgroundColor = .clear
      let scene = SKScene(size: CGSize(width: 500,
        height: 800))
      scene.backgroundColor = UIColor.clear
      guard let snow = SKEmitterNode(fileNamed:
        "Snow.sks") else { return SKView() }
      guard let blustery = SKEmitterNode(fileNamed:
        "Blustery.sks") else { return SKView() }
      //snow sks file
      snow.position = CGPoint(x: scene.size.width / 2, y:
        scene.size.height / 2)
      ///use the particlePositionRange property to spread
        the snow particles on the screen for the x and y
        axis
      snow.particlePositionRange = CGVector(dx: 500, dy:
        900)
      //blustery sks file
      blustery.position = CGPoint(x: scene.size.width / 2,
        y: scene.size.height / 2)
```

```
            ///use the particlePositionRange property to spread
               the snow particles on the screen for the x and y
               axis
            blustery.particlePositionRange = CGVector(dx: 500,
               dy: 900)
            ///add the snow to the scene
            scene.addChild(snow)
            scene.addChild(blustery)
            view.presentScene(scene)
            return view
        }
        func updateUIView(_ uiView: SKView, context:
          UIViewRepresentableContext<SnowView>) {
            /// Update the snow in this function if you need to
        }
    }
```

The code positions both nodes, the snow node and the blustery node, using the position property, and then sets the particlePositionRange property on both as well. particlePositionRange is the range of allowed random values for a particle's position. Finally, as we've done with our other particle files, we add them to the scene using the addChild function and passing in the view that we want to add to the scene.

Now, we can call this struct in ContentView to check out the blizzard, and in fact, let's also add a background snow scene too:

```
struct ContentView: View {
    var body: some View {
        ZStack {
            Image("background")
                .resizable().frame(width: 600, height: 900)
                .aspectRatio(contentMode: .fit)
            SnowView()
        }
    }
}
```

Now, run the previews and check out the blizzard effect:

Figure 15.11: Our blizzard scene

Now, let's continue with the project and add another animation to it. For this one, we want to make the branches of the tree blow in the wind.

Animating the tree branches

To animate the tree branches, we're going to wrap all the code up into several `ZStack`. Then, we will use one image of a snowy branch, replicate it many times with a `ForEach` loop, place the branch images over a portion of the tree, and put rotation animations on each of the axes of those images. We will also randomize the animation so that it doesn't follow a set pattern.

Let's start by creating the struct that we need to hold these views:

```
struct Branches: View {
  var body: some View {
```

```
        }
    }
```

Next, let's add the variables we need to keep track of the animations and set some initial values:

```
@State private var anglesX = [Double](repeating: 0,
   count: 25)
 @State private var anglesY = [Double](repeating: 0,
    count: 25)
 @State private var anglesZ = [Double](repeating: 0,
    count: 25)
 @State private var positions = [CGPoint](repeating:
    .zero, count: 25)
 @State private var durations = [Double](repeating: 0,
    count: 25)
```

This code defines five state properties in a SwiftUI view.

The anglesX, anglesY, and anglesZ properties are arrays of Double values, each with a length of 25. These arrays are used to store the rotation angles around the *x-*, *y-*, and *z*-axes, respectively. The repeating: parameter is used to initialize all the values in each array to 0.

The positions property is an array of CGPoint values, also with a length of 25. This array is used to store the positions of the views. The repeating: parameter is used to initialize all the values in the array to the zero point, (0, 0).

The durations property is an array of Double values, again with a length of 25. This array is used to store the durations of the animations associated with each view. The repeating: parameter is used to initialize all the values in the array to 0.

As we have seen, the @State property wrapper is used to make each of these arrays a mutable state property of the view. This means that whenever any of the arrays are modified, SwiftUI will automatically re-render the view to reflect the changes.

Next, let's move into the body property and add a ZStack that contains the image we want to manipulate and reproduce, as well as the animation we're going to put on it:

```
ZStack {
    ForEach(0..<8) { index in
        Image("branch")
            .resizable()
            .aspectRatio(contentMode: .fit)
```

```
                .rotationEffect(Angle(degrees: anglesX[index]))
                .rotationEffect(Angle(degrees: anglesY[index]),
                  anchor: .center)
                .rotationEffect(Angle(degrees: anglesZ[index]),
                  anchor: .center)
                .position(positions[index])
                .frame(width: 200, height: 700)
                .animation(
                    Animation.easeInOut(duration:
                      durations[index])
                        .repeatForever(autoreverses: true),
                          value: anglesX)
                .onAppear {
                    anglesX[index] = Double.random(in: 2...4)
                    anglesY[index] = Double.random(in: 2...3)
                    anglesZ[index] = Double.random(in: 1...3)
                    positions[index] = CGPoint(x:
                      CGFloat.random(in: 0...10), y:
                      CGFloat.random(in: 0...5))
                    durations[index] = Double.random(in: 3...5)
                }
        }
    }
  } .offset(x: 50, y: 200)
```

Here's what we're doing in here. We start off with a ZStack so we can stack our views on top of each other. Next is a ForEach loop, which iterates over a range of integers from 0 to 7; the index parameter is used to access the current iteration value in the loop.

Then, we add the branch image and the following modifiers:

- The resizable modifier resizes the image.

- The rotationEffect(_:) modifier is used to rotate the image around the *x*-, *y*-, and *z*-axes. The angle of rotation is specified by the corresponding value in the anglesX, anglesY, and anglesZ arrays, respectively. The anchor parameter is used to specify the center of rotation. In this case, .center is used for both the anglesY and anglesZ rotations, so the image is rotated around its center point.

- The position(_:) modifier is used to position the image on the screen. The positions array stores the position for each image instance based on its index.

- The `frame(width:height:)` modifier sets the size of the image.

- The `animation(_:, value:)` modifier is used to animate the rotation of the image. The duration of the animation is based on the value stored in the `durations` array, while the `value` parameter specifies that the animation should be re-evaluated whenever the `anglesX` array changes.

- The `onAppear` modifier is used to randomly generate new values for the `anglesX`, `anglesY`, `anglesZ` positions, and `durations` arrays whenever an image appears on the screen.

- Finally, the `offset` modifier applies an offset of 50 points on the *x*-axis and 200 points on the *y*-axis to the entire `ZStack`, which positions the tree branches in the middle-right portion of the tree.

To summarize, what we're doing is creating eight image views of snow-covered branches, each with a different rotation, position, duration, and animation. The views are stacked on top of each other within `ZStack` and have an offset applied to place them in the tree.

Now, I'd like to replicate the `ZStack` several more times so we can cover the whole tree with snowy branches, rather than covering only a portion of the tree. So, we'll make four more ZStacks but with slightly different values to make the wind-blowing effect seem more random and natural:

```
ZStack {
    ForEach(0..<10) { index in
        Image("branch")
            .resizable()
            .aspectRatio(contentMode: .fit)
            .rotationEffect(Angle(degrees: anglesX[index]))
            .rotationEffect(Angle(degrees: anglesY[index]),
              anchor: .center)
            .rotationEffect(Angle(degrees: anglesZ[index]),
              anchor: .center)
    .position(positions[index])
            .frame(width: 200, height: 700)
            .offset(x: 50, y: 200)
            .animation(
                Animation.easeInOut(duration:
                  durations[index])
                    .repeatForever(autoreverses:
                      true), value: anglesY)
            .onAppear {
```

```
                anglesX[index] = Double.random(in: 3...4)
                anglesY[index] = Double.random(in: 2...5)
                anglesZ[index] = Double.random(in: 1...4)
                positions[index] = CGPoint(x:
                    CGFloat.random(in: 0...10), y:
                    CGFloat.random(in: 0...14))
                durations[index] = Double.random(in: 2...6)
            }
        }
    }.offset(x: -80, y: -156)



    ZStack {
        ForEach(0..<15) { index in
            Image("branch")
                .resizable()
                .aspectRatio(contentMode: .fit)
                .rotationEffect(Angle(degrees: anglesX[index]))
                .rotationEffect(Angle(degrees: anglesY[index]),
                    anchor: .center)
                .rotationEffect(Angle(degrees: anglesZ[index]),
                    anchor: .center)
                .position(positions[index])
                .frame(width: 200, height: 700)
                .offset(x: 50, y: 200)
                .animation(
                    Animation.easeInOut(duration:
                        durations[index])
                            .repeatForever(autoreverses: true)
                    ,value: anglesZ)
                .onAppear {
                    anglesX[index] = Double.random(in: 1...3)
                    anglesY[index] = Double.random(in: 2...4)
                    anglesZ[index] = Double.random(in: 3...6)
                    positions[index] = CGPoint(x:
                        CGFloat.random(in: 0...10), y:
```

```
                        CGFloat.random(in: 0...8))
                durations[index] = Double.random(in: 4...6)
            }
        }
    }
}.offset(x: -120, y: 0)


    ZStack {
      ForEach(0..<7) { index in
        Image("branch")
          .resizable()
          .aspectRatio(contentMode: .fit)
          .rotationEffect(Angle(degrees: anglesX[index]))
          .rotationEffect(Angle(degrees: anglesY[index]),
            anchor: .center)
          .rotationEffect(Angle(degrees: anglesZ[index]),
            anchor: .center)
          .position(positions[index])
          .frame(width: 200, height: 700)
          .offset(x: 50, y: 200)
          .animation(
              Animation.easeInOut(duration:
                durations[index])
                  .repeatForever(autoreverses: true)
              ,value: anglesX)
          .onAppear {
              anglesX[index] = Double.random(in: 1...3)
              anglesY[index] = Double.random(in: 2...3)
              anglesZ[index] = Double.random(in: 3...5)
              positions[index] = CGPoint(x:
                CGFloat.random(in: 0...10), y:
                CGFloat.random(in: 0...12))
              durations[index] = Double.random(in: 4...6)
          }
        }
      }
    }.offset(x: -100, y: 160)
```

```
ZStack {
  ForEach(0..<7) { index in
    Image("branch")
        .resizable()
        .aspectRatio(contentMode: .fit)
        .rotationEffect(Angle(degrees: anglesX[index]))
        .rotationEffect(Angle(degrees: anglesY[index]),
          anchor: .center)
        .rotationEffect(Angle(degrees: anglesZ[index]),
          anchor: .center)
        .position(positions[index])
        .frame(width: 180, height: 700)
        .offset(x: 50, y: 200)
        .animation(
            Animation.easeInOut(duration:
              durations[index])
                .repeatForever(autoreverses: true)
            ,value: anglesY)
        .onAppear {
            anglesX[index] = Double.random(in: 0...2)
            anglesY[index] = Double.random(in: 0...3)
            anglesZ[index] = Double.random(in: 0...1)
            positions[index] = CGPoint(x:
              CGFloat.random(in: 0...10), y:
              CGFloat.random(in: 0...12))
            durations[index] = Double.random(in: 3...6)
        }
  }
}.offset(x: 10, y: 100)
```

All of these ZStack do essentially the same thing, except that the code uses different values. For example, in the ForEach loop, we're using a different range of values, and we're also changing the random values for the *x*-, *y*-, and *z*-axes, as well as the position and duration values. Also, each ZStack has its own onAppear modifier, so it could randomly move its set of branches at a different pace and on a different axis.

Now, let's call this struct inside `ContentView`. We will call it just before the `SnowView` call; this way, the snow will appear on top of the tree images:

```
struct ContentView: View {
    var body: some View {
        ZStack {
            Image("background")
                .resizable().frame(width: 600, height: 900)
                .aspectRatio(contentMode: .fit)
            Branches()
            SnowView()
        }
    }
}
```

Now, run the code and check out the really cool animation of the tree branches blowing in the wind as the snow falls.

Play around with all the values that we've used in the various parameters and customize them to your liking. Maybe you want fewer branches for a thinner-looking tree, maybe you want the wind to blow much stronger, or maybe you want to animate all the trees in the background image... you can change all the settings to do just that.

Let's continue our exploration of some interesting animations. Up next, we will look at the rain particle system.

Animating rain

In our next project, let's make it rain. We're going to create a realistic effect by creating rain from the **Rain** particle template and making it bounce off the ground as you would see in a rainstorm. We'll also create a puddle that will subtly grow and shrink, appearing to react to the falling rain, and it will also look like water, as we will add some blending options to it to give it a transparent look for a spectacular effect that even shows some of the ground underneath it.

Creating the Rain SpriteKit particle file

Let's get started. You know how to do this now – create an SKS file, choose **Rain** from the particle template list, and name the file `Rain` too. Now, configure the file to have the following attributes:

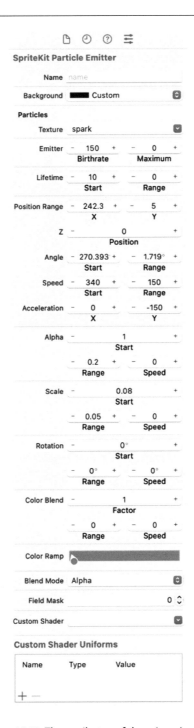

Figure 15.12: The attributes of the rain animation

Using the **Rain** particle template gives us rain right out of the box, but with some slight adjustments to the **Birthrate** and **Lifetime** options, we can alter how much of a rainstorm we want.

Let's now create another new file, this time, a SwiftUI file, which we will use to bring the rain effects into a SwiftUI view.

Creating the raindrops

To create the SwiftUI file, press *Command + N* and call this file `DropView`. The code we will add to this file will be responsible for creating the collision effect between a raindrop and the ground. We'll also alter the opacity and the blur to really help it blend into the scene.

Let's now add the following code inside the `DropView` struct:

```
struct DropView: View {
    @State private var dropScale: CGFloat = 0.1
    @State private var xOffsets = (0..<300).map { _ in
        CGFloat.random(in: -150...UIScreen.main.bounds.width)}
    @State private var yOffsets = (0..<240).map { _ in
        CGFloat.random(in: UIScreen.main.bounds.height/5...
        UIScreen.main.bounds.height)}
    @State private var durations = (0..<150).map { _ in
        Double.random(in: 0.3...1.0)}
    var body: some View {
        //Color.clear.edgesIgnoringSafeArea(.all)
            ForEach(0..<150) { index in
                Circle()
                    .fill(Color.white)
                        .opacity(0.6)
                     .blur(radius: 3)
                    .frame(width: 15, height: 15)
                    .scaleEffect(dropScale)
                    .rotation3DEffect(Angle(degrees: 80.0),
                      axis: (x: 1, y: 0, z: 0))
                    .offset(x: xOffsets[index] - 140, y:
                      yOffsets[index])
                    .animation(Animation.easeInOut(duration:
                      durations[index]).repeatForever
```

```
            (autoreverses: true), value: dropScale)
        .onAppear {
            dropScale = 0.8
        }
    }
  }
}
```

There's a lot going on here, so let's break it down line by line.

There are four `State` variables we need and each one has a specific task:

- The first variable is of the `CGFloat` type and gets an initial value of `0.1`. This variable is used to control the scale of the drops.

- The next two variables create arrays of `CGFloat` values, stored in the `xOffsets` and `yOffsets` state variables. The `map` method is used to generate random `CGFloat` values and the `CGFloat.random(in:)` method is used to generate a random `CGFloat` value within a given range. In short, these variables are used to set a random *x*- and *y*-coordinate position for each drop.

- The final variable is the `durations` variable, which randomizes the duration of the animation.

Let's take a closer look at the `map` method since it is being used by three of our properties. The `map` method is a higher-order function in Swift that transforms an array of values into a new array of different values. It takes a closure expression as an argument, which is executed for each element in the original array and returns a new value for that element. The resulting array is then the combination of all of these new values.

In the code, the `map` method is being used to transform the range of integers between 0 and <300 into an array of `CGFloat` values, by using the `CGFloat.random(in:)` method to generate a random value for each element in the range. The closure expression passed to the `map` method takes a single argument, `_`, which is a placeholder for the current element of the range, and returns a new `CGFloat` value, generated by `CGFloat.random(in: -150...UIScreen.main.bounds.width)`. The `map` method combines all of these new values into a single array, which is then assigned to the `xOffsets` variable.

The `map` method is an important and versatile function in Swift, as it allows you to easily transform arrays and sequences of values into new arrays and sequences. Additionally, the `map` method is often used in combination with other functional programming techniques such as filter and reduce, to perform complex operations on arrays and sequences in a more efficient and maintainable way.

Now, let's move into the `body` property and look at what the code is doing there.

We use a `ForEach` loop to iterate through a range from 0 and <150, and create a `Circle` view with each iteration – the circle will be the raindrop. Then, we set the `fill` color of the `Circle` view to `white`, the `width` and `height` values to `15`, and apply a `scaleEffect` with the value determined by the `dropScale` variable.

Next, we apply `rotation3DEffect` to the `Circle` view, with an angle of 80 degrees on the *x*-axis; we want to rotate the drop so that it appears more like a raindrop colliding with the ground. Following that, we set its offset using the `xOffsets` and `yOffsets` variables with a value determined by the index.

We then add the animation, setting the duration to be determined by the `index` constant, and repeating the animation with `autoreverse` set to `true` to create the realistic collision of the raindrop with the ground.

Finally, in the `onAppear` modifier, we give the `DropScale` variable a value of `0.8`.

Running that in the previews will be a little difficult to see because of the white background, but let's keep going and we'll check out the results shortly.

Let's now create a new view that will make a puddle of water that we can animate and add to the scene.

Creating the puddle

Let's now add a puddle to our scene, which we'll do in a new SwiftUI View file called `PuddleView`. I'm going to add all the code for this view and then we'll review how it works:

```
struct PuddleView: View {
  @State private var scaleX: CGFloat = 0.5
  @State private var scaleY: CGFloat = 0.5
  var body: some View {
    ZStack {
      Capsule()
        .fill(LinearGradient(gradient: Gradient(colors:
          [.white,  .black,.gray,  .white,.black]),
          startPoint: .topLeading, endPoint:
          .bottomTrailing))
        .opacity(0.5)
        .blur(radius: 5)
        .frame(width: 600, height: 500)
        .scaleEffect(x: scaleX, y: scaleY, anchor:
      .center)
```

```
        .animation(Animation.easeInOut(duration:
            8.0).repeatForever(autoreverses: true),value:
            scaleX)
        //creates the ripple
            .overlay(
                Capsule()
                    .stroke(Color.gray, lineWidth: 5)
                    .opacity(0.5 )
                    .frame(width: 350, height: 200)
                    .offset(x: 0, y: -15)
                    .scaleEffect(x: scaleX + 0.03, y: scaleY
                        + 0.03, anchor: .center)
                    .animation(Animation.easeInOut(duration:
                        8.0).repeatForever(autoreverses: true),
                        value: scaleY)
                    .onAppear {
                        scaleX = 0.54
                        scaleY = 0.6
                    }).rotation3DEffect(Angle(degrees: 81.0),
                        axis: (x: 1, y: 0, z: 0))

    } .offset(x: -50, y: 300)
        .onAppear {
            scaleX = 0.55
            scaleY = 0.6

        }
    }
}
```

This code defines a struct called PuddleView that has two properties, scaleX and scaleY, which are both CGFloat values. The body property of the struct is defined as follows:

- A ZStack view is created, which arranges views on top of each other.

- Inside ZStack, a Capsule view is created, which will be the shape of a puddle. The Capsule view is filled with a LinearGradient of colors and is then modified with several modifiers:

  - The opacity modifier is set to 0.5, making it partially transparent.

- The blur modifier is set with a radius of 5 pixels.

- The frame modifier sets the width property to 600 pixels and height to 500 pixels.

- The scaleEffect modifier is set with the *x* and *y* scale values set to scaleX and scaleY, respectively. The anchor parameter is set to .center, indicating that the scaling should be the center of the capsule.

- The animation modifier has a scaleX value, with an easeInOut timing function and a duration value of 8 seconds, and is set to repeat forever with autoreverses.

- Then, .overlay() is used to create a new Capsule view that is placed on top of the previous one. This new Capsule view is also modified with several modifiers:

  - The stroke modifier adds a gray stroke with a line width of 5 pixels.

  - The opacity modifier is set to 0.5, making it partially transparent.

  - The frame modifier sets the width property to 350 pixels and height to 200 pixels.

  - The offset modifier shifts the capsule slightly upward.

  - The scaleEffect modifier sets the *x* and *y* scale values, with scaleX set to + 0.03 and scaleY to + 0.03, respectively. The anchor parameter is set to .center, indicating that the scaling should be centered on the capsule.

  - The animation modifier has a scaleY value, with an easeInOut timing function and a duration value of 8 seconds, and is set to repeat forever with autoreverses.

  - The onAppear modifier sets the initial value of scaleX and scaleY to 0.54 and 0.6, respectively.

  - The rotation3DEffect modifiers set an angle of 81 degrees on the *x*-axis.

- The ZStack view is then modified with .offset(x: -50, y: 300) and .onAppear { scaleX = 0.55; scaleY = 0.6 }. This shifts the group view 50 pixels to the left and 300 pixels downward. This code block is executed when the view appears and sets the initial values of scaleX and scaleY to 0.55 and 0.6, respectively.

In summary, this code creates a view that looks like a puddle of water by using a gradient fill that's partially transparent and blurred, and with a ripple effect added. The ripple effect is created by applying a scale effect to the second capsule view and animating the scaleX and scaleY properties so that it appears to be moving. The ripple effect is also rotated on the *x*-axis to make it more interesting.

Putting it all together

With `PuddleView` done, let's just fill out `ContentView` and check out the animation. Add the following code to modify `ContentView`:

```
import SpriteKit
import SwiftUI
struct ContentView: View {
    var body: some View {
        ZStack {
            Image("street")
                .resizable()
                .scaledToFill()
            PuddleView()//.blendMode(.hardLight)
            RainView()
            DropView()
            RainView()
        }.edgesIgnoringSafeArea(.all)
    }
}
```

In `ContentView`, we added an image of a street, resized and scaled it, then called `PuddleView`. In `PuddleView`, `blendMode` is set to `hardLight`. Play around with the blend mode options for different looks and effects, but I think the hard light gives the best water effect so far, creating a glass-like look that is perfect for making a puddle of water where you can see some of the ground underneath.

Next, I called `RainView` to add the rain, then `DropView` to add the collision effect of the raindrops hitting the ground, and then `Rainview` again just to add a little more rain to the mix. This is the result:

Figure 15.13: The raindrops

This creates a nice effect of raindrops colliding with the ground and even with the puddle.

Let's continue and take a look at the **Magic** particle template and we will see how we can use an image to make the particles.

Animating a magic wand

In this project, we're going to use the **Magic** particle system, and we will display that magic from the tip of a wand. You will be able to move the wand around the screen with your finger, and as it moves, magic will emanate from its tip. We will also have a cemetery background including a gravestone, and when you tap on the gravestone, a skeleton will rise up from it.

So, let's get started with our spooky animation. Create a new project and call this one Magic. Next, add the resources for this project by dragging them from the Chapter 15 | Magic folder on GitHub into the Asset Catalog. Then, we can make our particle file.

Creating the magic SpriteKit particle file

As we've done before, create a new SpriteKit particle file, but select the **Magic** particle template, and simply call the file Magic. Now, let's do something a little different this time – using the **Texture** field in the **Attributes** panel, select the **star** image that you placed into the Asset Catalog. We're going to make the particle system based on that image, so all the particles will be stars. Next, change the rest of the fields so the values look like the following:

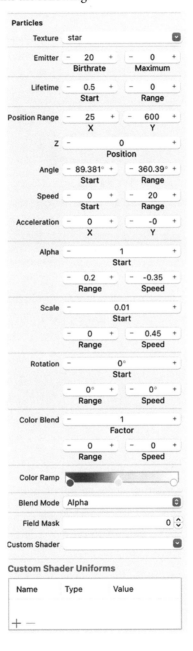

Figure 15.14: The attributes of the magic animation

Notice the **Color Ramp** field. It has three colors selected. If you would like to select a color for the **Color Ramp** field, simply click anywhere along the color selector, and then a pop-up color box will come up allowing you to choose a color. I've chosen three colors here: red will be the center of the animation, green will surround it, and the third color is yellow, which will be the outer part of the magic animation.

Next, we want to make this `Magic.sks` file available as a SwiftUI view. So, let's create a new Swift file, and call it `MagicView`. Then, add the following code to the file:

```
import SwiftUI
import SpriteKit
struct MagicView: UIViewRepresentable {
    func makeUIView(context:
      UIViewRepresentableContext<MagicView>) -> SKView {
        let view = SKView(frame: CGRect(x: 0, y: 0, width:
          400, height: 400))
        view.backgroundColor = .clear
        let scene = MagicScene(size: CGSize(width: 900,
          height: 600))
        scene.backgroundColor = UIColor.clear
        scene.scaleMode = .aspectFill
        view.presentScene(scene)
        return view
    }
    func updateUIView(_ uiView: SKView, context:
      UIViewRepresentableContext<MagicView>) {
    }
}
```

We've worked with this code in previous projects, so we're familiar with it by now.

The code defines a struct called `MagicView`, which conforms to the `UIViewRepresentable` protocol in SwiftUI. The `makeUIView` function creates an instance of an `SKView` with a given frame size and sets its background color to `clear`.

It then creates an instance of `MagicScene`, specifying its size, setting its background color to `clear`, and scaling it to `aspectFill`. Finally, the created scene is presented on `SKView`, and the `SKView` instance is returned.

The `updateUIView` function does not perform any actions for us, as we don't need to update anything, but it is a required method for the `UIViewRepresentable` protocol.

Now, the code will give us an error because of this line: `let scene = MagicScene(size: CGSize(width: 900, height: 600))`. This is because we're creating a scene and setting it to the `MagicScene` class, but we haven't created a `MagicScene` class yet.

So, let's do that now. Let's create the `MagicScene` class, which will contain the properties and functions we need to manipulate the magic coming from the wand, as well as making the skeleton rise up from the ground. Create a new Swift file and call this `Magic`. I'm going to place all of the code here and then I'll explain how it works:

```
import Foundation
import SwiftUI
import SpriteKit
class MagicScene: SKScene {
  var magic: SKEmitterNode!
  var wand: SKSpriteNode!
  override func touchesMoved(_ touches: Set<UITouch>,
    with event: UIEvent?) {
      let touch = touches.first!
      let touchLocation = touch.location(in: self)
      wand.position = CGPoint(x: touchLocation.x - 30, y:
        touchLocation.y + wand.frame.size.height / 2 - 20)
      ///make the skeleton appear
      if touchLocation.x < frame.size.width * 0.55 &&
        touchLocation.y < frame.size.height * 0.12 {
          let skeleton = SKSpriteNode(imageNamed:
            "skeleton")
          skeleton.position = CGPoint(x: frame.size.width /
            2 - 80, y: 175)
          skeleton.size = CGSize(width: skeleton.size.width
            / 2, height: skeleton.size.height / 2)
          addChild(skeleton)
          let moveAction = SKAction.move(to: CGPoint(x:
            frame.size.width / 2 - 50, y: frame.size.height
            / 2), duration: 2.0)
          skeleton.run(moveAction)
      }
      wand.zPosition = 2
      let trail = SKEmitterNode(fileNamed: "Magic.sks")!
```

```
        trail.particlePositionRange = CGVector(dx: 5, dy: 5)
        trail.particleSpeed = 50
        trail.position = CGPoint(x: wand.position.x - 40, y:
          wand.position.y + wand.frame.size.height / 2 +
          trail.particlePositionRange.dy)
        addChild(trail)
        let fadeAway = SKAction.fadeOut(withDuration: 1.2)
        trail.run(fadeAway) {
            trail.removeFromParent()
        }
    }
    override func didMove(to view: SKView) {
        let stone = SKSpriteNode(imageNamed: "stone")
        stone.position = CGPoint(x: frame.size.width / 2.3,
          y: frame.size.height / 2 - 150)
        stone.size = CGSize(width: 120, height: 175)
        stone.zRotation = CGFloat(Double.pi / 20)
        stone.zPosition = 2
          addChild(stone)
        guard let magic = SKEmitterNode(fileNamed:
          "Magic.sks") else { return }
        magic.particlePositionRange = CGVector(dx: 5, dy: 5)
        magic.particleSpeed = 50
        addChild(magic)
        self.magic = magic
        wand = SKSpriteNode(imageNamed: "wand")
        wand.position = CGPoint(x: frame.size.width / 2, y:
          frame.size.height / 3)
        wand.size = CGSize(width: 80, height: 180)
        addChild(wand)
    }
}
```

Okay, let's break down the code and see what it's doing here.

Inside the `MagicScene` class, there are two instance variables declared:

- `magic` is an instance of `SKEmitterNode`, which is a class from SpriteKit that represents an emitter that can create particles.

- `wand` is an instance of `SKSpriteNode`, which is a class from SpriteKit that represents a textured rectangle.

The `MagicScene` class overrides two methods from `SKScene`:

- The `touchesMoved(_:with:)` method is called when the user moves their finger across the screen. Inside this method, the position of the wand sprite is updated to follow the user's touch location. If the touch location is in a specific area of the screen, a skeleton sprite is created and animated to move to a specific location on the screen, straight up. Then, a new `SKEmitterNode` instance is created and added as a child of the `MagicScene` instance. This emitter is positioned relative to the wand sprite and emits particles that we created in the `.sks` file, and simulates the magic. After a duration of 1.2 seconds, the emitter fades away and is removed from the scene.

- The `didMove(to:)` method is called once when the scene is first presented. Inside this method, a stone sprite is created and positioned on the screen. Then, an `SKEmitterNode` instance is created and added as a child of the `MagicScene` instance. This emitter will also simulate magic particles. Finally, a wand sprite is created and positioned on the screen.

That completes the code for the `magic.sks` file. Let's continue and head into `ContentView` and add a little bit of code there so we can see the magic. All we need to do is add the graveyard background scene and call `MagicView`. To do this, change your `ContentView` to the following:

```
struct ContentView: View {
    var body: some View {
    ZStack {
        Image("graveyard")
            .resizable()
            .scaledToFill().frame(width: 500, height: 900)
        MagicView()
        }
    }
}
```

With that bit of code, the project is done. Run the animation and start making magic:

Figure 15.15: The magic wand and graveyard scene

Move the wand around and see the magic coming out of its tip, then tap on the gravestone to wake the skeleton!

Summary

With SpriteKit's extensive support for physics and particle systems, combined with SwiftUI's easy-to-use interface and modern design capabilities, you can create dynamic, engaging animations that bring your apps to life. As we have seen here, you can create smoke, rain, fire, snow, and magic, but there are even more particle systems to try and experiment with.

As always, alter each project to your liking, and add your own unique creativity and ideas. Add sound to various parts of each project if you want – for example, in the magic wand project, maybe when the wand is moving, play a wand sound effect. Enhance the animations by altering the values, changing the images, or building out more complex scenes using the tools you now have. Just have fun because the effects are only limited by your imagination.

And with that, we have completed the final projects, and also the final chapter.

Throughout the book, we delved into both implicit and explicit animations, exploring the differences between them and how to use them to achieve different effects. As we progressed through the book, we gradually introduced different modifiers and more challenging animation techniques, from basic bounces to more advanced moves. We also built two complete games that you can modify in many different ways.

You now have the knowledge, skills, and a deeper understanding of SwiftUI animations to be able to implement a wide range of effects that will take your app to the next level and create engaging and dynamic user experiences.

Happy animating!

Index

Symbols

Packt.com

Subscribe to our online digital library for full access to over 7,000 books and videos, as well as industry leading tools to help you plan your personal development and advance your career. For more information, please visit our website.

Why subscribe?

- Spend less time learning and more time coding with practical eBooks and Videos from over 4,000 industry professionals

- Improve your learning with Skill Plans built especially for you

- Get a free eBook or video every month

- Fully searchable for easy access to vital information

- Copy and paste, print, and bookmark content

Did you know that Packt offers eBook versions of every book published, with PDF and ePub files available? You can upgrade to the eBook version at packt.com and as a print book customer, you are entitled to a discount on the eBook copy. Get in touch with us at customercare@packtpub.com for more details.

At www.packt.com, you can also read a collection of free technical articles, sign up for a range of free newsletters, and receive exclusive discounts and offers on Packt books and eBooks.

Other Books You May Enjoy

If you enjoyed this book, you may be interested in these other books by Packt:

iOS 16 Programming for Beginners - Seventh Edition
Ahmad Sahar, Craig Clayton
ISBN: 978-1-80323-704-6

- Get to grips with the fundamentals of Xcode 14 and Swift 5.7, the building blocks of iOS development
- Understand how to prototype an app using storyboards
- Discover the Model-View-Controller design pattern and how to implement the desired functionality within an app
- Implement the latest iOS 16 features such as SwiftUI, Lock screen widgets, and WeatherKit
- Convert an existing iPad app into a Mac app with Mac Catalyst
- Design, deploy, and test your iOS applications with design patterns and best practices

SwiftUI Cookbook - Second Edition

Giordano Scalzo, Edgar Nzokwe

ISBN: 978-1-80323-445-8

- Explore various layout presentations in SwiftUI such as HStack, VStack, LazyHStack, and LazyVGrid

- Create widgets to quickly display relevant content at glance

- Get up to speed with drawings in SwiftUI using built-in shapes, custom paths, and polygons

- Discover modern animation and transition techniques in SwiftUI

- Add user authentication using Firebase and Sign in with Apple

- Manage concurrency with Combine and async/await in SwiftUI

- Solve the most common SwiftUI problems, such as integrating a MapKit map, unit testing, snapshot testing, and previewing layouts

Packt is searching for authors like you

If you're interested in becoming an author for Packt, please visit `authors.packtpub.com` and apply today. We have worked with thousands of developers and tech professionals, just like you, to help them share their insight with the global tech community. You can make a general application, apply for a specific hot topic that we are recruiting an author for, or submit your own idea.

Share Your Thoughts

Now you've finished *Animating SwiftUI Applications*, we'd love to hear your thoughts! Scan the QR code below to go straight to the Amazon review page for this book and share your feedback or leave a review on the site that you purchased it from.

`https://packt.link/r/1-803-23266-8`

Your review is important to us and the tech community and will help us make sure we're delivering excellent quality content.

Download a free PDF copy of this book

Thanks for purchasing this book!

Do you like to read on the go but are unable to carry your print books everywhere?

Is your eBook purchase not compatible with the device of your choice?

Don't worry, now with every Packt book you get a DRM-free PDF version of that book at no cost.

Read anywhere, any place, on any device. Search, copy, and paste code from your favorite technical books directly into your application.

The perks don't stop there, you can get exclusive access to discounts, newsletters, and great free content in your inbox daily

Follow these simple steps to get the benefits:

1. Scan the QR code or visit the link below

https://packt.link/free-ebook/9781803232669

2. Submit your proof of purchase

3. That's it! We'll send your free PDF and other benefits to your email directly

Made in the USA
Columbia, SC
27 February 2024

32331554R00265